Caen Controversy

The Battle for Sword Beach 1944

Andrew Stewart

Helion & Company

Helion & Company Limited
26 Willow Road
Solihull
West Midlands
B91 1UE
England
Tel. 0121 705 3393
Fax 0121 711 4075
Email: info@helion.co.uk
Website: www.helion.co.uk
Twitter: @helionbooks
Visit our blog http://blog.helion.co.uk

Published by Helion & Company 2014

Designed and typeset by Bookcraft Limited, Stroud, Gloucestershire
Cover designed by Euan Carter, Leicester (www.euancarter.com)
Printed by Gutenberg Press Limited, Tarxien, Malta

Text © Andrew Stewart 2014
Index prepared by Onderosa Indexing, email onderosa.indexing@gmail.com
Photographs © see Bibliography
The maps were produced by the Geographical Section, General Staff (GSGS)
operating under the Director of Military Operations and form part of the 1944
series specially produced for the D-Day landings. They were Crown Copyright but
are now in the public domain and, where applicable, have been adapted by George
Anderson for Helion.

Cover: Front – Leading companies of 1 South Lancs move inland supported by
tanks of 13/18 Hussars. Rear cover – The view from HILLMAN today looking
down towards the Sword beaches.

ISBN 978-1-909982-12-3

British Library Cataloguing-in-Publication Data.
A catalogue record for this book is available from the British Library.

For details of other military history titles published by Helion & Company
Limited contact the above address, or visit our website: http://www.helion.co.uk

Contents

List of Photographs

For sources see Bibliography

List of Maps

Maps in colour section.

The maps were produced by the Geographical Section, General Staff (GSGS) operating under the Director of Military Operations and form part of the 1944 series specially produced for the D-Day landings. They were Crown Copyright but are now in the public domain and, where applicable, have been adapted by George Anderson for Helion.

Acknowledgements

The analysis, opinions and conclusions expressed or implied are those of the author and do not necessarily represent the views of the Joint Services Command and Staff College, the UK Ministry of Defence or any other government agency. Any errors of fact are the responsibility of the author.

I would like to thank the staff of the following archives and libraries for their assistance whilst I was undertaking research for the project: the National Archives, London; the Imperial War Museum, London; the Liddell Hart Centre for Military Archives, King's College London; the National Army Museum, London; the Bodleian Library, Oxford University; Special Collections, David Wilson Library, University of Leicester; Suffolk Records Office, Bury St Edmunds; Staffordshire Record Office, Stafford; The Duke of Lancaster's Regiment Lancashire Infantry Museum, Preston; A Soldier's Life, Discovery Museum, Newcastle Upon Tyne; U.S. National Records and Archives Administration, Maryland; and finally both the King's College London Library and the Joint Services Command and Staff College Library. A number of other regimental archives have also been most generous with their time providing both information and advice on additional sources for study. Where relevant and appropriate I must thank the trustees or similar of those archives above that have kindly granted access and for permission for the use of selected brief quotations. The material examined has proven to be of considerable benefit to the study.

I am most grateful to Andrea Jackson and Luke Vivian-Neal who completed research for me in the National Archives.

The encouragement and support provided by Duncan Rogers, Managing Director of Helion and Company Limited, throughout the production of this book has been most welcome. This has been both in terms of advice and also, more generally, with his refreshingly positive attitude towards military history writing. I very much look forward to working with him and his expanding publishing enterprise over the coming years.

As with all of my projects there have been many friends and acquaintances that have offered assistance when required and to them I am also grateful. I must also express my gratitude to those military officers whose participation in my classes and seminar groups continues to provide the most effective environment for shaping ideas connected to the work in hand.

I consider myself to be extremely fortunate to have the continuing encouragement and support of both my parents and my wife Joanne. Without this it would not be possible to spend the hours in the archives and at my desk. This narrative is dedicated to them with the most sincere thanks.

Oxford, February 2014

Introduction:
The Battle for Sword Beach

See maps 1 and 2.

In the autumn of 1944 Sir Robert Ensor, an Oxford academic who wrote regularly in *The Sunday Times* about foreign affairs, authored a brief account of the Second World War up to that stage. Within this he could offer only two paragraphs by way of description of the invasion of France that had taken place that summer. Despite the limited reference he did highlight what already seemed to be perhaps the most disappointing outcome of this operation, "Caen with its port would have been an immense gain, if taken intact in the first onset; but the attempt on it failed. The Germans had their chief strength here; and it was not till after more than a month's fighting that the British occupied even part of the town".[1] Whilst the detail in his description was not entirely accurate, the assessment and questions Ensor hinted at have remained open to debate ever since.

This book examines Operation OVERLORD, the Allied plan to invade Europe, and offers a narrative of the first part of this invasion, Operation NEPTUNE, more commonly referred to as 'D-Day', which saw British, American, Canadian and French troops land along the Normandy coast. The specific focus of this account is the Sword sector, on the eastern flank of the Allied plan which ran from west of the small village of Luc-sur-Mer to the port of Ouistreham. The narrative details the story of 3 (British) Infantry Division and 6 Airborne Division as these troops fought throughout the day and into the evening of 6 June 1944 to secure their objectives. In so doing it reflects upon the importance of this sector to the wider Allied plan of effecting a lodgement and, in conclusion, considers in greater detail the role that was played both during the planning stages and throughout the subsequent fighting by the Norman city of Caen.

One distinguished British professor, in a recent book that examined what he claimed to be the twelve turning points of the Second World War, perhaps inevitably included the Allied invasion and noted that the very fact that the technical term 'D-Day' had "entered the English language is a lasting sign of the significance of the event".[2] Sword has, however, tended to be overlooked in the literature of the invasion, a surprising failure to recognise its significance both in terms of what took place during the initial invasion and events that were to follow. When it has been written about the results have often been controversial. Perhaps the best known account, and one which would influence

---

1   R.C.K. Ensor, *A Miniature History of the War – Down to the Liberation of Paris* (Oxford University Press; London, 1944), p.77.

2   The actual invasion only covers part of the relevant chapter, the remainder discussing the subsequent campaign that culminated with the liberation of Paris; P.M.H. Bell, *Twelve Turning Points of the Second World War* (Yale University Press; London, 2011), pp.166-179.

many of the later writers, was that produced by Chester Wilmot, the acclaimed wartime correspondent.[3] In *The Struggle For Europe* he asserted that in the Sword sector the British division, and more specifically its assault brigades, had been unduly cautious and had a defensive complex. Indeed he referred in the brief account he provided within his much larger review of the North-West Europe campaign, to a tendency on the part of these troops to dig in and consolidate instead of driving on to their objectives. This tendency, he argued, was based in large part both on the training the division had received and also the personalities of the officers who were in command. Wilmot reached these conclusions by drawing on interviews with senior British and German officers before arriving at his own conclusions on performance and effectiveness. Despite criticisms of his approach from some of those he had interviewed his flawed narrative has largely dominated the historiography ever since.

Amongst the many general histories of the Second World War and the Normandy campaign, there is generally some reference made to Sword but the historical accuracy can be varied and the length of the coverage tends to be extremely brief.[4] This is a great pity as this remains one of the most important aspects of the entire Normandy campaign. The fortieth and fiftieth anniversaries of D-Day saw new books published, most notably by Max Hastings, Carlo D'Este and John Keegan, which demonstrated how Wilmot's imperfect account had an extraordinary influence upon the subsequent historiography.[5] For the most recent series of authors to write on this subject two notable examples confirm this to still be the case reiterating the relative lack of interest that endures in this element of the Normandy campaign. In his highly acclaimed account of the war, which runs to more than six hundred pages, Andrew Roberts could only find a single paragraph to reference D-Day's Anglo-Canadian beaches and in this he includes an erroneous reference to the fate of Caen. Far better is Rick Atkinson who, in concluding his multiple prize-winning trilogy which has exhaustively scrutinised the wartime Allied campaigns in North Africa and Europe, also combines the story of Gold, Juno and Sword together but the last of these does receive two paragraphs.[6]

Fortunately there is a scrupulously researched account, Norman Scarfe's *Assault Division*, a 'semi-official' history prepared shortly after the war's end which provides a comprehensive study of the battle. The author had participated in the battle as a junior artillery officer and produced his initial version of the manuscript to detail the division's

---

3   Chester Wilmot, *The Struggle for Europe* (Wordsworth Editions; Ware, 1997), pp.276-280.
4   The following have included more extended references to events on the Sword sector: Stephen E. Ambrose, *D-Day: June 6, 1944 – The Battle for the Normandy Beaches* (Pocket Books, London, 2002), pp.549-566; Michael Reynolds, *Eagles and Bulldogs in Normandy 1944* (Spellmount Limited; Staplehurst, 2003), pp.63-93; Patrick Delaforce, *Monty's Iron Sides – From the Normandy Beaches to Bremen with the 3rd Division* (Sutton Publishing Limited; Stroud, 1995), pp.23-49.
5   Max Hastings, *Overlord – D-Day and the Battle for Normandy 1944* (Papermac; London, 1993), pp.121-125, 134-139; Carlo D'Este, *Decision in Normandy* (Konecky and Konecky; Old Saybrook, 1984), pp. 120-146; John Keegan, *Six Armies in Normandy: From D-Day To The Liberation Of Paris* (Pan Macmillan Ltd; London, 1995).
6   Andrew Roberts, *The Storm of War – A New History of the Second World War* (Allen Lane; London, 2009), p.476; Rick Atkinson, *The Guns at Last Light – The War in Western Europe, 1944-1945* (Little, Brown; London, 2013), pp.75-77.

experience; post-war he became an academic and the papers that he assembled during his research into the D-Day landings have proven especially useful.[7] Other than Scarfe's work D'Este's account offers an important addition and includes within it a reasoned and convincing examination not just of the battle but also of Wilmot's analysis.[8] Added to this the value of Ken Ford's many battlefield guides, at least two of which have focussed on the attack on the Sword sector, also needs to be recognised.[9]

In order to write this narrative it predominantly draws upon various service and regimental histories that were produced directly following the conclusion of the fighting, some of which were published and others which have remained unavailable. It has been fortunate to have been able to examine the papers of Eric Lummis, a young officer who landed on Sword on D-Day with 1st Battalion, The Suffolk Regiment, and who spent many years of his retirement studying his regimental history. It also includes the work of the Air Historical Branch, the Cabinet Office Historical Section, and the Admiralty. The British official history written by Major Lyle Ellis, which drew on these along with additional research including interviews with a number of those involved at the senior levels, offers a good basis for study although it has been suggested that its author deliberately refused to challenge the established narrative of events on the day of the invasion.[10]

This is intended to act as an introduction to the story of D-Day and the role played by 3 (British) Infantry Division on the Sword beaches and there is deliberately limited reference made to a number of other important themes connected to the wider battle. These include the role played by ULTRA and the intelligence battle as well as the deception and influence strategies which formed part of the FORTITUDE plans. There could also be a more expansive account of the role played by the British airborne forces and the commandos operating on the flanks of the divisional plan. The German contribution receives sufficient detail to support the narrative of the main British effort; this story has been expanded upon elsewhere. The controversy of whether OVERLORD sought to capture airfields in its first days also still requires further investigation.

Much of the inspiration for the project has come from having visited the area on numerous occasions, both on my own, with friends and family and with students attending the Joint Services Command and Staff College, a part of the UK's Defence Academy based at Shrivenham. As a member of the academic faculty teaching military history, being able to conduct battlefield studies provides an invaluable opportunity to study the terrain and compare this to the decisions that were made. During the last three years this has included the study undertaken with the senior attendees of the Higher Command and Staff Course. As part of the European visit this course makes there is some focus on the Normandy landings and the chance to reflect upon whether the Allies

---

7   Norman Scarfe, *Assault Division – A History of the 3rd Division from the Invasion of Normandy to the Surrender of Germany* (Spellmount; Stroud, 2006), pp.vii-xxii.

8   D'Este, *Decision in Normandy*, pp.132-133.

9   Ken Ford, *Sword Beach* (Sutton Publishing; Stroud, 2004) [Series Editor: Simon Trew, Battlezone Normandy, No.2]; Ken Ford, *D-Day 1944 (3) – Sword Beach and the British Airborne landings* (Osprey Publishing; Oxford, 2002).

10   Major L.F. Ellis, *History of the Second World War: Victory in the West – Volume I, The Battle of Normandy* (HMSO; London, 1962), pp.183-187, 201-206; D'Este, *Decision in Normandy*, pp.491-493.

could have captured Caen.[11] With this year also marking the 70th anniversary of the landings, and the official international commemoration taking place on Sword, there is all the more reason to examine what this book contends was a vital element to the broader NEPTUNE and OVERLORD plans and its impact on the subsequent, final phase of the conflict in Europe.

---

11 Only one of the student papers had been published to date but the analysis provided by those participating in this course has generated some fascinating debates; James Babbage, 'Montgomery's presentation of his plans for D-Day: a case of consent and evade?', *Defence Studies* (Vol.11, No.4; December 2011), pp.657-671.

1

Invading Europe

On Saturday 22 June 1940 at Compiègne, a forest north of Paris where twenty-two years earlier the Germans had signed the armistice documents ending the First World War, French representatives were ushered into the same railway carriage that their predecessors had used in much happier times. The campaign in France was over, only six weeks after it had begun, and for the victors it "represented one of the great military triumphs of history".[1] The French military had been compelled to accept abject capitulation while the second British Expeditionary Force although it had, to a large part, been evacuated, most if its equipment had been left behind on France's beaches. With what little remained the coastline of England was hurriedly fortified against a possible invasion while the initial main battle took place in the skies. Here the *Luftwaffe* proved unable to deliver the decisive defeat of the Royal Air Force that the other two German services had demanded as being critical if the English Channel was to be crossed. More significantly the German leader Adolf Hitler in turn quickly lost interest and Britain was not defeated that summer.

Its survival, however unlikely or parlous, in many respects represented the key moment of the entire war. Whilst German planners could dismiss it as a mere detail it was a military failure they failed to rectify; the longer term strategic outcome was that there would remain a persistent and enduring threat to their rear flank.[2] For even basic students of warfare this would be of some concern leading to a level of uncertainty and the potential to undermine planning and operations conducted elsewhere. As the war became truly global in nature and the protagonists increased, the incomplete nature of Germany's series of victories in 1940 would become all the more obvious. The entry of the United States into what had become a truly global conflict was quickly followed by the First Washington Conference, also known as the Arcadia Conference. Held in December 1941 the leaders of the United States and Britain and representatives from the other still fighting powers agreed that they would pursue a strategy which demanded the Axis forces accept unconditional surrender. It was also determined, albeit reluctantly on the part of some American military commanders, that the newly christened Allies would first focus on securing victory in Europe. To do this the Continent would have to be invaded.

The subsequent meeting of British and American military and political leaders that took place in Casablanca in January 1943 marked the formal beginning of what would in time become known as Operation OVERLORD, the Allied invasion of France. At

---

1   Williamson Murray and Allan R. Millett, *A War to Be Won – Fighting the Second World War* (The Belknap Press of Harvard University Press; London, 2000), pp.82.

2   Andrew Stewart, *A Very British Experience – Coalition, Defence and Strategy in the Second World War* (Sussex Academic Press; Eastbourne, 2012), pp.28-46; Norman Davies, *No Simple Victory – World War II in Europe, 1939-1945* (Penguin Books; London, 2007), pp.87-88.

this, and despite the British delegation's continued lack of firm support for the idea of a hurried attack somewhere on the European mainland, it was agreed to form a dedicated planning staff to examine how such an operation might be conducted. The lead for this would be a senior British officer, Lieutenant-General Frederick Morgan, referred to as 'Chief of Staff to the Supreme Allied Commander (Designate)', a long title shortened to 'COSSAC'. To emphasise the unity of the new coalition and drawing upon the several months work he had already conducted on broad invasion questions there was an American deputy, Brigadier-General (quickly promoted to Major-General) Ray W. Barker. With the Supreme Allied Commander, or 'SAC', yet to be nominated, Morgan's team were tasked with, as one of the many post-war official histories put it, examining systematically all of the potential problems that could possibly lead this huge undertaking to fail.[3] This meant that they were expected to prepare no more than an initial estimate and do so in the knowledge that when the SAC appointment was made this could be altered and they would be incorporated into an entirely new headquarters.

There had been previous planning groups that had undertaken similar work. The Combined Chiefs of Staff, which first met in Washington DC on Christmas Eve 1941, and the Combined Commanders who met from early 1942, had each considered how Europe might be invaded successfully and, in so doing, they had conducted various staff exercises. The start point was a 1941 British study, titled Operation ROUNDUP, which examined a possible invasion two years later, and another much more fanciful proposal – Operation SLEDGEHAMMER – which considered the possibility of an attack in 1942 in the event of a Russian collapse or a sudden weakening of Germany's position.[4] This was not a cursory process as the small staffs that had been tasked with conducting the studies looked far and wide for information and produced detailed recommendations. This even extended to a public request being made for photographs and postcards showing locations in France, Belgium and Holland and several million of these were received. Not including this huge visual resource, the folder of material that was handed over to the COSSAC staff following their appointment was "some inches thick" and provided a sound basis on which to begin.[5]

By this stage of the war there were already various other military operations which could be examined for ideas on how to plan an invasion of Europe. Amongst these the most obvious, not least due to where it had taken place, was the raid on Dieppe on 19 August 1942, much criticised by post-war historians for its apparent complete, costly failure, but which offered several important lessons.[6] Whilst the attack had convinced

---

3   Horst Boog et al, *Germany and the Second World War: Volume VII, The Strategic Air War in Europe and the War in the West and East Asia 1943-1944/5* (Clarendon Press; Oxford, 2006), p.490.

4   D'Este, *Decision in Normandy*, pp.24-35.

5   The Historical Sub-Section, Office of Secretary, 'History of COSSAC (Chief of Staff to Supreme Allied Commander), 1943-1944', General Staff, Supreme Headquarters, Allied Expeditionary Force, May 1944, http://www.history.army.mil/documents/cossac/Cossac.htm; Lieutenant-General Sir Frederick Morgan, *Peace and War: A Soldier's Life* (Hodder and Stoughton; London, 1961), pp.156-157, 162.

6   The raid was recognised, shortly over OVERLORD's success had seemed assured, as having been "the most important" trial that had been conducted in its preparation. 'Dieppe and Cherbourg: I – An Experiment against a Fortified Coast', *The Times*, 4 August 1944; 'Dieppe and Cherbourg: II – Experience Gained from Landings', *The Times*, 5 August 1944.

Lieutenant-General
Frederick Morgan –
COSSAC at his desk

the Germans that the Allies would need to capture a major port at an early point, it in turn made the planners recognise that "a frontal attack on a port was akin to butting our heads against a brick wall and that it was essential for us to take our port with us".[7] This resulted in the development of the Mulberry artificial harbour project which, in its own way, would play a central part in determining how the Normandy campaign progressed. Operation JUBILEE also demonstrated that the assaulting troops would need overwhelming fire support throughout every stage of an invasion and the availability of this would need to be factored in when assembling the forces. Perhaps most significantly it emphasised the critical requirement for a combined headquarters, something that was manifestly accepted, first with the establishment of COSSAC and then its successor, and their large, joint staffs who planned and prepared for the invasion.

These were conclusions that would all be arrived at in the months that followed once COSSAC had set to work. In the first instance Morgan was required to provide an initial briefing to the British Chiefs of Staff after just 24 hours of studying the work that had already been done.[8] In terms of better understanding his task the "somewhat hazy background" that had been given to him in the initial orders issued by the Combined Chiefs of Staff did provide a mission statement of sorts:

> Our object is to defeat the German fighting forces in North-West Europe. To this end the Combined Chiefs of Staff will endeavour to assemble the strongest possible

---

7   Robert Laycock to Ellis, 10 October 1956, CAB101/309, The National Archives, Kew (hereafter 'TNA').
8   Morgan, *Peace and War*, p.162.

forces (subject to prior commitments in other theatres) in constant readiness to re-enter the Continent if German resistance is weakened to the required extent in 1943. In the meantime the Combined Chiefs of Staff must be prepared to order such limited operations as may be practical with the forces and material available.[9]

Even so this was vague direction and lacking in any real guidance other than a requirement to provide three sets of plans. The first of these was to take the form of a deception piece pointing to the Pas-de-Calais area, the second a contingency should German forces in France disintegrate and the third, and most important, the details for the proposed full-scale assault. The deadline to complete the last of these was extremely tight with a draft report to be delivered by mid-July 1943 and an agreed version of the plan available by the month's end. This timeline had been arrived at even before a firm date for the actual landings had been provided. This came shortly afterwards at the Trident Conference, held in Washington DC from 12-15 May 1943, where there still remained some very obvious and significant British and American disagreement about wider questions of wartime strategy. It was, however, agreed that Europe would be invaded less than a year later on 1 May 1944 and the more expanded planning process could now begin under the designation of the next name on the code list MESPOT. Prime Minister Winston Churchill intervened to reject a title which "had no rallying sound about it" and so it was changed to the next on the list, OVERLORD.[10]

The most obvious, and indeed, vital task facing the planners as their task turned to considering the more detailed questions was to identify where the landings would take place. There were seven factors considered by the COSSAC staff in selecting the lodgement area: port capacities; beach capacities; naval considerations; air considerations; German coastal defences; German reserves and; Allied forces available.[11] They were looking for flat areas and open beaches across which troops and equipment could be landed. Added to this there needed to be large ports nearby that could be captured quickly and opened up as the supply hubs for the invasion force. Morgan saw his primary task as being to identify an area where approximately thirty divisions could be put ashore. This force would seize and secure a base which could then be used for future operations involving an army that expanded up to 100 divisions in size.[12] Having examined various possibilities, by mid-July the review process was already down to just two options, Caen and the Cotentin Peninsula and the Pas-de-Calais. The first of these was decided upon not merely because of its closeness to Cherbourg but also because most defences were already concentrated further north and these made it clear that this was where the Germans anticipated an attack taking place.[13]

---

9   Ibid., p.156.
10   Pamela Marsh, 'A funny thing happened on the way to D-Day: memories of the staff that drew up the plans', *The Christian Science Monitor*, June 1984.
11   For a detailed but concise discussion of the COSSAC plan see Colonel C.P. Stacey, *Official History of the Canadian Army in the Second World War: Volume III, The Victory Campaign, The Operations in North-West Europe 1944-1945* (The Queen's Printer and Controller of Stationary; Ottawa, 1960), pp.16-22.
12   Morgan, *Peace and War*, p.163.
13   'Preliminary notes on "Overlord"', 20 July 1943, WO205/33, TNA.

This decision may well also have been influenced by a February 1943 plan that had been produced by the Combined Commanders planning staff titled 'The Selection of Assault Areas in a Major Operation in North-West Europe'.[14] Concluding that a large scale assault would only be possible in the Caen area, this had included an outline scheme, known as Operation SKYSCRAPER. This involved four divisions which would assault the beaches between the mouth of the River Orne north of the city and the estuary of the Vire, and on the southern beaches of the Cotentin Peninsula. An additional four were to be employed in an airborne role and six further divisions would follow up. As the Canadian official historian has noted, although the proposal was quickly rejected by the British Chiefs of Staff, it "turned out to be very close to the actual plan finally followed in the invasion of Normandy; considerably closer to it, in fact, than the plan subsequently produced by COSSAC, who was working within the straitjacket of the limited resources prescribed by the Combined Chiefs of Staff".

In order for the invasion to succeed its scope and size would need to be vast but it would also need to concentrate in a specific area. Nonetheless COSSAC's selection was not an obvious one as the two potential options had both positive and negative factors that had to be considered. For the more southern of the two the proposed assault area was further from British airfields which would reduce the amount of time for fighter cover. There was also a longer sea voyage with all the associated risks this would incorporate. The attacking force would, however, be opposed by lighter German defences, both in terms of manpower and fortifications, and the beaches were better suited for landings with some protection from the wind and tides. The area behind the beaches was also better suited for the establishment of forward airfields. In terms of the Pas-de-Calais region, the invasion force would require a sea crossing of only 20 miles, there would be an extended period for air cover and a rapid turnaround for shipping. The critical negatives were the German defences which were extremely intimidating while the potential for further exploitation was also not good as the port of Antwerp was a long way north and the other possibilities of Le Havre and Rouen to the south were protected by a series of water obstacles. Weighing these factors against one another allowed Morgan and his staff to conclude that the chances of a successful attack in the Caen sector were "so much greater … than in any other case that it is considered that its advantages outweigh the disadvantages".[15]

COSSAC's plan was distributed to the British War Cabinet on 30 July 1943 prior to its presentation the following month at the Quadrant conference held in Quebec. As the American official historian described it:

> Outline OVERLORD, in the strict sense, was not an operational plan at all. It was not a blueprint for maneuver (sic). No field order could have been issued on the basis of it, and no troop dispositions made. It was a plan for planning, not a plan for action. Its tone was discursive, not precise and peremptory. It reflected the fact that it was drawn by a staff in the absence of the commander, and it made a patent effort to refrain from tying the commander's hand, especially in examining the later stages.[16]

---

14 Stacey, *The Victory Campaign*, pp.16-17.
15 'History of COSSAC', pp.27-28.
16 Gordon Harrison, *Cross Channel Attack* (Office of the Chief of Military History; Washington DC, 1950), p.71.

This document proposed that Normandy would need to be invaded by three divisions landed from the sea supported by two airborne brigades. Two more divisions, which had been pre-loaded on to landing craft, would provide an immediate follow-up force and it was calculated that eighteen divisions would land in the first fortnight. A main objective was the capture of Cherbourg by no later than 14 days after the initial landings; the whole of Brittany was to be cleared within six to eight weeks so that its various ports could be used to re-supply the invasion force. It was stressed that a full-scale landing could only succeed if heavy bombardment and a strict sea blockade had weakened German defensive capabilities. Added to this would be needed a Soviet offensive on the Eastern front and the possibility of a landing against the French Mediterranean coast. Morgan further stipulated that his plan could only succeed if, at its start, the Germans had a maximum of twelve mobile field divisions in France with no more than three of these in Caen and its surrounding area at the time of the initial landings. This number could not increase beyond a total of five by D-Day plus 2 (D+2) and nine divisions by D+8.

As had become clear during the few months available for the review of material, the focus on Caen was perhaps the key strategic consideration of the entire plan.[17] The COSSAC planners referred extensively to the city, an important "bottleneck in communications", with its early capture and development of the surrounding airfield sites being described as "key". Indeed they were quite clear in their assessment that it would be "essential for us to seize it if we are to avoid defeat in the early stages. It also provides a valuable pivot for operations to develop the bridgehead".[18] The latter was important; Caen controlled the major roads into the invasion area from the principal German concentration areas near the Pas-de-Calais and in the other direction towards Paris. As such it would be inevitable that any German response would head in its direction, a critical consideration within the estimate as the likely nature, speed and extent of the counter-attack was a vital factor. It would also soon become known that the boundary between the Seventh and Fifteenth Armies, the two principal defending forces, had been fixed along the River Dives just east of the city. This would have an additional significance and the Operation FORTITUDE deception campaign, which proved so important to the invasion's success, sought to keep in place the armies in the Pas-de-Calais region. In the process this also further increased the case for Caen's capture as early as possible, a potential pivot around which the Allied campaign could swing.

Whilst the decision about location might have been confirmed there were, however, many operational issues which needed to be addressed. A broad area had been identified for the assault beaches covering a 35 mile front from north of Caen to Grandcamp and between the rivers Vire and Orne and five potential targets had been initially discussed which had considerably weaker defences than existed elsewhere along the Channel coast.[19] Only three of them were deemed to be sufficiently free from serious obstacles and have large enough initial capacity to be used even with these; it was still assessed that there would be a delay in opening exits for vehicles. As a result a 20 percent reduction

---

17 'Operation "Overlord": Report and Appreciation (with Appendices)', COS(43) 416(O), 30 July 1943, pp.2-11, CAB80/72/16, TNA.

18 Ibid., p.21, para 96.

19 These three beaches were marked as '308' (Courseulles-Arromanches), the western end of '307' (Courseulles) and '313' (Colleville-Vierville).

was made on the theoretical capacity for the amount of vehicles that could be offloaded during the first 12 hours; this led to a maximum figure of 12,100 vehicles being put ashore during the first day of the operation. This might not have seemed a major consideration but it was actually critical. At this rate it meant that the invasion of Europe would have to be carried out by three assault divisions with approximately three tank brigades and an additional infantry brigade group following them on the same day plus the equivalent of approximately one follow-up division. Of greater concern, with the size and topography of the beaches the proposed assault force for each target sector could only cover at maximum a two brigade front, a limitation in fighting power which potentially could have serious consequences. There were also some logistics issues with the airborne element of the plan; an entire British airborne division had been initially assigned the mission of capturing Caen at the earliest opportunity. With it being quickly recognised that there was insufficient transport aircraft to allow for it to be moved to the target area this was reduced to two brigades. Even at this size three transport lifts would be required for it to reach its target meaning an estimated 16 hours would be needed until the entire airborne force was available.[20] This further restricted the potential likelihood of achieving the primary operational objective of capturing Caen.

With all of the caveats and warnings and despite Churchill and his senior military team continuing to have doubts the proposals presented at the Quebec conference were broadly accepted. The British leader's concerns about launching a major attack on the French coast had not diminished and he continued to favour greater emphasis being placed on the Allied effort in Italy and preparation of plans for landings in Norway. He was also bitterly opposed to the idea contained within Morgan's proposals that there should be a simultaneous diversionary landing in the south of France.[21] Some of the prime minister's fears drew their basis from the near-disaster that had befallen the Allied attackers at Salerno; three divisions had only just proven enough to overcome the defending force and he worried about "the prospect of corpses floating in the Channel".[22] There were also more general fears in London about how the United States viewed strategic priorities, specifically the need for a major invasion of Burma as part of ensuring China's continuing role in the war. The British response was to therefore demand that 25 percent more landing craft be made available for OVERLORD; this would both allow for a strengthening of the assault forces by approximately one extra division and scupper many of the other recommendations that were being put forward for operations that ran counter to Churchill's vision for how the war should develop.

As the autumn of 1943 progressed the American leader President Franklin Roosevelt did eventually agree that plans relating to Burma would be postponed and extra shipping would be provided but there was no commitment to the extra troops Churchill had wanted. There was also refusal to consider any cancellation of Operation ANVIL and the requirement for landings on the French Mediterranean coast became a fixed element of the wider invasion narrative. The compromises that had been arrived at did, however,

---

20 'Operation "Overlord"', 'Task Table', p36, CAB80/72/16, TNA.
21 F.H. Hinsley (ed.), *British Intelligence in the Second World War – Its Influence on Strategy and Operations: Vol 3/Pt II* (London, HMSO, 1988), pp.9-10.
22 Andrew Roberts, *Masters and Commanders: The Military Geniuses Who Led the West to Victory in World War Two* (Penguin; London, 2009), p.215.

also lead to a final agreement that the invasion of Normandy would represent the main Allied effort in 1944 and operations would commence in May.[23] This did not mean that the British prime minister's doubts were entirely resolved; indeed they persisted right up until he received confirmation on the evening of 6 June 1944 that the landings had succeeded.

Despite the higher level political disputes the actual planning and training processes connected with preparing for an invasion could not afford to be delayed. By July 1943 Sir Bernard Paget, the first commander of 21st Army Group and the principal author of SKYSCRAPER, had a functioning headquarters which included the Home Defence Command. This gave him responsibility for over-seeing all the functions associated with British expeditionary forces and made him a key actor in the OVERLORD arrangements. With Morgan and Paget's staff officers liaising closely with one another the latter formalised how training would be organised for those divisions which were set to join Second British Army, the British land-based component for the proposed invasion. This process began with a basic separation being made between those units that would conduct the initial assault and those that would follow them. The assault forces, not surprisingly, practised beach-landings, how to get ashore and, from there, how to establish the beachhead.[24] All the divisions who were to take part in the landings, in whatever capacity, were also drilled at length on the complex arrangements that would deliver them to their embarkation points.

At the same time, for the staffs working on the written plans there were other important tasks that needed to be completed. Amongst these an initial step had been the completion of a system of code-names which needed to be devised for every possible beach in Normandy. These stretched phonetically and extended from the Cotentin Peninsula to the mouth of the River Orne; included within this was 'How' starting at Port-en-Bessin running through to 'Roger' which ended at Ouistreham. What was later to be the 'Sword' sector comprised 'Peter', 'Queen' and 'Roger'. In turn each of the sectors, which comprised two or three beaches, was further divided and, based on simple geography, these were named 'Green' (west), 'White' (centre) and 'Red' (east). This allowed the planners to be specific in terms of how they referred to each of the target areas. Hence for the Caen sector, where the available frontage created limitations of size, the principal beaches would eventually be titled 'Queen White' and 'Queen Red'.

A good deal of work was also being undertaken on establishing a general idea of the characteristics of the Caen sector, open rolling cultivated land which was described as being not dissimilar to East Anglia. After a built-up area of villas spread along the coast there were three main ridges which stood between these and the city. The first was a half mile to the south of the village of Hermanville and the second two miles further to the south and with the village of Bieville at its summit. The final ridge was another mile and a half south, just three miles north of the city, and was marked by thick woods and the village of Lebisey. Each of these ridges was reportedly held by German troops but there was some doubt as to the strength at each location. There were various coast defence guns across the northern coastline, most notably at Le Havre, but the enemy was

---

23 Wilmot, *The Struggle for Europe*, pp.135-142.
24 David French, 'Invading Europe: The British Army and its Preparations for the Normandy Campaign, 1942-44', *Diplomacy and Statecraft* (Vol.14, No.2; June 2003), pp.280-281.

also reported to have batteries between the first and second ridges near the villages of Beauville and Périers-sur-le-Dan with further guns on the slope down to Caen.

Whilst some worked on a general picture other planners focussed on more detailed issues. In October 1943 the group tasked specifically with examining the coast running from the port of Ouistreham to Lion-sur-Mer received an engineer appreciation which considered how assault forces would fare against the existing enemy defences.[25] Drawing on the huge amount of information now available to them about the local terrain in this document the sector nearest Caen was not referred to by code-names but, instead, separated into three geographic sections. Of these the east was reported as not being satisfactory as a result of the challenges associated with clearing Ouistreham and the lack of good roads inland. The centre was also problematic because of the inundated areas behind the beaches which the Germans had deliberately flooded. The remaining section was, fortunately, "very favourable for the assault along a frontage of 1,500 yards". The 500 yards on the eastern edge of this favoured section had sand dunes that were 20-30 yards wide while the remaining beach frontage had a vertical sea wall that was seven to ten feet high and then cliffs that were 20-30 feet high; the comment was that "the dunes and sea wall constitute only minor obstacles". It was also noted that there was a good lateral road only 250 yards inland with another after approximately 1,000 yards. The number of exits available off the beaches was considered a real positive factor there being ten existing roads connecting to the first lateral road. Of these eight were adjacent to the sea wall or sand dunes hence the conclusion "the possibilities for beach exits in this section are good". Much the same was said to be the case for the routes running further inland as a result of which the overall favourable assessment seems to have been entirely reasonable.

Although great progress was being made the task facing the Allied planners was, however, still considerable. As such it was accepted at the Teheran conference held in late November 1943 that there would need to be a revision to the previously agreed invasion date. This was now shifted to no later than 1 June 1944 and the final confirmation of this was not given until a few weeks before D-Day.[26] The final month of 1943 was even more significant as, after nearly a year of uncertainty, President Roosevelt finally confirmed that General Dwight D. Eisenhower would take the critical SAC role and be the commander of the invasion forces. Completing the senior command appointments, he arrived in England the following month to take charge of the newly designated Supreme Headquarters Allied Expeditionary Forces (SHAEF). General Sir Bernard Montgomery had been appointed Commander-in-Chief 21st Army Group on Christmas Day 1943 and, since this included all land forces, both British and American, in the initial assault, he was also OVERLORD's Commander-in-Chief Land Forces. Admiral Sir Bertram Ramsay had been appointed as Allied Naval Commander-in-Chief in October of the

---

25 'Engr Appreciation Concerning the Landing of a Bde Gp on the Beaches from Ouistreham to Lion-sure-Mer', Neptune, BM6/21 A Gp/6774/E, 15 October 1943, Lt Col D.B. Rooke Papers, Documents 11348, Imperial War Museum (hereafter 'IWM').

26 Churchill had proposed a target of 6 June, based upon advice from his Chiefs of Staff that this was the most suitable date in terms of the moon's phases, the following month, in December 1943; Sir Winston Churchill, *History of the Second World War: Vol.V, Closing the Ring* (Cassell and Co.; London, 1951), pp.386, 397.

same year with Air Chief Marshal Sir Trafford Leigh-Mallory having been confirmed in the November as taking charge of the air component involved. Morgan, who had overseen the planning process without knowing who would take charge, was appointed as Eisenhower's Deputy Chief of Staff. The invasion of Europe would therefore have an American commander who was supported by three senior British officers.

The Land Forces Commander, 'Monty' as he was widely known, saw the COSSAC plan for the first time on 1 January 1944; Churchill had requested he provide some immediate initial comments and despite believing these would be of little real value, he was quick to make it clear that he did not agree with the proposals that he was shown.[27] According to General Morgan, following his arrival at the headquarters Monty was critical of an "impracticable" and unacceptable plan and "for several days the most strenuous efforts were made in pursuit of any and every alternative".[28] His immediate concern was about the chosen landing area which he concluded was both too small and on too narrow a front; the potential was for "appalling confusion on the beaches" and military disaster. As such he quickly provided an alternate plan for a British Army to instead land on a two or three Corps front in the Caen-Cherbourg area; a similar size American force was to assault the St Malo-St Nazaire-Brest area. Monty also believed it essential that the four available British airborne divisions and four American parachute regiments should all be used. He was, however, also disturbed by the limitations imposed on the planning process by the lack of transport aircraft; he stressed that it should be possible to lift at least the equivalent of half of this airborne force at the same time.

These were not entirely new concerns, Paget had held similar and said as much to the Chief of the Imperial General Staff, General Sir Alan Brooke, in November 1943 just before he had left for the Tehran conference:

> An assault by three divisions in this sector will use the beaches and beach exits to maximum capacity and leave no margin for failure … At most, we can expect to establish a covering position some three to five miles inland by the evening of D-Day, by which time, taking present dispositions, two Panzer divisions might be in a position to stage a counter-attack. We may be able to hold this attack, but hemmed in behind the shallow covering position, and with beaches within range of enemy field artillery, the landing and deployment of our follow-up formations is liable to be seriously hampered. Unless the scale of resistance is much lower than that envisaged in the OVERLORD plan, the operation will be very risky.[29]

---

27 'First impressions of Operation "Overlord" made at the request of the Prime Minister by General Montgomery', 1 January 1944, Sir John Kennedy Papers, Kennedy 4/8, Liddell Hart Centre for Military Archives (hereafter 'LHCMA'); Phillip Green, 'Frederick Morgan' in Major General David T. Zabecki, *Chief of Staff: The Principal Officers Behind History's Great Commanders, Volume 2* (Naval Institute Press; Annapolis, 2008), pp.110-111.

28 The post-war relationship between the two men was famously obtuse. Morgan later wrote, "Megalomania is a great driving force, no doubt, but it is not always easy to direct"; 'Victory in the West – Comment by "COSSAC" (General Sir Frederick Morgan)', 30 September 1956, p.5, CAB101/309, TNA.

29 General Sir Bernard Paget to General Sir Alan Brooke, 15 November 1943; cited in Nigel Hamilton, *Monty: Master of the Battlefield, 1942–1944* (Hamish Hamilton; London, 1983), p.494.

General Eisenhower surrounded by his senior
OVERLORD commanders

The Land Forces commander for D-Day,
General Sir Bernard Montgomery

Admiral Sir Bertram Ramsay who
oversaw the creation of the huge
NEPTUNE fleet

With the exception of the degree to which the beaches could actually be threatened, this astute assessment proved almost entirely accurate.

There was, however, some confusion about the role Caen occupied in this once again revised strategic vision. At the first conference the COSSAC planners had offered their advice that Allied forces should concentrate on a single primary objective, namely Caen. This came with a clear caveat, as one of those who later presented the plan to the Land Forces commander recalled. He had told Monty, "he couldn't take Caen the first day. He was very optimistic. After all it is nearly 12 miles from some of the beaches. It would take troops two days to move that far. Only larger airborne forces could have taken [Caen]".[30] Morgan was also adamant that Monty had not grasped the tactical or strategic significance of Caen writing later:

> Lip service, so to speak, was paid to the Caen problem by including the city in I Corps' objectives for the day and by the inclusion of suitable exhortatory phrases in directives. But nothing practical, such as the addition of special troops possibly airborne, was done to help … in the formidable task set.[31]

Despite repeated efforts by many of the planners to get across the degree to which "the communication centre" was a key objective, the landings in the Utah sector were seen as having "loomed bigger in [Montgomery's] mind than the necessity for the early capture of Caen". Added to this potentially critical consideration was that of the size of the forces to be used. Once again the Land Commander's critique was not providing anything really new as Morgan and his team had conceded even before the Quadrant conference that the assault force could be expanded by at least another division. To achieve even this would require a ten percent increase in the number of landing craft needed for the operation, a logistical requirement that he and his team had not been able to remedy effectively despite the decisions that had been conceded to at Teheran. It would be down to Eisenhower's staff within SHAEF, established in December 1943 at Camp Griffiss in north London, to now take the planning for the invasion forward and reach a workable consensus.

---

30 Ibid., Major-General C.A. West, p.491.
31 'Victory in the West – Comment by "COSSAC"', pp.17-18, CAB101/309, TNA.

2

The Allies Prepare

Whilst Monty was the overall commander for all Allied land forces he entrusted the leadership of the British component not to Paget but to General Sir Miles Dempsey. 'Bimbo' Dempsey had started the war as a battalion commander landing in France in September 1939 and enjoyed a rapid rise through senior appointments eventually commanding a corps in the latter stages of the North African campaign and during the subsequent invasions of Sicily and Italy. Monty, who was a strong and consistent patron, called him back to London in December 1943 and the following month he was appointed as the General Officer Commanding (GOC) of the Second British Army replacing Lieutenant-General Kenneth Anderson.[1] This formation included two corps and in the autumn of 1943 General Sir John Crocker, who had followed a similar previous pattern to Dempsey with senior brigade, division and corps appointments, was given command of I Corps. With an armoured background he was well thought of by Brooke and despite only limited operational experience he found himself with one of the most important OVERLORD roles.[2]

Crocker's command area included Sword and the assault force assigned to this part of the plan, 3rd British Infantry Division (3 Br Inf Div), described as such to differentiate it from 3rd Canadian Infantry Division which had been chosen to land in the neighbouring Juno sector.[3] This celebrated British division dated back to the Peninsular Wars and, having fought Napoleon's armies, its troops later served in the Crimea and in South Africa during the Boer War.[4] At the end of August 1939 it was Monty himself who had assumed command of what, as a result of its service during the First World War, was known to him and throughout the British Army as the 'Iron Division'. On taking charge he had implemented an instant, rigorous training programme to improve the

---

1   Nick Smart, *Biographical Dictionary of British Generals of the Second World War* (Pen and Sword; Barnsley, 2005), p.82. Despite his distinguished wartime record, as his obituary noted, "…he was comparatively unknown to the public. This was doubtless due to the fact that it never fell to him to hold an independent operational command. But he was also a man who never sought the limelight"; 'Obituary – Gen Sir Miles Dempsey', *The Times*, June 7, 1969.
2   In this role he is said to have done a good job "without attracting much attention to himself" and retained his command through until the end of the North-West Europe campaign. He went on to fill a number of senior post-war Army appointments before retiring in 1953; Smart, *Biographical Dictionary of British Generals of the Second World War*, pp.72-73.
3   In terms of the style adopted throughout this narrative military units are referenced in a standard abbreviated form – hence '1st Battalion, The Suffolk Regiment' becomes '1 Suffolks' – and all timings are written in 24 hour clock form.
4   Delaforce, *Monty's Iron Sides*, pp.1-5; Reynolds, *Eagles and Bulldogs*, pp.7-10; Scarfe, *Assault Division*, pp.xxv-xxix.

deficiencies he felt existed and was also responsible for devising a new divisional sign of three black triangles surrounding an inverted red triangle.[5] The division played a key role in the British Expeditionary Force's withdrawal through France and the holding of the Dunkirk perimeter after which it was assigned to defensive positions on the Sussex coast to await a German invasion. Before Monty's promotion and departure the following year to take command of a corps, it had been designated as a mobile counter-attack force. The few texts that refer to it all make a similar point, that by 1943 nearly three years had been spent training in the British Isles.

This static role was about to change. In December 1942 3 Br Inf Div was re-designated as a lead division for any invasion of mainland Europe and initially prepared for this new role under the command of Major-General William Ramsden.[6] An interesting analysis has been provided highlighting the relatively high percentage of regular soldiers within the division, somewhere between 30-40 percent of the men.[7] Mindful of this the GOC is supposed to have persuaded Brooke that this force would be well suited to lead any assault, and in the process avenge the defeat at Dunkirk, and the men were moved to Scotland where they trained for the proposed invasion of Sicily.[8] For political reasons this operation was eventually given to Canadian troops leading to a dip in morale amongst the British troops about the continued lack of opportunity to put their training to use. Ramsden, who was not particularly well thought of by Monty, was soon after sent to take charge in the Sudan and Eritrea and Major-General Tom Rennie replaced him. The new GOC had previously been captured at Saint-Valery-en-Caux during the 1940 retreat from France but escaped nine days later while being taken to Germany, and made his way on foot and by bicycle through France into Spain and back from Portugal to England. From here he went on to serve in North Africa where he commanded the 5th Battalion of the Black Watch in 1942, leading the battalion at the Second Battle of El Alamein in October, and then becoming Commander of the 154th Brigade back in the 51st Division. He had led the same formation for the Allied invasion of Sicily in July 1943 before, in December of that year, being appointed to take charge of 3 Br Inf Div and arriving in Scotland on Christmas Day. Following some further final revisions over the coming weeks to the order of battle, under his command he had three infantry brigades – 8, 9 and 185 – which were made up of nine battalions drawn from around the country plus the normal supporting units from the Royal Artillery, Royal Engineers and other arms as well as the men and vehicles of 27th Armoured Brigade (27 Armd Bde). In addition there were a variety of more unusual units which had specific invasion tasks relating to the capture and maintenance of the beaches with specialist vehicles from 79th Armoured Division (79 Armd Div) which would help with the initial assault and subsequent operations. His division would also be working closely with the Royal Marines and airborne forces both of which would be operating on the flanks where they would provide protection for the infantry's anticipated line of advance.

---

5   A copy of this, which can be seen today prominently displayed outside the castle in Caen, was worn on the sleeve of every soldier who landed with the division in June 1944.
6   French, 'Invading Europe', p.288.
7   Reynolds, *Eagles and Bulldogs*, pp.9-10.
8   Ibid.; Delaforce, *Monty's Iron Sides*, p.5.

General Sir Miles Dempsey, GOC
Second British Army

Major-General Tom Rennie,
commanding 3 Br Inf Div

Well before he arrived to take charge the division had already spent several months preparing for the coming invasion. With a headquarters at Cameron Barracks in Inverness it had spent the summer of 1943 practising at Burghead Bay on the Moray Firth. In November an area of about 15 square miles, from east of the village of Frearn to just outside Portmahomack was requisitioned by the Admiralty for military purposes and between 800-900 people including the entire village of Inver were given a month to leave.[9] OVERLORD planners had sought to identify suitable practise areas and with beaches to the north and steep cliffs to the south the Tarbat Peninsula was ideal. Its use as a live firing range for the infantry, armoured vehicles and the naval vessels that would support them during the actual landings was kept a secret with neither those who were evacuated nor their neighbours discovering why they had been moved out of their homes. Other training and experimental areas were established such as Linney Head in South Wales where assault training took place during August and September 1943. Another site was west of Orford in Suffolk where, amongst the heathlands, replicas of German beaches and inland strongpoints were constructed. Elements of the Second British Army conducted exercises at each of these but most of the men who would attack the beaches around Caen completed the majority of their training in Scotland, about as far away from their actual target as was possible.

9   Susan Mansfield, 'The secret beach where Britain rehearsed D-Day', *The Scotsman*, 29 May 2004.

With the bulk of the OVERLORD ground forces having been assembled during October and November, throughout the winter that followed around 15,000 troops of what was termed 'Assault Force S', or 'Force S' as they were more commonly referred, with its target the Sword sector, were based around Inverness and Invergordon. New arrivals continued in the New Year bringing the specialist armoured formations to join the training. For the joint naval and army staff overseeing this hugely complex process they found themselves having to tackle "the trials and tribulations consequent on trying to make bricks without straw".[10] According to one of those involved with the training exercises in Scotland, central to their activity was the production of "…a veritable mountain of paper [as they] prepared and executed between them a series of combined exercises-cum-rehearsals which were in their way masterpieces, and certainly gave a very fair idea of what we are in for".[11] The same officer recorded that, "…the chaos on the beach itself was on each occasion quite unbelievable, but this strangely enough was an asset for on the day itself chaos reigned and our experience had taught us that it was the normal thing".[12] There were seven-mile runs which had to be completed in one hour in full gear and longer outings carrying 90 pound sacks.[13] The training exercises always used live ammunition from machine guns and mortars along with controlled but realistic explosions. Another veteran interviewed fifty years later recalled that his unit lost about 20 men during the training.[14] This period of intense preparation was, however, judged to have been a great success; it was written in one of the many post-invasion reports that, throughout the Scottish experience:

> …sailors and soldiers alike exercised in more arduous weather, and in worse conditions, than they experienced in the Channel. During last winter and spring they learned to improvise and fend for themselves, and so, somehow, to keep running as long as they remained afloat. As a result, when they reached the Far Shore, they found that life was not so very difficult after all.[15]

Every month from January to March 1944 all of the NEPTUNE assault divisions had taken part in two large-scale exercises. By the time 'Force S' readied to leave the training grounds of Scotland it had participated in a total of five exercises although only the last of them – Exercise LEAPYEAR – had been conducted at a scale allowing for close support fire on the same beach as the troops were assaulting. The reality was that, despite the quest for authenticity, limitations were imposed on the training exercises most notably relating to the tanks which had still yet to be waterproofed. This meant that their landings

10   Rear-Admiral A.G. Talbot, 'Report by the Naval Commander Force S', 22 July 1944, p.7, U.S. National Records and Archives Administration, Maryland (hereafter 'NARA').

11   Julius Neave, 'The War Diary of Julius Neave' (Winter 1942/3 to May 1945), privately published (1994), pp.21-26, http://www.lightdragoons.org.uk/downloads.html. This was an updated version of his initial post-war account published in the regimental journal; Major J.A.S. Neave, 'D-Day', *The 13th/18th Royal Hussars Journal* (Vol.VII, No.2; Spring 1946).

12   Ibid., p.26.

13   Gillian Harris, 'D-Day heroes return to Highland training base', *The Times*, 30 April 2004.

14   Bert Hardy, cited in Edward Pilkington, 'Home from hell with a cup of tea', *The Guardian*, 2 June 1994.

15   Talbot, 'Report by the Naval Commander Force S', NARA.

were 'assumed' and, at the first full-scale exercise in Burghead Bay the armour joined the infantry only after the first waves had come ashore. LEAPYEAR was therefore the first occasion where the now specially prepared and adapted tanks took part in a full dress rehearsal and, coming at the end of March, it meant there were only a few months for the men to master the entirely new techniques involved with their effective use.[16]

April and May were taken up with three final exercises and the completion of the production of the final operation orders. With these issued on 23 May four days later final briefings commenced for the commanding and senior officers who would be involved in transporting the invasion force to Normandy.[17] The division was assembled in its entirely in southern England and marshalled in Areas A and J for embarkation at their designated ports. These areas were described as embracing "an inverted U shaped stretch of Sussex country with a coastal base: Littlehampton – Cuckmere Haven and the most northerly point of the bend of the U taking in Burgess Hill".[18] Of the three main infantry formations 185th Infantry Brigade (185 Inf Bde) was in Area J for embarkation at Newhaven; 8th and 9th Infantry Brigades (8 Inf Bde/9 Inf Bde) were in A, in the vicinity of and including Portsmouth. The final exercise had been run from 24 April to 4 May and was codenamed FABIUS. During this the landing craft that the men used were the same as for the invasion proper and the crews manning them became an actual part of the team. One participant later wrote of his "hazy recollection" that "we sailed rather perilously far out towards France – with I'm sure very dense air cover. We quite certainly seemed to be 'going for it', on my LCT we weren't entirely sure that this was an exercise and wasn't the real thing. I wonder how many naval forces were in Fabius: was it all of us? Presumably it was only our Sword beach group that landed near Littlehampton?"[19]

The training period had been, for the most part, one of great activity as the men learnt about the use of landing craft and invasion tactics and familiarising themselves with their often new equipment. During this key phase many of the units involved had similar experiences and these offer an idea of just how prepared they were for what would follow on D-Day. A good example is provided by the Staffordshire Yeomanry which had arrived back in Britain from North Africa in December 1943 and moved to a camp near Ely in Cambridgeshire. With leave being given to the men who had all been overseas for an extended period it was mid-January before full training could begin. By mid-February the regiment had moved to Gordonstoun camp near Elgin in Scotland to continue their training as part of 27 Armd Bde. On 10 April 1944 the leading elements began the move southwards to a new camp at Wykehurst Park in Sussex; once arrived they participated in the FABIUS exercise and worked on the water-proofing of all the vehicles. By 26 May the camp was sealed and closely guarded and 'Operation Order No.1' for NEPTUNE had been published. Two days later the commanding officer, Temporary Lieutenant-Colonel James Eadie, briefed the entire regiment with details of the coming invasion and the

16 Paul Mace, *Forrard: The Story of the East Riding Yeomanry* (Pen and Sword; Barnsley, 2001), pp.105-112.

17 Christopher D. Young, *Gators of Neptune* (Naval Institute Press; Maryland, 2006), p.155.

18 Lieutenant-Colonel H.A. Pollock, 'Overlord: Plans and Preparations – 1940 to the "Touch Down"', CAB44/242, TNA.

19 Norman Scarfe to Eric Lummis, 9 January 1995, Lummis 6/6, LHCMA.

role that they would play.[20] For one of the infantry battalions, 1st Battalion, The South Lancashire Regiment (1 South Lancs), it was much the same with training initially at Carron Bridge in Dumfriesshire before moving to Inverary. The troops then moved to Forres, Aviemore and Grantown "for realistic landing exercises in Scotland's bitter winds, snows and heavy seas" before being transported one last time in the first week of April 1944 to Cowplain near Portsmouth. It was at this stage that the commanding officer Lieutenant-Colonel L.L. Lane was replaced by Lieutenant-Colonel Richard Burbury and two other senior officers from within the battalion were also moved.[21]

Perhaps the most interesting experience was that of 2nd Battalion, King's Shropshire Light Infantry (2 KSLI). The troops had spent the early part of the war on garrison duties in the Caribbean and returned to Britain in March 1942 travelling home via the United States and Canada. Lieutenant-Colonel Jack Maurice, who had been praised for his role with the 1st Battalion during its retreat to Dunkirk and his subsequent command of 1st Divisional Battle School, took charge that summer. The regimental histories highlighted his knowledge, charm and patience and the degree to which he "had a genius for getting the best out of his company commanders and his staff" and he was responsible for overseeing preparations for D-Day.[22] The battalion had transferred to join the 185 Inf Bde, at this stage as a lorry-borne force that was part of the newly formed 79 Armd Div. Following the decision not to send 3 Br Inf Div to Sicily, it transferred to Scotland where it also moved between seven different training areas, "a tedious and exhausting business". Again it was noted post-war that the actual landings did not match up to the discomfort and hardships experienced during the pre-invasion exercises when the weather and the use of live ammunition had highlighted the dangers in the task ahead. In February the move was made to a tented camp at Chailey in Sussex. The final camps were at Haywards Heath and these were sealed on 13 May before the troops moved on to the marshalling areas and then, on 2/3 June, embarked on their transport craft at Newhaven. Generally these were the common experiences of the training and preparations prior to the invasion of Europe.

The briefing Monty delivered at St Paul's on 7 April 1944 to an assembled audience of senior British and American officers confirmed the D-Day plan of operations. For 3 Br Inf Div its specific role had been revealed some weeks before following Exercise CROWN, held on 8-9 February after which it had been decided that a single brigade would conduct the initial landing, and a final series of revisions which were trialled during Exercise ANCHOR held later in the month. With these complete the planning staff had gathered at Aberlour House, a specially prepared venue in Scotland, where a series of briefings given to this select audience had revealed some of the details behind SAC's intention "to secure a lodgement on the Continent from which further offensive operations could be developed". For Dempsey's Second British Army, providing

20 'War Diary', Vols.48-53, D1300/4/5, part 2/4, Staffordshire Yeomanry Archives, Staffordshire Archives (hereafter 'SYA').

21 'The South Lancashire Regiment – Regimental Chronicle, 1st Battalion Notes', n.d., p.4, The Duke of Lancaster's Regiment Lancashire Infantry Museum (hereafter 'LIM').

22 *The History of the Corps of the King's Shropshire Light Infantry*, Vol.3: 1881-1968 (KSLI, 1970), p.226-231; G.L.Y. Radcliffe, *History of the 2nd Battalion, the King's Shropshire Light Infantry (85th Foot): in the campaign in N.W. Europe, 1944-1945* (Basil Blackwood; Oxford, 1947).

protection for the First United States Army which was to capture Cherbourg and the Brittany ports, it was to land on the left of the attacking Allied forces – all of the directions and references in the plans were determined on the basis of point of origin – and would consist of XXX Corps on the right of the British Commonwealth line and I Corps on the left. For this second corps, on its right would be 3rd Canadian Division landing at Juno sector and 3 Br Inf Div on the left.[23] As has already been noted, although termed as Sword, the British division's assault area was actually a series of beaches each of which had in turn been subdivided again. Even in the original COSSAC plan these had been described as being rocky in places and only suitable for landing infantry near high water; with the exception of two short stretches of sand – one of which was Queen – it was thought that they were unsuitable for landing the vehicles needed by assault divisions.[24] These same beaches were now, however, described to the divisional planning staff as 'good' with the sand "smooth and firm, except for a possible soft strip above high water" and a clear approach from the sea.[25] The briefings also confirmed that the warnings which had been registered from the beginning of the planning process still remained true. The restricted beach width meant that the initial attack would have to be restricted to a single brigade. Operating in such a confined space there was considerable risk attached, both during the potentially hazardous landing phases and as the troops sought to exit the beaches. Almost inevitably bunched together they would be impeded in terms of the amount of fighting power they could deploy and a concerted response from the defending forces could present a considerable challenge to the landings. Nonetheless the importance attached to Caen meant that these previously identified limitations had been accepted and worked around.

The staff at both the divisional and brigade level spent more than a week at Aberlour House, an isolated country property on the Spey, studying all the available air photographs of the assault area and working on their respective plans which were then to be submitted to General Rennie for his approval. Sword sector covered a total of 3,000 yards running from Lion-sur-Mer on the west to La Breche on the east.[26] Full details were given to them about the area which fixed the exact landing to two beaches, Queen White and Queen Red, each offering just 800 yards to attack. At low water these averaged 400 yards in width; in high water it was believed that this reduced to as little as 30 yards. The beaches were backed by sand dunes running in strips 10 to 20 yards wide and 10 to 15 feet high with a forward facing slope of about 45 degrees. Along either flank the ground was unsuitable for landing; to the east the mouth of the River Orne produced soft flat sandbanks which extended out at low water for about 2,000 yards seawards and were full of runnels. Peter sector to the west was backed by steep limestone cliffs rising up to 25 feet high and with only a small number of exits leading up them. At Lion-Sur-Mer there was also a masonry sea wall which was almost vertical and varied from four to ten feet in height. A positive factor was that the sector was "well provided" with exits leading to a

23 Scarfe, *Assault Division*, pp.15-16.
24 This was the eastern end of '307' and beach '306' (Ouistreham).
25 '76th Field Regiment RA Intelligence Summary', n.d. (May 1944), Norman Scarfe Papers, D8/1/2, University of Leicester Special Collections (hereafter 'ULSC').
26 'Opposition Encountered on the British Beaches in Normandy on D-Day', Army Operational Research Group, Report No.264, p.101, DEFE2/490, TNA.

20 foot lateral road about 150 to 200 yards inland. All the proposed invasion sectors had to contend with eastward drift resulting from the prevailing winds and currents; Sword was best protected as the mudflats of the Caen Canal – River Orne estuary disrupted the drift pattern.

The operation orders that were made available to all of the NEPTUNE forces in May 1944 provided additional details on topography and terrain.[27] These began by offering the positive assertion that the area being assaulted was "for the most part good going". The country was almost entirely arable with woods and orchards found in valleys and around the villages. Elsewhere the terrain was very open and bare and offered little cover. Roads were narrow by English standards with banks and ditches rather than hedges most commonly found. The contours were gentle with the highest ground rising only to about 250 feet. Directly behind the beaches there was a marshy area and this was clearly of some concern; when the 27 Armd Bde order was published on 18 May 1944 it stated that the waterlogged land had decreased appreciably and the ground had become firmer. It was also noted that these areas could, be flooded at any time and if this were the case tanks would have to make their exit following a specific route. This gap between the two inundated areas was a worrying potential choke-point, spanned by a single eight-foot wide road that was flanked on one side by a 15 foot dyke and on the other by another marsh. There was no large areas of woodland to restrict tank movement; much was the same in terms of rivers and canals, certainly north of Caen, although it was stated that these could not be crossed by the first wave of tanks because of their muddy banks. Aside from a small stretch immediately west and south-west of Ouistreham there was well-drained limestone which it was believed would make the going off the roads good. There was also reference to the intense cultivation in the countryside with intervals in the fields consisting of lines of trees and occasional hedges and large numbers of orchards. It was also highlighted that there were few obvious recognition points on what was "a featureless flat coast" but it picked out seven build-ings the profiles of which could offer some help to the approaching troops.[28] These were a mixture of churches, houses, water towers and even a lighthouse which were marked on the maps carried by each officer.

Even at this late stage a greater level of detail was still needed and a last series of beach inspections on 8 May 1944 helped complete the final intelligence summary given to the assaulting forces later in the month.[29] This task was primarily once again undertaken by Combined Operations Pilotage Parties (COPP), small teams which were deployed to conduct physical reconnaissance of the beaches and the shallows that guarded them. Formed in December 1942 and trained at Brancaster in Norfolk which was similar to the Normandy targets, each team had a Royal Navy navigation expert and an officer from the Royal Engineers. Having been transported across the Channel in small craft or submarines they made their way ashore in the darkness using small collapsible canoes. For each beach they were tasked with providing information on a range of key terrain

---

27 'Overlord 27 Armd Bde Operation Order', May 1944, WO171/623, TNA.
28 '3 Br Inf Div Briefing Intelligence Summary', n.d., Scarfe Papers, ULSC.
29 Ibid., '76th Field Regiment RA Intelligence Summary', n.d. (May 1944), D8/1/2.

factors, from the slope and the width through to measurements of the tide and currents and the actual material construction.[30]

Their work during the months prior to the invasion had also confirmed the type and number of German lines of defence across the Queen beaches. These began with two rows of ramp obstacles which had been sited about 300 yards from the back of the beach with an average distance of about 50 feet between them. Next was a double row of stakes running continuously across the beach at a distance of 30 to 60 feet between each and 30 to 70 feet between the rows. The stakes were reported as being eight to ten feet high and probably made of timber about a foot thick with the top sloping slightly towards the sea. About 180 yards from the back of the beach iron hedgehogs had been laid in straight rows about 100 to 110 yards in length with 14 to 17 of them in each. It was noted that these rows overlapped and ran continuously across the beaches with the hedgehogs being measured at five-and-a-half feet high. Although these obstacles were described as less dense than on the neighbouring beaches in the Juno sector it was assumed that more of them could be planted in the coming weeks. There was no evidence of mines attached to the stakes but it was to be assumed, correctly, that these were present. There was also the anticipation that mines would be found almost continuously along the back of the beach and amongst the houses and gardens behind. An appendix to the operational order issued for 27 Armd Bde which discussed at some length the likely German defences and how, specifically, these could impact on British tanks, also made specific reference to mines.[31] These, it was reported, could be safely assumed as being across the beach, the exits, roads leading inland and around all wire defences.

Whilst there was a growing mass of information available its distribution was tightly controlled and the regular troops were given no indication during their training of where they would be going. The brigade level instructions relating to the issue of the operation order, which was dated 21 May 1944, went into some detail about what today would be termed as OPSEC or 'Operational Security'. Those within 9 Inf Bde who viewed the document, there only being 28 copies of this made available, did so in the Brigade 'Overlord' Room and there was clear instruction that, whilst extracts could be copied there needed to be a clear operational purpose. Even then only portions that were indispensable were to be carried on board ships or aircraft and whilst these could be taken ashore they were not to include details of any tasks or intentions for other units. At the same time whilst maps could be marked to show relevant details this was to be done with pencil on trace paper so that it could be quickly erased. It was stressed that no complete copies of these orders were to be carried and the top of each page was stamped with this warning.[32]

This last point was significant for an operation of such complexity as the maps inevitably were a critical element. Once Normandy had been confirmed as the target the mapping project alone was unlike anything previously undertaken. Starting with the aerial survey programme – codenamed BENSON after the Oxfordshire airfield from where the

---

30 'Combined Operations Assault Pilotage Parties – COPP', http://www.combinedops.com/COPPs. htm.

31 Ibid., 'Overlord 27 Armd Bde Operation Order', May 1944, WO171/623.

32 '9 Br Inf Bde – Operation Order No.1, Operation Overlord', 21 May 1944, WO171/616, TNA. A further eight copies were printed to be retained as permanent records.

reconnaissance aircraft flew – and involving all of the Royal Engineer survey units in the UK and the staff of the Ordnance Survey along with Canadian and American survey units who arrived later, this produced 170 million maps. These ranged from 1:12,500 for the immediate invasion area though to 1:250,000 series covering north-western Europe. Working from a central Map Depot in Hanwell these maps were distributed around the units but not opened until the assault waves had moved into their pre-invasion concentration areas and were sealed off from the outside world.[33] For briefing purposes, indeed until only a few hours before the invasion began, special 'Bogus' maps were used on which the grid lines were re-numbered and all of the key towns and villages were shown but with entirely fictitious names. Hence Luc-sur-Mer became 'Vienna'; Hermanville was 'Mexico'; Colleville was 'Brazil'; Ouistreham was 'Oslo'; and the key target of Caen was 'Poland'.

Contained within one of the divisional intelligence briefings was a detailed description of 'Poland'. With its wide main cobbled streets and numerous bridges this warned that, "in that part of the town between the castle and the river buildings are high and compact. Here the preliminary bombing will probably create a shambles of burning houses and debris-littered streets".[34] The pre-war population was recorded as having been 54,000 but was believed by May 1944 to have been reduced to about 35,000: the hope was that the vast majority of these would leave once the invasion began but, even then, as many as 7,000 civilians could still remain. This assessment also contained within it an especially interesting insight into the attitude of the "mass of the population in the whole of France" which, it was claimed, "hates the Germans, and will greet our landings with great enthusiasm and will do their best to impede the enemy in this area". Yet at the same time it was also noted that there were only small numbers of organised resistance groups and that "once the initial excitement caused by a landing has died down, all Frenchmen must not be expected to be as friendly to the allies, or to one another, but they are hostile to the Germans". A German intelligence summary by way of comparison reported three weeks prior to the invasion that "the majority of the population expects invasion – in a depressed state of mind. National Socialist propaganda has no effect; the rest are expectant and guided by self-interest".[35] Just a week before the population was "in a state of expectant tension and reserved as before" but there was also "considerable feeling against the Anglo-Americans … amongst the section of the population affected by air raids".

Even with the security precautions and false details every possible effort was still made to ensure that thorough briefings were provided to the British troops. In light of the task facing 3 Br Inf Div, "the principle had been laid down that, despite the risk from the point of view of security, the fullest possible information was to be passed on to the men who had to do the fighting. It can safely be said that no army had ever before had such a wealth of information made available to help it to fight".[36] In many cases these were

---

33 Alan Gordon, 'Mapping and Charting for the Greatest Collaborative Project Ever', *The American Surveyor* (June 2005).

34 '3 Br Inf Div Briefing Intelligence Summary', n.d., pp.3, 18, Scarfe Papers, ULSC.

35 'Situation Reports by German Army Commanders in Normandy: Weekly Report, May 21-27, 1944', LH15/15/31, LHCMA; ibid, 'Weekly Report, May 28 – June 3, 1944'.

36 'History of the 2nd Battalion the Royal Ulster Rifles in NW Europe 1944-1945' (The Regiment, n.d.), Chapter 1.

carried out in special marquees which, aside from the bogus versions, contained "map enlargements scaled one foot to a mile, models, stereoscopic photos of the whole area and enlargement of all places of particular interest to us like Caen [presumably with its bogus name], the beaches, assembly and concentration areas and anti-tank ditches". An entire day was given over to the Commanding Officer's Orders and briefing all officers including those within the supporting arms. The following day these same marquees were then allotted on a Company and Platoon basis, and briefing continued for the next three days under the supervision of the Intelligence Officer and the Intelligence Section. By this point everybody involved had reviewed the information and, whilst they might not have known where they were going, how they would get there and what they would be doing had been fully explained. In the case of 2 KSLI it was not until the first two weeks of May that the commanding officer, his second-in-command, adjutant and intelligence officer were allowed to know the whole of the divisional plan and to study the real maps. All that was still lacking at this late stage was the actual date of the attack although this was apparently not difficult for them to guess.[37]

Special attention during these briefings was paid to sites that were considered as presenting the greatest potential danger. The appendix to the operational order issued to 27 Armd Bde had drawn attention to four locations across the Sword sector which it was believed would present the greatest challenge for the armoured forces.[38] One of these was opposite a beach exit and the other three surrounded specific strongpoints. In addition there was reference to anti-tank ditches which covered the principal roads leading into Caen from the north and north-west although the report also stated "there is, in fact, very little evidence that the enemy intends to use this … as the basis for the defence of [the city]". For the infantry there were a number of strongpoints which would need to be tackled and neutralised. Using aerial photographs and large-scale models two of these, referred to as MORRIS and HILLMAN, were closely studied by all of those who had a role to play in their capture. Intelligence reports indicated that the first of them, nearer to the beach, held four 10.5cm coastal defence guns with supporting entrenchments, deep concrete shelters and even a small quarry containing ammunition. A further half mile inland was HILLMAN which covered an area of approximately 600 yards by 400 yards and consisted of pillboxes, deep concrete shelters, three cupolas and a complete system of interconnecting trenches which were about seven feet deep. This second strong defensive position was believed to contain two guns, several machine guns for both anti-aircraft and ground roles and a garrison of approximately one platoon. Around the site were two belts of barbed wire with anti-tank and anti-personnel mines sown between them. The position was reported to be battalion headquarters for the German forces holding this area of coast and it was believed to be in touch by telephone with MORRIS and other positions elsewhere. Subsequently it was discovered that there were even underground transport bays, concrete corridors leading to mess rooms, sleeping accommodation and one of the cupolas housed a heavy calibre gun. This particular weapon was reached by an underground passage that ran about 50 yards from the main complex. The cupola had a narrow slit and the gun, mounted on a fixture, could be rotated in any direction with ease. This field of fire

---

37 Radcliffe, *History of the 2nd Battalion, the King's Shropshire Light Infantry.*
38 'Overlord 27 Armd Bde Operation Order', May 1944, WO171/623, TNA.

covered all approaches to the site and it was sufficiently strong to withstand all forms of British firepower including 17 inch armoured piercing rounds which bounced off during the actual attack. This was an especially daunting obstacle and the assault that took place on it on the afternoon of D-Day would prove critical.

It was a 17-hour crossing from the English coast to the Normandy beaches. The assault craft had begun to move out of harbour about midday on 5 June at which point the 'Go' signal was given and the sealed packages of genuine maps were opened and targets and enemy defences examined in full detail for the first time. In one battalion each officer had fourteen maps and two folders of aerial photographs which showed a wave-top view of the coast, the assembly area, the immediate area of the beachhead, and, finally, the approach to and the town of Caen.[39] The photos were pasted onto a sheet of thin card-board which could be carried in officer's battledress pockets. The second-in-command for W Company 2 KSLI later wrote that "there was sadly little time to get the details of 'our' area imprinted on our minds – and an unfamiliar map in a poor light at dead of night, on tossing craft, looked widely different from a sand table model seen once in a Nissen hut in peaceful Sussex surroundings".[40] These final briefings were made especially difficult by the level of seasickness experienced by some of the men for their final move; in one of the Royal Engineer assault squadrons the orders group had to be cancelled as the men passed a bucket round.[41] Fortunately, for the majority of the troops, what additional details there were did not appear too different from the scenarios in LEAPYEAR and FABIUS. Going into battle the men were confident.[42] Some who had travelled in France pre-war guessed where they were heading but only the French commandos who would take part in the landings on Sword, some of whom came from Normandy, could do so with any certainty. One of the histories of an armoured Regiment involved records that the first impression was one of "unfamiliarity": "Caen, Bayeux, Falaise – the names had undertones of schoolroom lessons half forgotten, of invasions to and from the Normandy coast that once had occupied a sheet or two of paper in barely remembered examination halls".[43] Now there would be one more.

---

39 'History – 2nd Battalion the Royal Ulster Rifles…'.

40 Major R.R. Rylands, '"W" Coy, 2nd Bn. K.S.L.I. in Normandy', KSLI Regimental Journal, http://warchronicle.com/ksli/soldierstories_wwii/wcoynormandy.htm.

41 Lieutenant I.C. Dickinson, 'Obstacle Clearance with 3 Tp 77 Assault Squadron on Queen Sector White Beach', Brigadier E.E.E. Cass Papers, Documents 1471, IWM.

42 '33 Field Regiment Royal Artillery – 6 June 1944 to 8 May 1945', June 1945, p.2, Scarfe Papers, ULSC.

43 Raymond Birt, *XXII Dragoons 1760-1945, The Story of a Regiment* (Gale and Polden Limited; Aldershot, 1950), p.155.

3

Defending Normandy

On 13 May 1944 an order of the day from the *Führer* was issued to the soldiers of all services and those of the *Waffen-SS* serving in Western Europe. Instructions were given that this document was to be stored and its contents kept secret only to be issued once the invasion had started. Even then once read it was to be destroyed and not published in newspapers or read over the wireless. It was a momentous order:

> In this historic hour I appeal to your courage, to your proven bravery and to the steadfastness of your hearts. Your task is to forbid the enemy entry into Europe whatever the circumstances ... Here there can be no withdrawal and no manoeuvring; here you must stand fast, hold or die ... Wherever the enemy attacks, he must be annihilated. He will not succeed in gaining a firm foothold on the coast which we defend. Victory will thus be ours! You are summoned to fight and win, and thus to fulfil the legacy of our fallen comrades.[1]

Despite considerable efforts to prepare, both in terms of constructing fortifications and training, the Allies were coming. For the German troops in Normandy the greatest test of the entire war was upon them.

Attempts to defend the coastline of the occupied European countries began in 1940 almost as soon as the fighting in France had stopped.[2] Following the French surrender almost immediately 30 guns had been installed in the Pas-de-Calais to shell Dover along with a few coast defence batteries, mostly covering smaller ports. It was not until December 1941 that Hitler issued orders confirming the entire Atlantic coastline was to be fortified. Within a matter of months a large number of light and medium gun batteries had been installed and all vulnerable areas were protected by minor defences. British raiding operations that same year, which included not just the failed assault on Dieppe but also the more successful attack at St Nazaire, had added to concerns about the potential for the opening up of a 'second front' in Western Europe. The Commander-in-Chief West, Field Marshal Gerd von Rundstedt, had been tasked in March 1942 with strengthening coastal defences and establishing what was termed as the 'Atlantic Wall'. When completed this was intended to run from the far north of Norway to the Franco-Spanish border, 2600 km of coastline but much more if all of the bays and inlets were included.

---

1 EDS/Wheatley, 'Hitler's Order of the Day, 13 May 1944', 6 September 1957, CAB146/336, TNA.
2 Alan F. Wilt, *The Atlantic Wall 1941-1944 – Hitler's Defenses for D-Day* (Enigma Books; New York, 2004), pp.107-126; Patrick Delaforce, *Smashing the Atlantic Wall – The Destruction of Hitler's Coastal Fortress* (Pen and Sword; Barnsley, 2005), pp.17-43; 'The "Atlantic Wall" – An Historical Summary', MI14h, 14 July 1945, CAB146/329, TNA.

Increasingly, as German manpower was drained to fight in the east leaving France and the Low Countries as more of a training ground, the perceived threat of invasion grew. Hitler's Directive No.51, which he issued on 3 November 1943, specified that this could be expected at any time from the middle of the following February onwards and highlighted his determination that the threat should be met. Field Marshal Erwin Rommel and the staff of Army Group B were sent to France, initially to assess the defensive readiness of the coastal areas. Following an extensive tour to inspect progress, on 15 January 1944 Rommel was given command of the area covered by Seventh and Fifteenth Armies running along the coast from the Netherlands down into Brittany; this appointment also provided some level of influence over the use of armoured reserves. This re-organisation was intended to galvanise the defensive preparations in the region that was believed to be the most threatened and this was exactly what happened. Already existing defences were improved and a system of secondary positions was introduced 15 to 25 miles inland from the coast. Most significantly, Rommel focused on the fortifications that had been placed on or near the beaches and made their strengthening a priority. This would lead to the establishment of the *Perlenschnur*, a string of fortified defensive positions spread along the entire coast which were designed to be mutually supportive of one another and produce an overwhelming amount of firepower. The basic element was the *Widerstandsnester*, or 'Resistance Nests' (WN), which were formed into *Stuetzpunkt*, several WN acting as strong points, and the more complex *Stuetzpunktgruppe*. In addition to these there were 'Defended Areas' and, finally, the harbour 'Fortresses'.

Rommel inspects the Atlantic Wall

The German defensive plan was based entirely on the Atlantic Wall absorbing the initial shock and containing any assault on or near the beachhead for a sufficient period of time to enable armoured reserves to move up and push the invaders back into the sea before they could establish anti-tank defences. This strategy, in many ways, led to a battle based around the production of cement. From January to April 1944 the number of cubic metres of concrete laid doubled from 357,000 to 722,100 per month; about 8,500 fortifications had been largely completed by the beginning of 1944, but by the day of the invasion an additional 12,247 had been built along the northern French coast.[3] In addition to machine gun nests and gun posts there were added beach obstacles, minefields, both real and dummy, barbed wire and anti-tank ditches. Aside from the approximately 160,000 volunteers and the pressed labour force employed by *Organization Todt*, which had been working on the construction of the Atlantic Wall for some years, local commanders also reduced the number of hours their troops spent in training and had them assist with the effort. As the programme expanded artillery positions were moved to make them less susceptible to Allied air and ship bombardment whilst dummy positions were constructed to deceive reconnaissance efforts.

Lord Lovat later provided a detailed description of the kind of fortifications he and his fellow commandos had encountered upon landing in the middle of Queen Red:

> They were not, as it were, a continuous row of grouse butts, but rather a system of ingeniously interlocked defence works equipped with every weapon, from underwater obstacles and devices to set the sea on fire to wire and minefields at the water's edge, ranging back through strong points laced with machine guns and anti-tank guns to distant artillery and self-propelled half-track cannon – all bearing on the beach. Beyond lay German infantry dug into weapon pits – again with interlocking fields of fire.[4]

Information before the attack indicated that in terms of obstacles across the Sword sector there were 522 Hedgehogs, 267 Stakes, 76 Timber Ramps and 46 Element 'C' making a total of 0.3 obstacles for each yard of the beach. In a detailed post-battle analysis that was produced by the British Army it was calculated that these 911 obstacles had required approximately 245 tons of steel, 124 tons of wood and an unknown amount of concrete for their construction. As the COPP reports had suspected, most were armed with an explosive charge, either tellermines or captured French or British anti-aircraft shells. In terms of the other British and Canadian beaches this figure was considerably lower than the totals encountered almost entirely as a result of the much reduced beach frontage that existed at Sword along which the defenders could make preparations.[5] Nonetheless for each yard of the two beaches it was estimated that there was one pound of explosives.

In this sector the Germans also fortified the houses all along the front and established two major strongpoints which were given the codenames on the bogus maps of TROUT and COD; of these the latter, which was at the junction of the two assault beaches and

---

3 Boog et al, *Germany and the Second World War – Volume VII*, p.512.
4 Lord Lovat, *March Past – A Memoir by Lord Lovat* (Weidenfeld and Nicolson; London, 1979), p.314.
5 'Opposition Encountered…', pp.120-122, DEFE2/490, TNA.

covered about 500 yards of frontage, would have to be attacked immediately. Once again, Lovat later provided some sense of what these were like:

> Each pill-box was a citadel of reinforced concrete, sunk hull-down and half-buried in the ridges of the dunes. Walls two feet thick stood six feet above ground level, their height made up by a very solid roof giving further feet of concrete head cover. They were certainly bomb – if not blast – proof, and made equivalent precautions at home appear inadequate. Positions cited in depth, 100 to 150 yards apart, were surrounded with barbed wire, with minefields in between. No pill-box based directly to the front, but each … sited to enfilade the wire and deal effectively with approach from the flanks. Each was manned by a crew of half a dozen men firing 75 mm cannon and light automatics. In support to the rear were heavy machine guns set in less solid foundations equipped with revolving turrets.[6]

The subsequent analysis concluded that the two Queen beaches had seven guns protecting them – of which three were 75 mm – and the same number of mortars in addition to which there were 14 or 15 machine guns; the majority of these were in the strongpoints. Of these approximately 28 major weapons just over a quarter of them were knocked out by bombardment during the assault and initial follow-up stage. The amount of weapons facing the attackers at Sword was in fact greater than for any other British or Canadian beach.[7]

A key element of the defensive plans was the apparently impressive size of the German garrison. Allied intelligence reports at the end of May 1944 noted that there were 58 divisions stationed in France and extending into the most threatened areas of the Low Countries. Ten were armoured formations and one estimate suggested a maximum total strength of 1,900,000 troops and 1400 tanks which increased to 1860 armoured vehicles of all types. Amongst this huge force some 37 divisions were reported as being deployed directly along the coast.[8] There was, however, considerable disparity in the figures, and the earlier figure was certainly the maximum number of troops; another source reported on 1 July the army strength as being 892,000 men, a significant difference even allowing for casualties by this stage. At the same time just two days before the invasion Rundstedt's staff reported that out of 11 motorised divisions, six of them had considerable shortages of equipment and personnel and none had even 100 tanks. On the planned invasion day it was calculated that there would be 187 German divisions in the Soviet Union, 12 in Norway, four in Denmark, 26 in Italy and 21 in the Balkans: none of these could be moved towards the assault area at short notice.[9] A much greater cause for concern was the degree to which the German land forces would have little in the way of support from the air. At the end of May *Luftlotte 3* had barely 900 aircraft which, from their bases mainly

---

6 Lovat, *March Past*, pp.314, 316.
7 'Opposition Encountered…', pp.133, 136, DEFE2/490, TNA.
8 On 1 June 1944 there were 156 divisions in the east, 12 in Norway, 27 in and 25 in the Balkans; Boog, *Germany and the Second World War*, p.522.
9 Ibid., pp.568-569.

With the tide out the height of the defences can be clearly seen

in north-eastern France and Belgium, were expected both to prevent Allied bombers from reaching Germany and support the defensive plans.[10]

Despite the apparent improvements a fundamental issue weakened the chances of mounting a successful defence. This was the differing strategic approaches adopted by the two principal German commanders about how this should be conducted.[11] Von Rundstedt recognised that the data being provided on troop numbers were actually misleading with large concentrations of troops in some areas and hardly any in others. He therefore considered it essential that there should be numerous mobile forces made available, especially armoured divisions, which would be used to defend the coast. This was the last line of defence: at the beachhead, if the enemy had not been defeated at sea, it was to be counter-attacked by local reserves, after which corps and army reserves would have to be called upon before finally, if the attack still continued, the large armoured divisions directly under his command would be deployed. Or as one assessment has put it, his was a strategy which called for "using an offensive defensive by operating behind the coast strong armoured divisions, strictly controlled and flexibly led".[12] At the same time Rustedt remained convinced that the most likely area for an invasion was the Pas-de-Calais. He had reached this conclusion because it was the shortest sea route from Dover, the launch sites for the new German rocket weapons which would target London and the south-east of England were in this area and, finally, it was the shortest route to

---

10 Ibid., pp.528-529.

11 Dieter Ose, 'Rommel and Rundstedt: The 1944 Panzer Controversy', *Military Affairs* (Vol.50, No.1; January 1985), pp.7-11.

12 Ibid., p.9.

the Ruhr, the industrial heart of the Reich which the Allies would need to capture if they were to win the war.[13]

Rommel held a very different view, believing that the only possibility of defeating an invasion was to annihilate the enemy at the point of its greatest weakness when the Allied troops tried to come ashore. As part of the series of reviews that had been conducted in December 1943, and based upon an analysis of the successful amphibious operations the Allies had conducted in Italy, it was concluded that any attack would begin with heavy bombing, followed by landings along a broad front with cover provided by accompanying warships. Tanks would be used early on with a focus on attacking and seizing control of major ports.[14] This convinced him that infantry and artillery had to be placed directly on the coast with the armoured divisions in reserve but as close as possible to where they could take part immediately in the defensive battle. He also recognised that Allied air superiority would dramatically reduce his ability to move his forces forward once the battle had begun hence his desire that none of them should be more than three hours away. In a letter he wrote on 22 April 1944, following further inspection of the coastal defences, he offered the assessment that:

> … the enemy most likely will try to land at night and by fog after a tremendous shelling by artillery and bombers. They will employ hundreds of boats and ships unloading amphibious vehicles, waterproofed and submergible tanks. We must stop them in the water, not only delaying him but destroying all enemy equipment while still afloat. Some units do not seem to realise the value of this type of defence.[15]

This was the enduring theme of this long letter, one that was both positive in recognising the work that had been done but also openly critical about the deficiencies that still existed particularly in regard to the failure to have active minefields planted along all of the beach areas.

There were also great differences of opinion within the German intelligence community which were exacerbated by the increasing bitterness of the political dispute then raging within the military forces which would soon lead to an attempt on Hitler's life. In terms of the situation in Normandy these tensions undermined the defender's fighting cohesion. At the end of December 1943 an assessment provided wildly over-inflated figures for the number of divisions in Britain, indeed far greater than was ever available even during the invasion period, helping skew calculations about how the defence would be mounted.[16] In large part this was the reward for the Allies for all of the time and resources that had been spent on the FORTITUDE deception strategy. By May of the following year the total number of troops waiting in Britain was reported to have risen to around 80 divisions, or over two million men, the

---

13 'Special Interrogation Report – Field Marshal von Rundstedt', (H.S.) 981.023 (D6), cited in Canadian Historical Section (G.S.), 'Canadian Participation in the Operations in North-West Europe, 1944', Field Report No.54, (Directorate of History; Ottawa, 1986).

14 Boog, *Germany and the Second World War*, p.500.

15 General Rommel to Unknown, 22 April 1944, CAB146/329, TNA.

16 Boog, *Germany and the Second World War*, pp.498-499.

overwhelming majority of which were stationed south of a line running from London to Liverpool.[17]

Whilst German naval and air analysts openly wondered why the enemy would attack in areas in which they knew defence forces were concentrated and the greatest efforts had been spent on building fortifications, the senior military leadership had little doubt that the invasion would be in the area covered by the Fifteenth Army. Officers in the Naval Group West Command questioned twice, in late April and early May 1944, whether the information available, specifically that the bulk of the Allied fleet was concentrated around and to the west of the Isle of Wight, in fact suggested that the landing area would be further west than was believed. Fortunately the assessment that this might be somewhere between the Somme estuary and the Cotentin Peninsula, and a later similar assessment by intelligence officers in *Luftlotte 3*, were both ignored.[18] The degree to which the German Navy had little influence over the senior planners was indeed fortunate; the same naval analysts reviewing tide tables and the limited intelligence available to them had pointed to an invasion taking place at dawn, two hours after the lowest water level. This would mean that if the landings were not attempted in May – and there was a general consensus that this was too soon – the next period when conditions would be similar to those in the Allied trails which had been monitored was 5-7 June.[19] The time and the location of D-Day had been correctly identified and ignored.

As part of the failures associated with the German assessment of Allied intentions the potential significance of Caen was also overlooked by many of those involved. According to one senior officer, Lieutenant General Rudolf Schmetzer, who was the Inspector of Fortifications from 1940 to February 1944 for the area which included the sector of coast including the Orne estuary, there was never any sense that this could be a target due to its perceived general lack of suitability for large-scale landings:

> … and the disadvantage that the invading forces would first have to fight their way across the entire country of France to reach the German border, where they could begin the decisive thrust into Germany. For such an operation, the Channel coast further north (south of Boulogne as far as the mouth of the Somme river and the flat and extensive Flemish coast beyond the Scheldt river) was much more favourable besides being suitable for large-scale landings. Therefore they were considered as more immediately endangered. [20]

As a result the area that the Allies had, to a large degree, gambled on as their principle target was "the least developed of all the sectors along the Channel coast".

On D-Day the defence of the coastal area which included the Sword beaches was the responsibility of 716th Infantry Division (716 Inf Div) and it would be these men who would have to deal directly with the results of the failures that had taken place amongst

---

17 Ibid., p.502.

18 Ibid., p.505.

19 Ibid., p.507.

20 Cited in Historical Section (G.S.) Army Headquarters Ottawa, 'The German Defences in the Courseulles-St. Aubin Area of the Normandy Coast – Information from German Sources', Report No.41, pp.5-6, CAB146/482, TNA.

those planning for the Allied invasion. It was a static, garrison formation, one of the many that had been created during the war and, eventually, designated as *Bodenständige*, with little access to the best equipment or recruits. Established in May 1941, after almost a year of moving around France by the following March it was based in the Caen-Carentan area of Normandy where it had responsibility for a 90 kilometre front split into four sectors with the 'Orne' the most easterly. With a listed strength in August 1942 of approximately 6,000 all ranks and 1,600 horses, from the late summer onwards it had continued work on strengthening the Atlantic Wall. Of the sectors for which it had responsibility only the Orne was graded as being a priority and in September some 40 specific installations were identified in this category, 28 for the division, two for the Navy and the remaining ten for the Air Force. Despite this apparent prioritisation the division's first commander, Lieutenant General Matterstock, had issued a comprehensive directive in December 1942 relating to defence preparations in which he concluded that, "major landings in the sector are improbable" and this assessment appears to have remained fundamentally unchanged until shortly before the Allied invasion.[21] The division's basic task, as listed in this directive, was "prevention of any enemy landing, and in the event of a successful landing, complete destruction of the enemy force".[22] Despite this much of the following year was spent still focussing on defensive works as opposed to conducting training; it was recorded in June 1943 that 13,400 mines had been laid across its four sectors but of these about half had been rendered ineffective by the corrosion of the detonators.[23] Perhaps the key development during this period was the appointment of a new commander on 1 April 1943, only the second since the division's establishment, who established a tactical headquarters in a former stone quarry at La Folie, three kilometres north of Caen. Major General (later Lieutenant General) Wilhelm Richter was a 45 year old professional soldier with an artillery background and took charge of a division which, by the year's end, had grown in strength to 9343 all ranks. Included within this were five artillery batteries, designated as 1716th Artillery Regiment (1716 Arty Regt), and a single anti-tank company.

As the invasion drew closer there was further anxiety about the security of Normandy as Rommel continued with his drive to strengthen the area's coastal defences. The ability of the Allies to land their invasion force remained a key concern for the German planners: eventually, between January and March 1944, fourteen ports, most of which had been termed 'Defended Areas' nearly two years before, were now declared by Hitler as 'Fortresses'. For 716 Inf Div, now part of 84th Corps (84 Corps), the coastline for which it was responsible was reduced by two-thirds with a focus on the 'Caen Sector' running from Asnelles in the west to east of the Orne river. At the extreme right of the corps area, this was once again split into four subgroups and of these the Orne still remained a priority. This should have meant more numerous and better equipped defences but by 6 June it was a mixed position in terms of what had been completed. Good progress had been made on planting strips of anti-personnel and anti-tank mines behind the beaches and around strong points and battery positions in the rear of the likely battle zone. There were, however, few mines in the offshore waters, partly as a result of lack of time

---

21 Ibid., p.5.
22 Ibid., p.6.
23 Ibid., p.10.

The beaches of the Orne estuary show their defences

and heavy seas but also because the German Navy did not expect there to be any major landing in this sector. There had also been only partial work undertaken on placing anti-airlanding posts to destroy Allied gliders. Richter, in a post-war interview, concluded that "the fortifications were in no way sufficient to repel the attack of a modern army ... Two years (1942 and 1943) had been lost during which nothing or just simple field positions had been constructed...".[24] He also worried about the lack of aerial reconnaissance and support, and the overstretched area he had to cover. Added to this tensions existed between the Navy and the Army about how the coastal batteries were to be best employed leading to an artillery plan lacking in sufficient agreement or detail.[25]

Five weeks before the Allied invasion Richter had an available strength of 7771 all ranks with the division being listed as virtually at its fully authorised strength although the reality was very different. There were two infantry Grenadier Regiments, 726th Grenadier Regiment (726 Gren) and 736th Grenadier Regiment (736 Gren), each of which comprised three battalions. Between them in total the two regiments had a listed strength of 96 machine guns, eleven five cm mortars and thirteen of the larger eight cm mortars. There was also an *Ost-Bataillon* mostly comprising Poles and described in a post-war German account as "not yet fully trained for major fighting, and with their reliability not proven in the West".[26] Another source, a captured German NCO,

24 Ibid., pp.15-16.
25 Samuel W. Mitcham, 'Richter, Wilhelm' in David G. Chandler and James Lawton Collins Jr (eds.), *The D-Day Encyclopaedia* (New York; Helicon, 1994), p.458.
26 Lieutenant General Schimpf, 'Coast Defence Sector Caen 6 June 1944 – State of Defences', cited in 'The German Defences in the Courseulles-St. Aubin Area of the Normandy Coast'; 726th Grenadier Regiment (*Ost-Bataillon* 439 assigned as *IV. Bataillon*); 736th Grenadier Regiment (*Ost-Bataillon* 642 assigned as *IV. Bataillon*).

later indicated that this form of manpower was actually much more prevalent across the division with as many as 20 percent Poles in each company of the first battalion.[27] In addition to 1716 Arty Regt, which was equipped with French and Russian guns, there were now two anti-tank companies and various anti-aircraft batteries although there were no tanks. Defending the Sword beaches and the most heavily exposed to the Allied assault was 736 Gren with its first battalion, its headquarters at Colleville and based around Hermanville, and third battalion, headquarters at Cresserons and based around Plumetot although one company had been detached and was at Merville; the 10th Company under Captain Heinrich Kuhtz would endure a particularly torrid experience defending the beaches.

For the Allies their intelligence services continued to provide assessments on the German military position through the weeks prior to the invasion adding new details of the likely dispositions right up to the last moment. It was revealed, for example, that a number of additional defence works had appeared in the Sword sector with mobile 88 mm guns being reported as having moved up to the south of Hermanville. On the evening of 5 June the Brigade Major for the Suffolks had informed the men that an extra division had been added to the enemy defences. There was, however, one question that remained largely unanswered and this would have significant consequences. The divisional intelligence summary produced for 3 Br Inf Div on 14 May noted that 21st Panzer Division (21 Pz Div) "may now be stationed in an area 10-30 miles south of Caen and could therefore intervene against us on D-Day".[28] Directly prior to the landings it was believed to be stationed to the south-east of the city with the evidence of recent manoeuvres, tank tracks visible in aerial photographs, suggesting that its primary task would be Caen's defence. As Brigadier Copper Cass, commanding the British assault brigade, later wrote, "[we thought] it might be distracted by the airborne landings but it seemed certain that early on D-Day its main force would head straight for the rising ground between Caen and the beaches".[29]

In fact, and largely unknown to the Allied commanders, by May other than its armour, 21 Pz Div was already firmly established in and around the city. It comprised 22nd Panzer Regiment (22 Pz Regt), 200th Assault Guns Battalion and the 125th and 192nd Panzer Grenadiers (125/192 Pz Gren). On Rommel's orders its flak battalion was in the centre, one of the motorised infantry battalions was on the western outskirts, another was covering the eastern approaches, while a third along with twenty-four 88 mm guns of the anti-tank battalion had been moved up on to the ridge at Périers-sur-le-Dan. The two Panzer battalions, one with Mark IVs and one with French tanks, supported by 40 assault guns, by D-Day were able to deploy a maximum of 127 tanks and none of the guns.[30] Its exact composition was unknown to the Allies although the best estimate – that it might have as many as 160 tanks and 40 assault guns – was, fortunately, well off the mark. This potentially critical armoured division was commanded by General Edgar Feuchtinger who had fought during the 1940 campaign, commanding an

---

27 'Opposition Encountered…', p.157, DEFE2/490, TNA.

28 There is some debate as to whether this was in fact the last explicit reference made to this unit; Scarfe to Lummis, 19 April 1989, Lummis 6/6, LHCMA.

29 Cass to Miss Isaacs, 8 September 1958, Brigadier Cass Papers (87/28/1), IWM.

30 Hinsley (ed.), *British Intelligence in the Second World War*, pp.839-842.

artillery regiment, and on the Eastern Front where he had been wounded; in July 1943 he had been given command of the division and promoted shortly afterwards to brigadier general.[31] According to one assessment he was "the poorest divisional commander in France" who owed his position entirely to his Nazi party connections.[32] Definite orders had been given that in the event of an invasion he was not to make any move until told to do so by Army Group B but there was considerable confusion in terms of the chain of command. He also later noted that the area he was effectively covering was approximately 300 square miles. This unit had dual tactical roles of both supporting 716 Inf Div and acting as a more general reserve force. On 2 June 1944 his armour had moved from their concentration areas near Falaise and Vimont to the high ground on the Périers-sur-le-Dan ridge and from here they laid down fire onto the beaches in front of them watched by a senior general staff audience. According to the general, in a postwar interrogation, these exercises lasted for 24 hours at which point the tanks returned to their rear areas having left huge numbers of tracks in and around the Sword sector; it was these which had caused considerable anxiety for the Allied intelligence analysts.

Whether Feuchtinger was capable or not his troops and armour represented a potential significant German force only three miles inland from the beaches, sitting directly astride the axis to be followed by 3 Br Inf Div and about which they knew little. None of this, however, was known prior to the invasion beginning, a critical omission which was described in the final pre-D-Day report as among "the chief gaps in our knowledge of the enemy in the 'Neptune' area"; hence the May assessment that the invading force should anticipate meeting armoured elements "in the forenoon of D-Day and be joined by the whole Panzer Division by last light".[33] Indeed there were no further intercepts or information from air reconnaissance until late on the evening of 5 June by which point the airborne forces were already on their way.

For the defending forces, however, the lack of agreement about how the Allied invasion would develop, up until the final hours and beyond, effectively negated whatever slim advantage was gained by the Allied failure to track 21 Pz Div. According to reports from the German Admiralty, in mid-April Hitler feared attacks on central and southern Norway. By the beginning of May a "reliable agent" was warning of a raid on the Côte d'Azur followed by a main operation in Perpignan. Throughout that same month there were numerous references to an imminent attack on northern France but there was also still some obvious doubts about the Allied strategy; it was even suggested on 4 June that there would be an imminent American attack, including airborne troops, against Heligoland.[34] The German naval commander responsible for the area, Admiral Theodor Krancke, Commander Naval Group West, had written in late May that he thought the Allied activity was "a well calculated mixture of bluff and preparations for invasion at a

31 'Special Interrogation Report – Genlt Edgar Feuchtinger, Comd 21 Pz Div', Wilmott Papers, LH15/15/146/1, LHCMA.
32 Samuel W. Mitcham Jr., *Retreat to the Reich: The German Defeat in France, 1944* (Stackpole Books; United States, 2007), p.80.
33 '21st Army Group Intelligence Summary', 4 June 1944, WO171/129, TNA; ibid., JIC(44)215(0), 25 May 1944, CAB121/394.
34 Ibid., 'EDS Comments on Admiralty List', January 1956, CAB146/336.

later date".[35] Much the same view was evident in the last weekly situation report issued before D-Day by the German Army Command in the West (O.B. West); released on 5 June this concluded that despite the continuing evidence of the Allied build up "as yet there is no immediate prospect of the 'invasion'".[36]

In the days immediately prior to the attack only one senior official, a Gestapo officer in Paris, showed any real sense of urgency about the threat but his efforts to convince those above him that invasion was imminent were dismissed as "fantastic".[37] FORTITUDE had worked. When Fifteenth Army issued the first invasion alert at 2300 on 5 June, Naval Group West recorded in its war diary that the invasion would hardly be announced beforehand in signals to the resistance forces, that nothing had happened after similar signals, and that the chief intelligence officer of O.B. West "appreciated the situation in the sense that invasion at this time was not particularly probable".[38] Not everybody had been taken in, Richter held a conference at 1700 on 5 June for his commanding officers at which he reportedly said, "Gentlemen, it may start at any moment, they will come by the 10th at the latest".[39] Within a matter of hours his assessment was proved to be entirely correct.

35 Ibid., 'Marinegruppenkommando West, Review of the Developments in May', p.3, Appx to W.D. 16-31 May 1944, O.N.I., cited in 'The Campaign in North-West Europe – Information from German Sources: Part I, German Defence Preparations in the West', Report No.40, n.d., pp.42-43, CAB146/481.

36 Ibid., 'The Campaign in North-West Europe', pp.41-42.

37 Ibid., p.43.

38 Ibid., 'O.N.I. Naval Group West, W.D., 1-7, June 1944', p.6228, night 5/6 June 1944, cited, p.42.

39 POW interrogation, CO 736th Grenadier Regiment, cited in 'Opposition Encountered', p.151, DEFE2/490, TNA.

4

The Assault Begins

The final Allied decision to launch the invasion was determined by a series of key factors which went beyond considerations of terrain in the target area and the likely responses of the defenders. As General Eisenhower later described it:

> We wanted to cross the Channel with our convoys at night so that darkness would conceal the strength and direction of our several attacks. We wanted a moon for our airborne assaults. We needed approximately forty minutes of daylight preceding the ground assault to complete our bombing and preparatory bombardment. We had to attack on a relatively low tide because of beach obstacles which had to be removed whilst uncovered. These principal factors dictated the general period: but the selection of the actual day would depend upon weather forecasts.[1]

A combination of moonlight, tides, wind and cloud were all critical but for a landing in Normandy taking place during any four-day period in June 1944, the calculated odds were just under 100-1 against the right conditions being met.[2] For the planners the advice given to them was that the minimum weather should be: no morning mist or fog; generally quiet period followed by a sequence of three days with winds less than Beaufort Force 3 (eight to 12 miles per hour) onshore and Force 4 in the Channel; have cloud cover of less than three-tenths below 8,000 feet and visibility more than three miles with the possibility of a cloud base above 3,000 feet; and a full moon within one day before to four days after.[3] There is certainly much to be said for the claim, made nearly 40 years ago in one of the first books to discuss the intelligence gathering secrets of ULTRA, that "of all the natural factors, of all the schemes of men, that would unfold to influence the success of the invasion, Allied knowledge – and German ignorance – of weather conditions on D-Day would prove to be the most important".[4]

So great was the importance of this aspect of the wider plan that considerable resources were set aside to try and achieve something that few thought could be done. Forecasts were produced by consolidating material supplied by three forecasting cells or centrals – the US Army Air Forces central at Widewing (the United States Strategic Air Forces (Europe) headquarters at Bushy Park), the British Meteorological Office at Dunstable

---

1   Dwight D. Eisenhower, *Crusade in Europe* (Little, Brown and Co.; Boston, Massachusetts, 1950), p.239.
2   The Met Office's contemporary calculation was 13-12 for wind and weather, this figure being trebled when the need for a low tide was added this trebled the figure, a full moon doubled it again; 'D-Day: The Role of the Met Office', *The Met. Office* (1995).
3   Ibid.
4   Anthony Cave Brown, *Bodyguard of Lies* (New York; Bantam Books, 1975), pp.670-677.

and the British Admiralty weather office at Portsmouth. Within these three different teams there were six different meteorologists often producing diametrically opposed forecasts. Great responsibility therefore fell to Group Captain James M. Stagg, who had arrived at the COSSAC headquarters in November 1943, and his deputy Army Air Force Colonel Donald N. Yates, the senior USAAF weather officer in the European theatre, to agree upon a compromise that could be presented to Eisenhower. Stagg was a meteorologist from the British Meteorological Office and apparently amongst the large group of people who were surprised by his appointment. American officials were unhappy that this vitally important role should have been given to a civilian so the decision was taken to appoint him as a Group Captain providing the sufficient rank necessary to work in the high-level COSSAC planning environment. Despite the initial suspicion his "ability to work under pressure coupled with tact and, above all, character", which had led to him getting the job, quickly removed any doubts.[5]

Weekly meetings gradually increased in frequency until, from April 1944, the three centrals were in daily conference; as the planned assault date approached these in turn gradually increased to three meetings each day with Stagg and Yates still focussed predominantly on trying to produce a common forecast for delivery to the SAC. One study describes meetings involving "strong personalities" – or "primadonnas" as Stagg referred to them – which progressively became "a knockdown, drag out fight among strongly opinioned professionals".[6] The assembled meteorologists were not helped by the complex nature of the weather as early June proved to be exceptional. Cyclonic disturbances stretching back as far as the Rocky Mountains in the United States, what might more normally be referred to as 'Polar Fronts', were producing unseasonably unsettled westerly winds and low pressure areas. There were two deep depressions, designated L5 and L6, and it was these that were the focus of the forecasters' discussions as the invasion date drew closer. As Stagg put it "each by itself was a mid-winter phenomenon" and conditions were more like April than the start of summer. The really vital issue was not so much the depressions as what would happen in the ridge of space between them. Having recommended a last-minute cancellation from the original target date of 5 June, a consensus emerged that there would be "a fair interlude" on the following day.[7]

The forecast issued for Tuesday 6 June 1944 highlighted a new front forming to the south-west of Iceland leading to 36 hours of unsettled weather. Stagg famously gave his optimistic advice despite the fact that when Eisenhower and his commanders convened on the Sunday evening for their briefing at Southwick House, the location on the south coast of England where the final stages of the planning for D-Day took place, driving rain was rattling the windows. Ultimately the right decision was reached; Montgomery's own view was that cancellation on 5 June saved the Allies from disaster and he was

5   R. J. Ogden, 'Meteorological Services Leading to D-Day', *Occasional Papers on Meteorological History*, (No.3; July 2001), pp.13-14.

6   Colonel Gene J. Pfeffer, 'Weather and Overlord: Contemporary Lessons', *Air War College Research Report* (Maxwell Airforce Base, March 1985), pp.14-17; C.C. Bates and J.F. Fuller, *America's Weather Warriors, 1814-1984* (College Station, Texas; Texas A&M University Press, 1985), pp.5-47.

7   J.M. Stagg, *Forecast for Overlord* (London; Ian Allan, 1971), pp.111-112.

undoubtedly correct. Had the invasion gone ahead on the day it was originally scheduled to happen winds of Force 6 to 7 were measured in the English Channel blowing a steady Force 4 to 5: Force 4 was deemed sufficient to swamp landing craft although Admiral Ramsay was prepared to accept Force 5 as marginal with the possibility of the occasional Force 6.[8]

Intercepts available to the senior Allied commanders had also provided confirmation of the *Luftwaffe* meteorologists predicting disturbed conditions persisting in the English Channel.[9] It is worth considering the degree to which this proved crucial. The neutral Swedes apparently were able to read American coded weather observations although they were unable to crack the British transmissions; this has led to some claims that German meteorologists may have been given access to this information but there is only limited evidence.[10] One of those involved in the Allied forecasting group described the German long-range forecasts as "scientifically unsound and operationally naïve".[11] Certainly by the summer of 1944 a principal task for German U-boats was to make and transmit weather forecasts; this information, along with *Luftwaffe* weather flights, was in turn often intercepted and added to Allied charts. Whatever the exact case, the critical forecast that was offered on 5 June "gave no fewer than five of the [German] High Command an excuse to absent themselves in body and spirit from Normandy".

The weather was potentially key but, as Eisenhower had made clear in his post-war analysis, tides were also important. To this end the 'Swell Forecast Section', which was activated in February 1944, existed to provide analysis and forecasting of the likely sea, swell and surf heights across the entire assault area.[12] The SHAEF 5-day wave forecast issued on the evening of 4 June from within the section recorded: "Swell – In Western approaches to English Channel, and south of 50 degrees N up Channel as far as the Cherbourg Peninsula: 6 to 7 feet Monday, decreasing to 4 to 5 feet Tuesday, 3 to 4 feet remainder of period, westerly direction throughout".[13] For 6 June the forecast was for a three to four foot mixed sea and swell along the Normandy beaches. Allied planners' knowledge of the extent to which these had been fortified meant that the invasion

8 James R. Fleming, 'Sverre Petterssen, the Bergen School, and the Forecasts for D-Day', *Proceedings of the International Commission on History of Meteorology* (Vol.1, No.1; 2004), pp.75-81; Field Marshall, TheViscount Montgomery of Alamain, *Normandy to the Baltic* (Hutchinson; London, 1947) pp.51-52.

9 Brown, *Bodyguard of Lies*, p.634.

10 Anders Persson, 'Right for the Wrong Reason? – A New Look at the D-Day Forecast', *History of Meteorology and Physical Oceanography Special Interest Group, Royal Meteorological Society* (Newsletter 3, 2009), p.12; Persson, 'World War II Weather Maps', *History of Meteorology and Physical Oceanography Special Interest Group, Royal Meteorological Society* (Newsletter 3, 2010), p.9.

11 Letter from Lawrence Hogben, 18 August 1994 (Vol.16, No.16; 1994), *London Review of Books*. Lieutenant Commander Lawrence Hogben RNZN was a 28 year-old New Zealander and part of the British Admiralty forecasting cell. Much of the credit is given to him, using two-day forecasts, for arguing against an invasion on 5 June.

12 Lieutenant Colonel (Retd.) Charles C. Bates USAF, 'Sea, Swell and Surf Forecasting for D-Day and Beyond: The Anglo-American Effort, 1943-1945', unpublished MS, pp.3-9, (2010); Ron Cowen, 'The Tides of War', *Science News* (Vol.145, No.23; June 4, 1994), pp.360-361.

13 It was prepared by 1st Lieutenant John Crowell, a US air force oceanographer; Bates, 'Sea, Swell and Surf Forecasting for D-Day and Beyond', p.16.

force would need a low tide to ensure that the full extent of the Atlantic Wall was exposed. With this occurring just after dawn it meant that the maximum amount of light would be available for delivering subsequent waves of the Allied invasion forces on to the beaches. At the same time the airborne assault needed bright moonlight to assist the pilots delivering the paratroopers and glider-borne troops. In any given month there is only one day when a low tide at dawn coincides with a bright moon; in June 1944 this fell on the sixth but tidal and lunar conditions would still be acceptable the day before and the day following. A contingency existed during the period of 19-21 June but whilst the tide would be ideal there would be little or no moonlight. This made the decision for the SAC relatively simple and to maximise the available options he initially chose that the assault on Europe would take place on 5 June, just one day different from Churchill's recommendation of several months earlier. It was the day following, however, which was optimum as all of the preferred conditions existed with a full moon, low tide scheduled for around 0600 and approximately 15 hours of light. The uncertainty about the weather and tides and the focus attached to getting it right would ultimately provide a decisive advantage to the Allies.

Three meetings had been held in the space of 24 hours to confirm D-Day would take place; it was at 0415 on 5 June that the final decision was taken. With this signal the long-planned invasion timetable could finally commence and the vast force that had been assembled begin their assigned roles. It depended on the co-operation of all three services and each had a massive commitment to ensuring OVERLORD's success. Following his appointment as Allied Naval Commander Expeditionary Force (ANCXF) in October 1943, Admiral Ramsay and his staff had been responsible for the organisation of Operation NEPTUNE, the maritime elements that formed part of the invasion of France. Two task forces had been created, each including a series of bombarding forces, various assault vessels, minesweeping flotillas, and a follow-up force. The Western Task Force was mainly American ships, the Eastern Task Force, under the command of Rear-Admiral Sir Philip Vian, was largely a mix of British and Canadian vessels. Other Allied countries were represented across these two forces with Free French, Norwegian, Dutch and Polish warships and crews involved but approximately 60 percent of all shipping used for the invasion was British. In light of this complexity it is not surprising that the Operation Orders issued in mid-April 1944 contained 22 separate actions and covered 1100 pages.

The combined fleets were huge, a total of 285 warships, 4100 landing craft and 1600 support vessels. They assembled in 'Area Z', about 20 miles to the south-east of the Isle of Wight, the day before the scheduled start of the landings; the assembly area was more commonly known as 'Piccadilly Circus', because many of the vessels kept on going round in circles. From here ten separate groups would sail under cover of darkness included within which were a total of 579 landing ships, landing craft and ferry service landing barges assigned to the Sword beaches. This was 'Force S' commanded by Rear-Admiral Arthur Talbot, a long-serving officer who during the war had already acted as the captain of a destroyer and three aircraft carriers, before being appointed as King George VI's naval ADC. He was apparently well thought of by Ramsey although in one account he was described as "a stern disciplinarian with a voice to match, [who] was known to the lower deck as 'Noisy'". Along with the men and vessels under his command he had spent several months working alongside 3 Br Inf Div and honing the skills needed to make a success of the invasion.[14] Now 'Force S' headed towards the Normandy coast following the swept approach channels marked nine and ten.[15] As these ships moved forward each had a distinctive green band around the bridges and upper works while on the bowels or funnels there were the black and red triangles which General Montgomery had designed, the divisional sign confirming the identity of the troops that were being transported to Europe.

'Force S' and its transports were split into the assault, intermediate, and reserve groups, the first of which got underway at 0945 on 5 June sailing from berths at Spithead. At the front, designated as 'S3', was Captain Eric Bush who was commanding HMS *Goathland*, followed by 'S2', led by Captain Renfrew Gotto on HMS *Dacres*, and then the reserve brigade, 'S1', with Captain Leggat on HMS *Locust*. The command vessels were an interesting mix, specially fitted out for the role; the last of these was a flat bottomed Chinese river gunboat which had been selected due to its ability to move in close to the shore. Admiral Talbot was on his headquarters ship HMS *Largs* along with General Rennie and various other senior headquarters staff. Built in 1938 this vessel had started life as a fruit carrying passenger boat sailing between France and Jamaica under the name of MV *Charles Plumier*. In 1940 she was requisitioned by the French Navy and converted to an armed cruiser and when France surrendered it was sailed to Dakar and refitted. The following year the vessel was 'arrested' by the destroyer HMS *Faulknor* and sailed first to Gibraltar before heading to England where it was fitted out once again and converted to become a Combined Operations Headquarters Ship. Anchored in Largs Bay a new name was easily selected and the *Largs* took part in virtually every major seaborne assault of the war, beginning in North Africa in November 1942 with Operation TORCH and ending off the coast of Malaya nearly three years later with Operation ZIPPER.[16] As the first convoy left the force commander ordered a signal spelling the words 'Good Luck: Drive On' to be hoisted and this remained until 2145 when the headquarters vessel itself departed for the French coast.

In many respects the key components of this invasion armada were the landing craft about which, as has already been highlighted, there had been considerable confusion and anxiety throughout the planning period. As one of the planners put it, such was the uncertainty about the numbers that would be available he and his colleagues felt they were "building on sand"; this meant that "instead of being able to say 'We intend to assault with 'x' divisions; how many landing craft does this require'. We were forced to say 'We have 'y' landing craft; what sized assault can we manage with them'".[17] After Churchill's remonstrations and the subsequent interventions from Monty and General Eisenhower, the issue had only eventually been resolved by the agreement to postpone plans elsewhere and push the assault date back to the beginning of June. Aside from ensuring NEPTUNE would be recognised as the focus of activity this had allowed for

14 Pollock, 'Overlord: Plans and Preparations – 1940 to the "Touch Down"', CAB44/242, TNA; Andrew Lambert, 'Talbot, Arthur G.', in *The D-Day Encyclopaedia*, pp.535-536.

15 'Operation Neptune – The Normandy Landings, June 1944', Battle Summary No.39, Vol 1 (1947), p.37, ADM234/366, TNA.

16 The only exception to this was the landing on Madagascar, Operation IRONCLAD, in May 1942.

17 Admiral Sir Maurice Mansergh to Ellis, 12 September 1956, CAB101/309, TNA.

Rennie's command vessel HMS *Largs*

another vital month's production which would be available for immediate use. In truth there was still little spare capacity particularly with the need to support the Southern France landings.[18]

To deliver the invasion force to the Sword beaches the planning tables programmed 22 different groups of craft which, by H+360, would put ashore all three of 3 Br Inf Div's brigades plus the armoured brigade and all the supporting arms. Within the first 20 minutes the landing schedule called for a total of 18 Landing Craft Tank (LCT) and 69 Landing Craft Assault (LCA) to have delivered their tanks and assault troops onto the beachhead.[19] There were three main types of landing craft used during the invasion, the LCT, the LCA and the Landing Craft Infantry (LCI), also referred to as Landing Ship Infantry (LSI). The wooden LCAs, which were based on a design from the Thorneycroft shipbuilding firm, acted as the mainstay of the landings. Prior to the start of invasion 60 were being produced each month. Oblong shallow craft, with a crew of four controlled by a Royal Marine at the stern, they had a ramp at the front and were armed with mortars and machine guns. They could make a top speed of six knots and transport a maximum of 35 troops. These were slung alongside the LCIs on davits like lifeboats. Described by one of the infantrymen as "looking like a giant shoebox with

18 Ellis, *Victory in the West – Volume I, The Battle of Normandy*, p.65-67; David Eisenhower, *Eisenhower At War 1943-1945* (Random House; New York, 1986), p.102.

19 Lieutenant-Colonel A.E. Warhurst, 'Overlord: D-Day 6 June 1944, Book Two', CAB44/244, TNA.

an engine" their flat bottoms and shallow drafts men that they could be run directly onto the beaches and, in theory, provide a dry landing.[20] Their flimsy construction was, however, a factor behind the decision to land at low tide as there was thought to be no chance of them withstanding the German beach defences. There were three versions one of which, the LCA(FT), was fitted with flame throwing equipment. Another, the LCA(HR) and referred to as a 'Hedgehog', was designed specifically with a strengthened hull frame and contained four rows of six spigot mortars which fired a spread of explosives intended to destroy enemy minefields. The final version, the LCA(OC), was equipped for clearing beach obstructions.

The major movement across the Channel was done by the LCIs, former US naval craft which had been given to the Royal Navy under the Lend Lease programme. Much larger vessels displacing 384 tons and with a top speed of 14 knots, these were crewed by 24 men and armed with four 20 mm anti-aircraft guns and two machine guns. They could carry a maximum of 188 troops and were described as being roomy with the luxury of rations which included real white bread, something that virtually all the men on board had not seen for years. Aside from the transport of troops there were a wide range of other uses for these landing craft; one was fitted out specifically as a press facility, others laid smokescreens, while the LCK served a floating mobile kitchen. Finally, there were seven different models of LCT which was described as "nothing more than a large wooden box with a pointed nose; the back lets down forming a run up for the tanks".[21] The most numerous was the LCT(4) which had a displacement of 586 tons, a top speed of 10 knots and a complement of 12 crew. Later models were armed with two 20 mm guns and could carry shackled down to the deck for the crossing six 40 ton tanks or nine smaller 30 ton armoured vehicles. In a calm sea they could take the maximum of nine but rougher weather was meant to reduce this load; in reality many LCTs sailed overloaded with men and equipment.

Providing the transport and safeguarding the security of the invasion armies was only one of the NEPTUNE roles for the assembled Allied maritime forces. Because of its proximity to the heavy batteries in the vicinity of Le Havre and the light craft based at that port, Sword sector was assessed by the planner as being the most vulnerable to enemy attack. For this reason a powerful bombardment force, 'Bombarding Force D', the largest of the three similar forces within the Eastern Task Force, had been earmarked to offer additional protection on the eastern flank. This consisted of the battleships, monitors and cruisers HMS *Mauritius, Warspite, Ramillies, Roberts, Arethusa, Frobisher, Dragon* and *Danae* supported by 13 other destroyers, a total of 21 vessels and a range of additional heavy landing craft providing artillery fire. This was a powerful force and included amongst its armaments eighteen 15 inch guns and 49 of the smaller six inch guns. The plan called for the cruisers to fire on the enemy coastal batteries which were thought to hold 155 mm guns while the destroyers would be firing on the beaches right up to the moment of touch down.

For the air component there were also a huge number of missions and roles during the opening phases of the invasion. In order to adhere to the limitations imposed by

20 Lieutenant-Colonel Edward Jones (Rtd), 'Wartime Service with the 1st Battalion, the South Lancashire Regiment 1941-1945', 21 June 2007, p.16, LIM.

21 J.D. Downer, 'A Personal Account', p.11, A Soldier's Life, Discovery Museum (hereafter 'SLDM').

the FORTITUDE deception plan, throughout the months prior to the assault for every Allied air attack that was made in the NEPTUNE area two were conducted outside. The heavy day bombers of the US VIIIth Air Force spent the period immediately prior to D-Day attacking military camps, ammunition and fuel dumps, transport parks and coastal defences of various types across not just the target area but the whole of northern France. As an example of the strategy being employed, on 5 June six objectives were attacked in the invasion area and 12 in the Pas-de-Calais; with 14 of these targets being coastal defence batteries; it was assessed that throughout this period the element of surprise had not been lost. For the day of the invasion this American air force, consisting of both bombers and fighters, was given a variety of missions designed to support the ground assault. This would lead, over a period of 18 hours, to a total of 4,647 aircraft being dispatched, only three of which were lost, and nearly 5,000 (US) tons of bombs being dropped. This was an exceptional level of activity and intensity leading the post-campaign narrative to term the day of the invasion as one "of records"; a single bomber force had not previously dropped such a tonnage of bombs in a 24-hour period nor had a single command dispatched so many aircraft.[22]

At least initially it was intended that the air component would remain under central control in England with requests been transmitted back to it from the beachhead.[23] To ensure a speedy response there were formations of aircraft at various states of readiness and the planning orders indicated that, at best, it would take 1 hour 45 minutes for fighters/bombers to arrive over target and 2 hours 30 minutes for light bombers; these figures could, however, extend by as much as an additional 90 minutes. There were also formations permanently in the air which were within wireless range of the *Largs* and it was estimated that these could be on target within just 30 minutes; such support was restricted though, both in terms of scale and duration which was likely to be no more than 20 minutes at any one time. In addition the plan called for a continuous patrol to be maintained over the shipping lanes throughout daylight hours by four squadrons of Lightnings, 64 aircraft operating between 3,000 to 5,000 feet or just below the cloud base.[24] Over the whole assault area a continuous fighter cover of nine squadrons in strength was also to be maintained with Spitfires providing low cover and Thunderbolts higher cover. During the night of D-Day, with the troops hopefully ashore, six Mosquito squadrons were available to cover the assault areas and shipping lanes; a total of 24 British and American squadrons of fighters had been specially trained to take off and land in darkness and were available during the critical periods of first and last light.

As 'Force S' moved forward in the darkness its leading elements looked for a guiding beacon coming from the direction of the Sword target ahead of them. Fitted with radar equipment they were searching for the deployment point marked with special buoys that had been laid by a midget submarine positioned approximately 7,000 yards offshore and emitting signals that only they could pick up. The narrow strip of beaches available in this assault zone had resulted in a decision to reinforce the number of available navigational aids and HM Midget Submarine X23, commanded by Lieutenant George Honour

---

22 RAF Narrative, 'The Liberation of North-West Europe: Volume III, The Landings in Normandy', *Air Historical Branch*, JSCSC Archives (hereafter 'JSCSC'), p.220.

23 'Overlord 27 Armd Bde Operation Order', May 1944, WO171/623, TNA.

24 Ibid., 'Battle Summary – Operation Neptune', p.105, ADM234/366.

RN, set sail on 2 June arriving in her position two days later where she bottomed and remained undetected for the following 48 hours.[25] The craft, which weighed less than 30 tons, was just 51 feet long and five feet wide and the crew were not able to stand whilst on-board. Normally painted grey and black, the X23 "sported an exotic camouflage scheme of yellow and green, because experts had assured [the captain] that this would hide her from the air while she lay on the bottom, in shallow water and well within the range of German shore artillery".[26] Range was supposed to be a maximum of about 1,000 miles but this was only at very slow speed and using diesel engines that were the same as those in London buses; midget submarines were normally towed into action and, for X23, HM Trawler *Sapper* provided the necessary assistance.

For this often over-looked element of the Sword plan, which lasted for a total of 74 hours, all except ten of these were spent submerged as the limited summer darkness allowed only the briefest of periods on the surface. The crew of five, cramped together in a vessel that had been designed for one less person, spent much of the time resting waiting for what they initially believed would be the launch of the invasion in the early hours of 5 June; only at the last minute did they receive the signal informing them of the delay. Operation GAMBIT was later judged to have been a complete success. The 18 foot high navigation beacon flashing a green shade to denote that it was within 300 yards of its planned position was seen clearly by the LCT lowering the first waves of tanks and infantry into their launch position.[27] And at daybreak large flags were hoisted to provide an additional marker. With the mission completed a motor launch escorted the midget submarine back to *Largs* where the crew were treated for exhaustion and allowed a brief rest before being towed home.

The successful sighting of X23 was entirely in keeping with the progress being made by NEPTUNE. During 5 June the wind blew from the west at Force 5; overnight it eased slightly to Force 3 to 4 and changed direction slightly with the previous low cloud lifting to between 4-5,000 feet by dusk. The moon was within a day of offering full visibility and the swell was also average, coming from the west initially four to five feet but also decreasing as the night wore on. The conditions were much as Stagg and the other specialists had predicted. As Talbot himself later wrote, "such was the weather which, set down in bald terms of Beaufort scale, does not sound as bad as press reports have made it out to be. But, as we all know, any sea or wind over 3 is a cross to landing craft and much more to sea-sick soldiers".[28] One of his commanding officers, Lieutenant Commander A.J.R. White RN who was captaining HMS *Virago*, wrote that "…the passage went without a hitch and was a triumph for the organisation. It was like driving to a race meeting, with the AA controlling the traffic". When *Largs* arrived off the coast of France, bringing up the rear of the convoy, the highly experienced naval commander of 'Force S' felt that there was a real sense that:

---

25 Another vessel, X20, also crossed the Channel and remained off Juno beach, the concern here being that there was a lack of clearly defined markers on the beach which might lead to landing craft failing to transport the troops to their designated targets.

26 'Obituary – Lieutenant George Honour', *Daily Telegraph*, 3 June 2002.

27 Talbot, 'Report by the Naval Commander Force S', NARA; 'Operation Neptune – Employment of X20 and X23, Operation Gambit', ADM179/475, TNA.

28 Talbot, 'Report by the Naval Commander Force S', p.11, NARA.

…we had achieved a large measure of tactical surprise … No air attacks, no E-Boat attacks, no Radar or W/T jamming … The air plot showed enemy aircraft on patrol away to the eastward in the Pas-de-Calais area. A glance to starboard showed the assault convoys on time as far as could be judged. The operation was proceeding with unreal precision.[29]

NEPTUNE did not, however, go entirely according to plan. Aside from firing at targets onshore 'Bombarding Force D' also laid down a heavy smokescreen to act as a shield. It was through this that German torpedo boats were able to conduct an attack on the approaching fleet as it neared the French coast before making good their escape back into the smoke. The *5-T Flotille* had been at Le Havre since 24 May when it had moved along the coast from Cherbourg. During the transfer a number of vessels had been damaged by Allied air and naval attacks and as a result only four E-Boats remained operational. At 0535 on D-Day three of these put to sea and just under an hour later at 0630 they came into contact with the invasion fleet. Under cover of the artificial smoke and with Allied radar screens effectively blinded by the thousands of echoes from the vessels surrounding them they approached unseen and launched their attack. Commanded by *Korvetten-Kapitän* Heinrich Hoffmann the three German E-Boats managed to fire 15 torpedoes. Two of these passed between the *Ramillies* and *Warspite* before hitting the Norwegian destroyer *Svenner* immediately under a boiler room and it quickly sank although most of the crew were rescued. A fourth torpedo was on course to hit *Largs* but the ship went into a rapid reverse and was narrowly missed. All three E-Boats made it back to their base and the captain was decorated for his action the following day; during the sorties that followed no further success was achieved. Other than the *Svenner* which, with its up-ended bows in clear view was an enduring memory recorded by many of the troops who landed in the initial waves, the only other significant casualty for 'Force S' came shortly afterwards, at 0745, when HMS *Westler* struck a mine and, about the same time, an LST was also sunk. This was the extent of the damage done out to sea and beyond the littoral. There was worse to follow near the beaches but nowhere near as bad as had been feared.

Watching all of this the German defenders on shore knew that something was happening but, even now, there still remained considerable confusion and disagreement about what was unfolding before them. An intelligence report prepared for *Luftlotte 3* at some stage on D-Day, and detailing the day's events, confirmed that at 2100 on 5 June a signal had been picked up from the BBC which was recognised as giving instructions to the Maquis to carry out a series of planned attacks within the following 48 hours. The objectives included railway lines, roads, canals and telephone and telegraphic communications and seemed to confirm that something significant was imminent.[30] There had been other warning signs during the hours immediately prior to the invasion, such as an increase in the number of meteorological recce flights been conducted by American aircraft. A report written in July 1944 stated that, "as these had never been

---

29 Ibid., p.15; Young, *Gators of Neptune*, pp.177-183.
30 'Field Headquarters, Gruppe Ic (intelligence), 6 June 1944', Wilmot Papers, LH15/15/32, LHCMA.

Heinrich Hoffmann, who commanded the E-Boat attack on the invasion fleet

noticed before at these times [2300] units were advised to be on the alert".[31] A warning was issued at midnight to the Fifteenth Army and at 0111 the signal was passed around the 84 Corps area, reportedly at General Fuechtinger's initiative, 24 minutes before it was issued by the Seventh Army. The general later claimed that just an hour later he had already identified the Cotentin Peninsula and the area being covered by 716 Inf Div as where the Allies were concentrating their forces. In reality Feuchtinger was most likely away from his post on the night of the invasion in Paris with his mistress; for his absence he would later be relieved of his command and condemned to death although his sentence was never carried out. He was able to contact his headquarters at St-Pierre-sur-Dives by telephone at around 0200 and arrived back there about three hours later. Much of the key decision-making during the initial period was made by Colonel Hans von Luck who was in command of the 125 Pz Gren.[32]

The war diary for General von Rundstedt's headquarters confirms that the first reports of "parachute descents" were received at 0130 but according to this same source it was not until 0410 that the warning order 'Alarm Priority II' was issued for both army groups and Panzer Group West and all troops were from that point sitting in their vehicles

31 Ibid., 'The Luftwaffe and the Invasion', OKL Special Post Mortem (15-30 July 1944).
32 Samuel W. Mitcham Jr, 'Feuchtinger, Edgar' in *The D-Day Encyclopaedia*, p.231; 'Normandie 6 juin 1944', *Historica* (No.75; avril-juin 2003), pp.151-153.

prepared to move.[33] Various sightings were reported throughout the night starting 30 minutes after the initial alert and nearly all of them made reference to airborne landings in the area between the Seine and Orne estuaries. Just before 0500 General Richter ordered 716 Inf Div to begin countermeasures and, as the light improved, the reports of sightings of assault craft heading for the French coast grew. The first reports of actual landings came at 0630 in the American sectors. At 0642 Naval Group West confirmed that this was the start of the invasion and that multiple warships were being sighted off the Normandy coast. Even so, it could not be determined whether this was "a diversion attempt on a large scale or the main attack". By 0700 there were now continued reports of the approach of large enemy naval formations; two minutes later a battleship and 20 destroyers were said to be north-west of Le Havre. Throughout the morning the message log in the diary continued in a similar vein, a progression of information charting the escalation of the attack along with repeated requests to release the armoured reserves.

Absent from his headquarters was Field Marshal Rommel who had accepted the weather forecast given to him suggesting there was little chance of an invasion and had returned to his home in Bavaria to celebrate his wife's fiftieth birthday. This proved to be critical as his Chief of Staff Lieutenant-General Hans Spiedel, who was effectively acting as the temporary head of Army Group B, assessed that the reports indicated that there was no more than a local attack taking place. Despite the best efforts of Major-General Max Pemsel, the Chief of Staff for Seventh Army, to convince his superior that he was wrong, a debate which had begun as early as 0215 with warnings that a major attack was taking place, Spiedel demanded more evidence. It was not until 0730 that he finally telephoned Rommel and informed him of events. Hearing the news the Field Marshal immediately cancelled his plans and set off back to his headquarters in the castle at La Roche-Guyon, some 40 miles north of Paris on the banks of the River Seine, where he arrived at 2130 on D-Day. By this stage the battle for the beaches had already been decided.

---

33 There were two alarms: Alarm I confined all ranks to their barracks; 'AL1636/1, Commander-in-Chief West's War Diary, June 1944: 6 June 1944', EDS Notes, CAB146/337, TNA.

5

Airborne Prologue

Whilst the fleet moved towards the French coast the men of 3 Br Inf Div knew that the invasion had in fact already begun some hours before. In many respects the airborne assault that formed a key part of the OVERLORD plan, with its two principal targets on the extreme west and east of the assault area, is perhaps the most well-known part of D-Day.[1] There were several reasons why for the men heading to the Sword sector beaches the role played by the British 6 Airborne Division (6 AB Div) was absolutely critical to their chances of success. The left flank of the area being attacked was bounded by a double water obstacle, consisting of the River Orne and the Caen Canal, and this, in turn, was overlooked by high ground to the east. From this area and the coast in front of it the invasion fleet and the landing beaches could potentially be fired upon.[2] The beaches in this sector, referred to as 'Oboe', had been reviewed during the planning process but the lack of landing craft and their vulnerability to fire from the German coastal battery at Le Havre meant that landings here were never really considered. With the east bank of the Orne also more or less covering the boundary between the two German Army groups that were based in northern France and which Rommel had taken under his control there was an added reason for why it needed to be occupied. The Fifteenth Army based around the Pas-de-Calais was larger in size and much the stronger force and the potential for reinforcements of men and armour moving from it, both in the period immediately following the initial invasion but also during the days and weeks that followed, was a great concern for the Allied planners. The FORTITUDE deception plan proved far more successful than could ever have been anticipated in terms of fixing the German strategic assessment to the wrong area but this would only become clear once the troops were ashore.

The flanks of the invasion force needed to be secured if OVERLORD was to have any hope of achieving success and the decision was therefore reached that the best approach was to use an airborne assault to seize the dominating ground to the east of the Orne.[3] On 17 February 1944 orders were therefore issued to 6 AB Div to place elements of its force under the command of 3 Br Inf Div and to plan for an operation providing flank protection for the whole of I Corps.[4] Major General Richard 'Windy' Gale was given

---

1   Flint Whitlock, *If Chaos Reigns – The Near-Disaster and Ultimate Triumph of the Allied Airborne Forces on D-Day, June 6, 1944* (Casemate; Newbury, 2011), pp.192-228.

2   Indeed by 1 July the German defenders had effectively managed to close the two original assault beaches such was their ability to fire on them both from positions along the coast and also from concealed points within the original airborne assault area.

3   Joshua Levine, *Operation Fortitude – The Story of the Spy Operation that Saved D-Day* (Collins; London, 2011), pp.288-294.

4   Warhurst, 'Overlord: D-Day 6 June 1944, Book Two', p.169, CAB44/244, TNA.

three primary tasks: firstly, the capture of bridges at Benouville and Ranville which spanned the double water obstacle, if at all possible intact, followed by the establishment of a bridgehead which the defenders could hold until additional support arrived; the destruction or neutralisation of the coastal gun battery at Franceville Plage, more commonly referred to as the Merville battery, before the approaching seaborne assault craft came within range, a point calculated as being dawn minus 30 minutes; finally, his forces would destroy a series of bridges at four locations over the River Dives to delay any enemy attempt at reinforcement from the north or the east. As soon as additional resources became available, but only if these primary missions had been successfully completed, two additional secondary tasks were also indicated: the area between the Orne and Dives rivers was to be secured with the towns of Sallenelles and Franceville Plage being captured and as much of the coastal strip up to Cabourg cleared of defending troops as possible; with this base secured the airborne forces and their reinforcements were to 'operate offensively' against any German moves towards them coming from the east and south-east. To assist in the completion of what was a wide-ranging set of orders, the commandos of 1 Special Service Brigade (1 SS Bde) would

Major-General Richard 'Windy' Gale in his airborne smock

land on the extreme left of Sword and move quickly to support the airborne forces, in the process coming under Gale's command.[5]

Referred to as Operation TONGA, the airborne operation was to be carried out between midnight and dawn on D-Day and all the main objectives, if possible, had to be secured before the assault forces approached the beachhead. There were two parachute and one airlanding brigades within this division but the total aircraft available was insufficient to allow for it all to be lifted at full strength so care had to be taken to select the forces needed for the initial assault. To secure the right flank of the area being assaulted, this task was given to 5 Parachute Brigade (5 Para Bde), commanded by Brigadier J.H.N. Poett, consisting of three parachute battalions – 7, 12 and 13 – along with specialist engineer, artillery, and medical units who would jump with them. In addition men from 2 Oxfordshire and Buckinghamshire Light Infantry (2 Ox Bucks) would carry out a special mission, a *coup de main* assault designed to capture the two bridges on the double water obstacle. For the attack on the Merville battery and operations on the left flank 3 Parachute Brigade (3 Para Bde), commanded by Brigadier S.J.L. Hill and consisting of a similar force to the other brigade, the main elements of which was 1 Canadian, 8 and 9 Parachute Battalions (1 Can Para Bn, 8 Para Bn, 9 Para Bn). On the evening of D-Day 6 Airlanding Brigade (6 AL Bde), commanded by Brigadier The Hon. H.K.M. Kindersley, with that the best part of two specially trained infantry battalions along with an Armoured Reconnaissance Group, was to land by gliders. The planned sequence called for troops from 3 Br Inf Div to arrive at the captured bridges on the east bank of the Orne at H+5 to relieve troops holding them, only an hour after the bulk of 1 SS Bde had passed through.

As the post-battle airborne narrative described it, "the task of seizing bridges was one which required a rapid concentration of effort if they were to be secured intact, while the business of holding bridgeheads on both sides of the obstacles would be more suitable for airlanding battalions with their heavier equipment".[6] The first detailed plan saw 6 AL Bde being deployed initially along with one of the parachute brigades and a few specialist engineer and artillery troops. During the course of the COSSAC planning Caen had been confirmed as ideal for airborne landings with groups of very large, clear and almost flat fields and few problems in terms of agreeing potential target zones for the parachute and glider forces. Flak and other ground forces were also relatively few while plentiful and distinctive map features meant that the pilots of the tugs and carrier aircraft could anticipate a good flight.[7] The gliders, while they were the strongest element of an airborne division and could be on the ground almost instantly, absolutely required this type of cleared secure terrain. Both sides understood this to be the case and a reconnaissance photo taken on 13 April 1944 revealed extensive anti-air-landing obstacles being erected throughout the area that had been identified by the Allied planners as potential landing zones. The result was a change in plan and the substitution of

5   T.B.H. Otway, *Airborne Forces: The Second World War 1939-45* (Imperial War Museum; London, 1990), pp.172-173; RAF Narrative, 'Volume III, The Landings in Normandy', pp.93-94, JSCSC.
6   Warhurst, 'Overlord: D-Day 6 June 1944, Book Two', p.170, CAB44/244, TNA.
7   Ibid.

the second airborne brigade which was given the task of removing these obstructions to allow gliders to land on the evening of D-Day.[8]

The revised plan called for the division to be lifted by four squadrons of Albemarles, four of Stirlings and two of Halifaxes belonging to No.38 Group, and five squadrons of Dakotas from No.46 Group. There was a total of 423 aircraft available across these squadrons located at eight operational bases; on 1 June 406 of these aircraft were listed as being available. The division also used about 350 gliders the majority of which were for the airlanding brigade; these were Horsas whose load was 29 soldiers or three tons of freight. Added to these were a much smaller number of Hamilcars, 70 in total, all based at Tarrant Rushton with No.298 Squadron. Each could carry 40 soldiers or eight tons of freight and just under half of these also were used by the airlanding brigade.[9] For the paratroopers there were 6,000 man-dropping (X-type) parachutes available along with 3,000 supply containers which would be used as part of the main operation. An additional 10,000 of these carriers were intended for the various planned re-supply missions. Air support was deemed to be vital with the Merville battery being attacked by 100 Lancasters carrying 4,000 pound bombs as part of a raid programmed to commence 20 minutes before 3 Para Bde began its drop but last only for ten minutes. Searchlights and flak were also to be targeted in and around the Caen area with all of these aircraft clear before the first landings began. For the arrival of 6 AL Bde a close escort of 15 fighter squadrons was also made available.[10]

To accomplish its tasks three main Dropping (DZ) and Landing (LZ) Zones were selected for 6 AB Div's use each of which was convenient to the primary objectives. As was standard with this form of operation, the intention was that these would allow the airborne forces to attack before their opponent was able to appreciate what was happening. Prior to the landing Pathfinders would drop who would set up ground navigation aids to ensure that the main force landed in the right areas. One zone, DZ V, was within reach of the Merville guns and one of the Dives bridges. Another, DZ K, was near the road connecting Troarn with Colombelles and a third larger combined landing and dropping point, DZ N, was between the villages of Ranville and Breville. In addition two other small landing zones between the River Orne and the Caen Canal were referred to as LZ X and LZ Y and had been set aside for 2 Ox Bucks and their assault on the two critical bridges. This would represent the start of the airborne operation at approximately 0020 with all of the remaining paratroopers scheduled to commence jumping 30 minutes later. The final part of the force, a second glider-borne detachment who had trained specifically to provide support to the attack on the Merville guns, was to land at approximately 0430.

During the planning phase and because the time of the seaborne assault was variable, the key consideration was light and all operations were expressed as plus or minus Civil Twilight which was called 'P-hour'. An extremely accurate model of the area of operations, to a scale of 1:5000, was constructed and set up at the secure planning headquarters near Netheravon. All aircrews were given some opportunity to study this in

---

8   'Staff College Camberley 1947 Course', pp.2-3, JSCSC.
9   There is some difference in terms of the figures quoted. These are taken from RAF Narrative, 'Volume III, The Landings in Normandy', p.94, JSCSC.
10   Warhurst, 'Overlord: D-Day 6 June 1944, Book Two', p.178, CAB44/244, TNA.

addition to which a colour film was made, both of it and of even larger scale models. This film, in which the camera moved above the model at the appropriate height and speed simulating the actual runs in from the coast to the target area, were shown repeatedly at all the air stations involved in the operation. In addition to the latter a huge number of photographs were made available showing the appropriate DZ/LZ with a copy of the full packs given to each aircrew and glider crew taking part. Steps were also taken to simulate night operations including the production of a special target map. Ease of map reading and the ability of the tugs to use ground navigation aids for as long as possible were considerations for the glider crews; the avoidance of flak and small arms fire and wind forecasts were probably viewed as being more important. The latter was to be provided at the final briefing which began for the crewmen and glider pilots three days before the operation. As part of the preparations a height of approximately 1,500 feet was chosen in nearly all cases for the release of the gliders but pilots were given considerable freedom to make their own decision. Exceptions were made for the *coup de main* assault and the attack on Merville; these gliders were both to release at 6,000 feet, the former to ensure the element of surprise and the latter to allow a carefully planned approach to try and achieve a landing on top of the German fortifications.[11]

By this stage of the war British airborne troops formed part of an experienced, well-trained and well-resourced elite. A paratroop battalion had a jumping strength of 550 men with three rifle companies, each of three platoons, a headquarters company including six three-inch mortars and four medium machine guns and two jeeps and trailers to provide transport. The men of 6 AB Div landed in France with 48 hours of rations, the water they could carry in their own bottles and enough ammunition to last for about 24 hours. In addition there was three-inch mortar and machine gun ammunition but only enough for short actions. The very limited transport that had been brought in had enough petrol for about 200 miles of travel per vehicle.[12] The more heavily armoured airlanding force had an additional rifle company and four platoons per company along with the mortars and machine guns, and there were also eight six-pounder anti-tank guns. Each airborne brigade had three 'Forward Observer, Bombardment' (FOB) each of whom was dropped by parachute or glider. This was in addition to the four FOBs accompanying the commando brigade who landed on the beaches. The intention was that these naval officers would be able to direct fire from the vessels in 'Force S' detailed to provide specific support to the airborne assault.[13] Along with artillery rounds provided by 3 Br Inf Div, this was seen as a means of overcoming the lack of heavier firepower which could be brought in by air, a result of a shortage of tug aircraft.

The departure of the first groups of airborne troops, the Pathfinders, Advance Parachute Parties and the *coup de main* force, was timed so that their aircraft would arrive over their target areas at P-5, approximately 0020 on 6 June. Each had a critical role to play but the mission given to the latter remains the most celebrated. The six gliders piloted by crews of No.1 Wing, Glider Pilot Regiment carrying the *coup de main* force were actually the first to leave Britain setting off at 2256 from RAF Tarrant Rushton. During the planning phase on the bogus maps the Caen Canal was referred to as 'Portugal' and the River Orne was

---

11 Ibid., p.181.
12 Ibid., p.183.
13 This was intended to increase by an additional two to four destroyers once the commandos arrived.

'Prague' but they were now codenamed 'Rugger' and 'Cricket'. Referred to as Operation DEADSTICK, the force consisted of D Company, 2 Ox Bucks, less supporting Bren and three-inch mortar detachments, plus two other platoons from the battalion, a total of 130 men.[14] The commanding officer was 31 year-old Major John Howard who, pre-war, had served as a non-commissioned officer for six years before joining the Oxford police and had been recalled following the war's outbreak. In order to neutralise any demolition charges on the two target bridges a detachment 249th Field Company RE (249 Field) commanded by Captain Neilson and Lieutenant Bence plus 28 other ranks were distributed amongst the gliders, five sappers on each. If it was the case that the bridges had been blown the plan was to establish four small bridgeheads on the banks of the canal and river for which purpose four of the gliders carried an assault boat each. The follow-up force included on board rafts for anti-tank guns and five dinghies; an additional 30 dinghies were to be dropped with 7 Parachute Battalion (7 Para Bn).

The available pre-invasion intelligence offered a great deal of technical information about the two bridges, which were said to form "an excellent anti-tank obstacle, further strengthened by the low marshy land lying between them".[15] The Caen Canal bridge was lock controlled with an average width of 150 feet and steep banks on either side of about six feet in height with small roads running along both of them; it was described as "a steel girder rolling lift" with a road width of about 12 feet and a length of 190 feet. The neighbouring bridge over the river, which was tidal but slow flowing, was about 100 feet wide with banks of about six to ten feet above high water. Constructed from steel lattice girders, it had a two span swing with a length of 350 feet and a width of 20 feet when the sidewalks were included. During their training every platoon had been trained on how to capture the canal bridge: the pillbox guarding it was to be put out of action by the leading section throwing smoke bombs on the road and using this as cover to then approach and put short fuse grenades through the gun slits. In May 1944 the men had conducted a rehearsal attacking two bridges at Countess Weir near Exeter which, entirely unknown to them, were very similar to their actual targets.[16]

The attacking force was split with three gliders targeting the bridge at the canal and the other three at the river. As one of the glider pilots described it, "what we were required to do had never been done before, nor to the best of my knowledge was ever required again in the subsequent airborne landings of Arnhem and the Rhine, namely to navigate various courses on a 45-degree angle of descent, dropping at the rate of 2,000 feet per minute in the dark and without aids of any kind".[17] Three flight corrections were made with the pilots using only a map, stop-watch, airspeed, altimeter and basic gyro-compass and relying on their training which had made the approach almost instinctive; as one of them put it, "it all looked so exactly like the sand-table that I had the strange feeling that

14 'Report by Major R.J. Howard, DSO – Capture of Pegasus Bridge 5/6 June 1944', Staff College Camberley 1947 Course, JSCSC.

15 '76th Field Regiment RA Intelligence Summary', n.d. (May 1944), D8/1/2, Scarfe Papers, ULSC.

16 Denis Edwards, *The Devil's Own Luck – From Pegasus Bridge to The Baltic, 1944-1945* (Pen and Sword; Barnsley, 2001), p.26.

17 Staff Sergeant Roy Howard (1994), cited in *D-Day: Then and Now, Vol.1* (After the Battle, 1995), pp.224-225.

List of maps

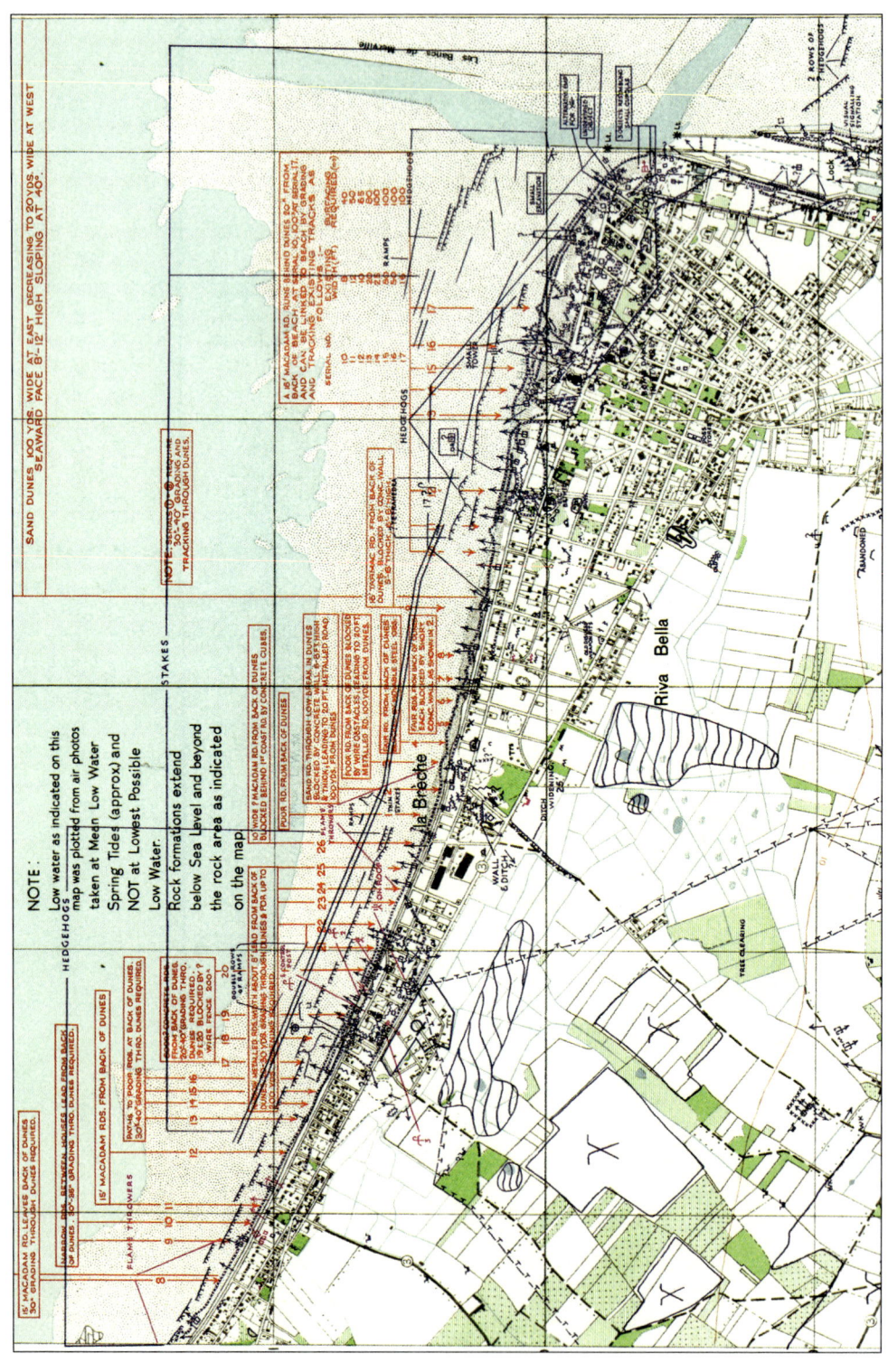

1. One of the series of maps issued on 5 June 1944 to the troops in 3 Br Inf Div showing the area of operations

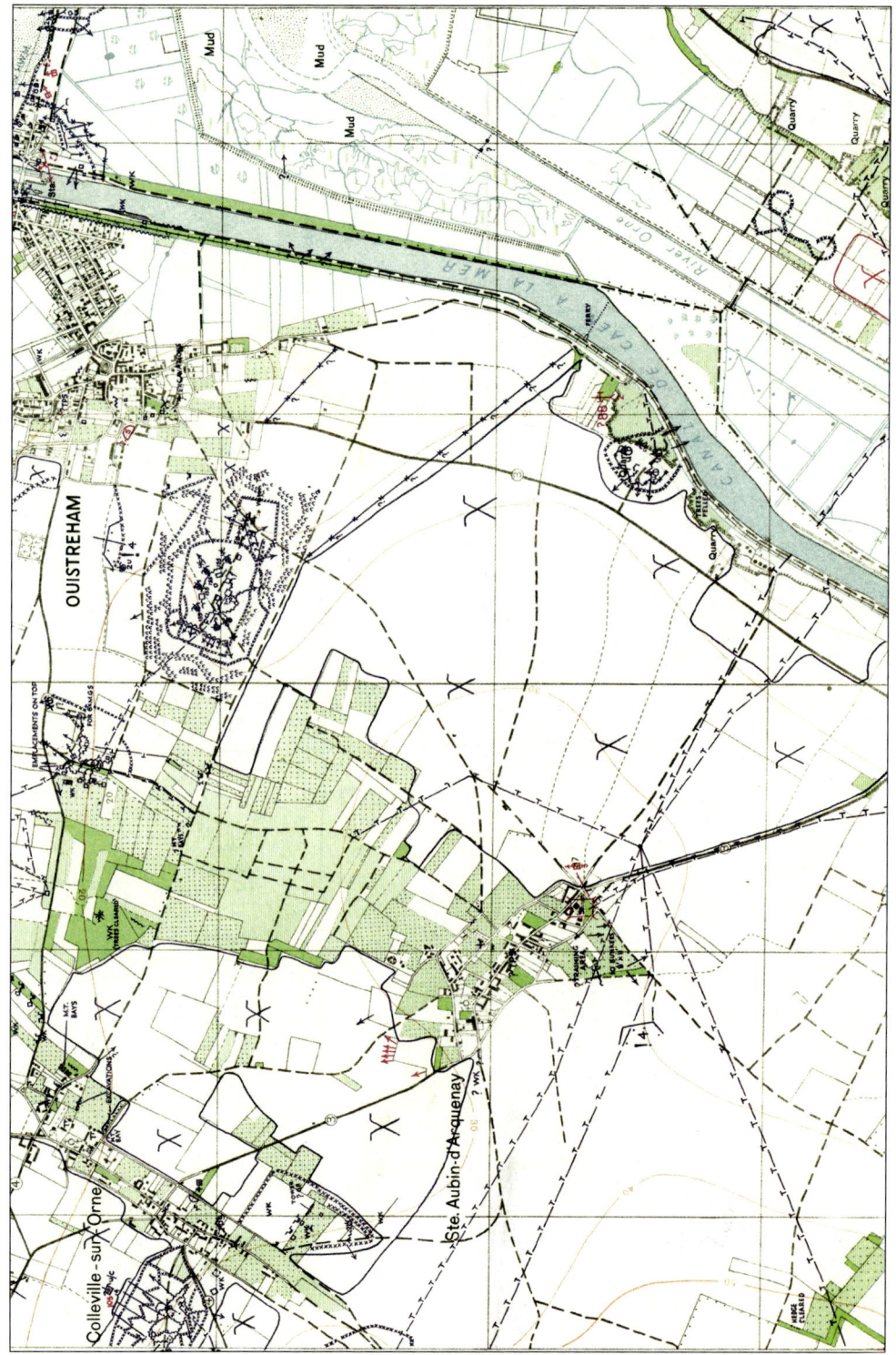

OUISTREHAM

River Orne

Mud

Mud

Mud

Quarry

Quarry

Quarry

CANAL DE CAEN A LA MER

FERRY

QUARRY

QUARRY

PELLES

Colleville-sur-Orne

Ste. Aubin-d'Arquenay

HEDGE CLEARED

HEDGE CLEARED

M.T. BAYS

WK.

WK. HEDGE CLEARED

EMPLACEMENTS ON TOP FOR GUNS?

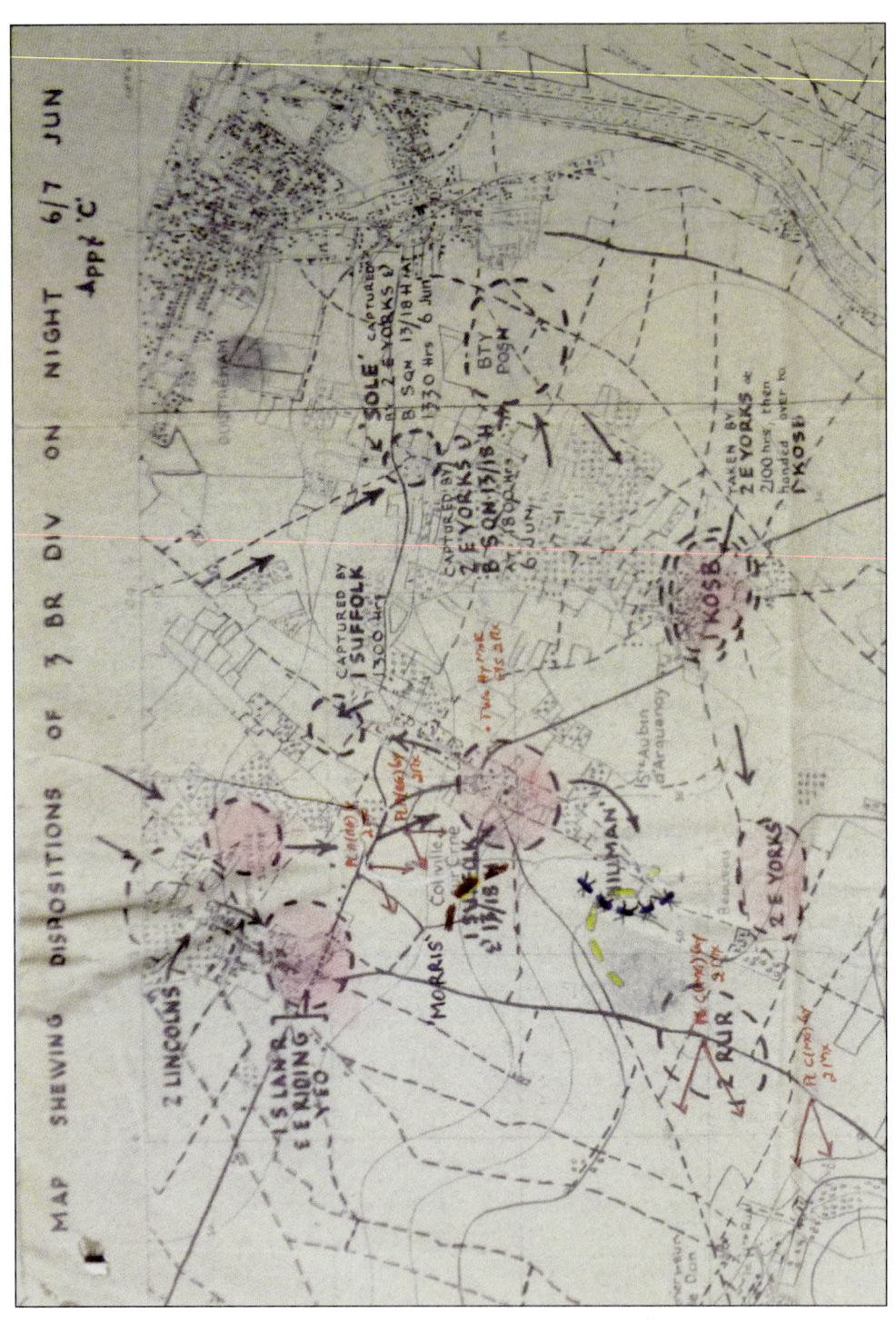

2. An annotated map showing the final D-Day positions for each of the battalions from 3 Br Inf Div

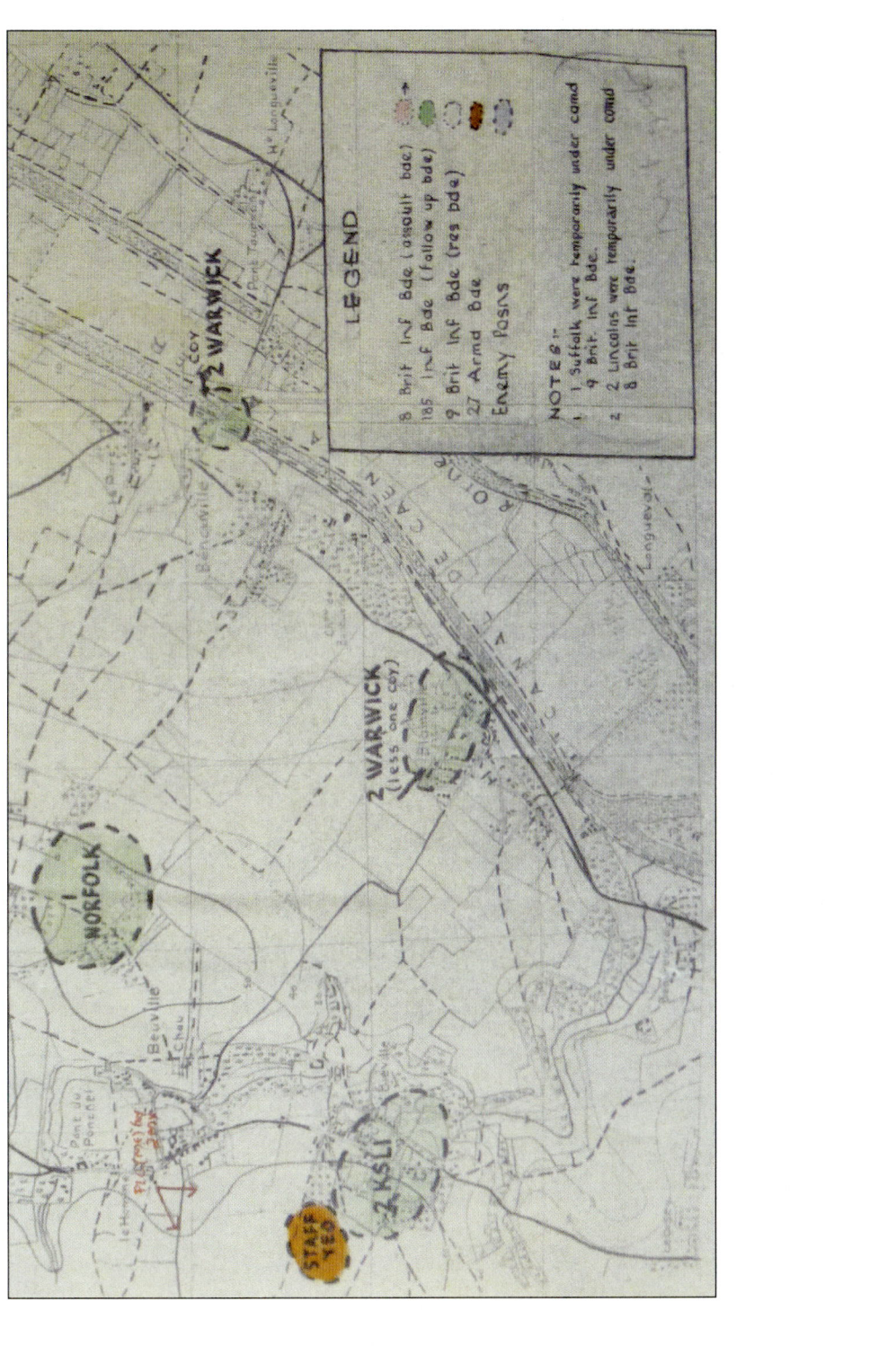

LEGEND

8 Brit Inf Bde (assault bde)
185 Inf Bde (follow up bde)
9 Brit Inf Bde (res bde)
27 Armd Bde
Enemy Posns

NOTES:-
1. Suffolk were temporarily under comd
   9 Brit Inf Bde.
2. Lincolns were temporarily under comd
   8 Brit Inf Bde.

H^t Longueville

Pont Tournant

1 coy

1 2 WARWICK

Bénouville

CANAL DE CAEN

ORNE

Longueval

2 WARWICK
(less one coy)

Blainville

NORFOLK

Beuville

Chau

Bieville

Pont du Pontaria

PLATOON (Inf)

STAFF YEO

2 KSLI

le Hauger

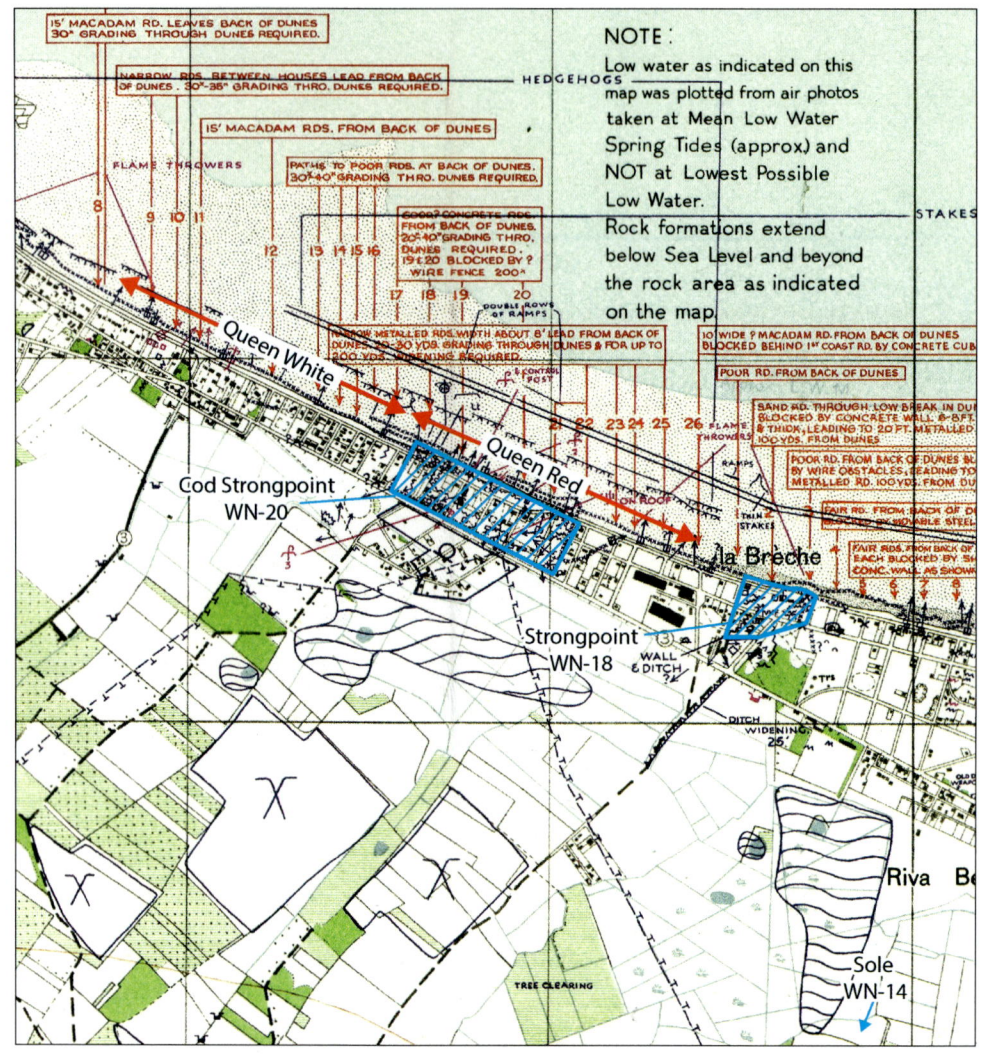

3. The British assault area for Sword sector centred around La Breche and the strong-point COD (Chapter 7)

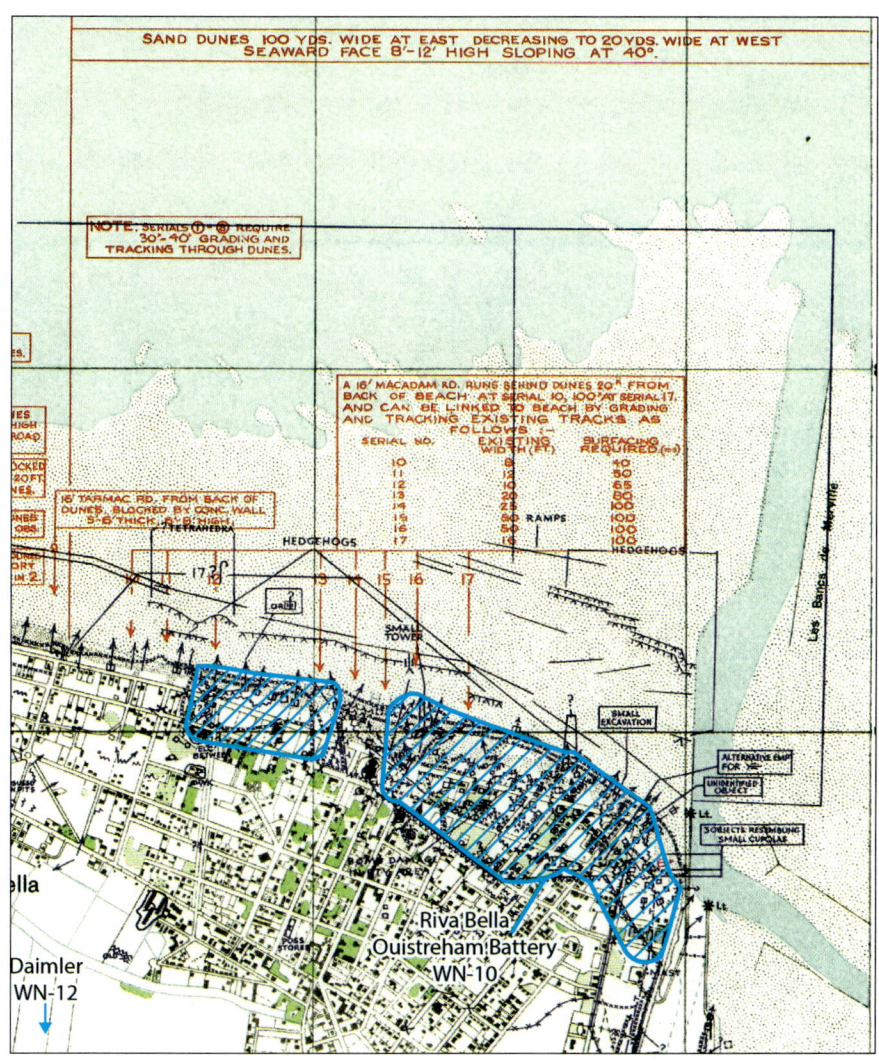

SAND DUNES 100 YDS. WIDE AT EAST DECREASING TO 20 YDS. WIDE AT WEST
SEAWARD FACE 8'-12' HIGH SLOPING AT 40°.

NOTE: SERIALS ⑪ - ⑰ REQUIRE
30'-40' GRADING AND
TRACKING THROUGH DUNES.

A 16' MACADAM RD. RUNS BEHIND DUNES 20' FROM
BACK OF BEACH AT SERIAL 10, 100'AT SERIAL 17,
AND CAN BE LINKED TO BEACH BY GRADING
AND TRACKING EXISTING TRACKS AS
FOLLOWS :-

SERIAL NO.	EXISTING WIDTH (FT)	SURFACING REQUIRED (YDS)
10	8	10
11	10	50
12	10	65
13	20	80
14	8	100
15	8 RAMPS	100
16	50	100
17	10	100
		HEDGEHOGS

16' TARMAC RD. FROM BACK OF
DUNES, BLOCKED BY CONC. WALL
5'-6' THICK, 5'-6' HIGH

HEDGEHOGS

SMALL TOWER

SMALL EXCAVATION

ALTERNATIVE RAMP FOR ?

UNIDENTIFIED OBJECT

? SCHELDE RESEMBLING SMALL CUPOLA

Lt.

Lt.

Les Bancs de Merville

ella

Daimler
WN-12

Riva Bella
Ouistreham Battery
WN-10

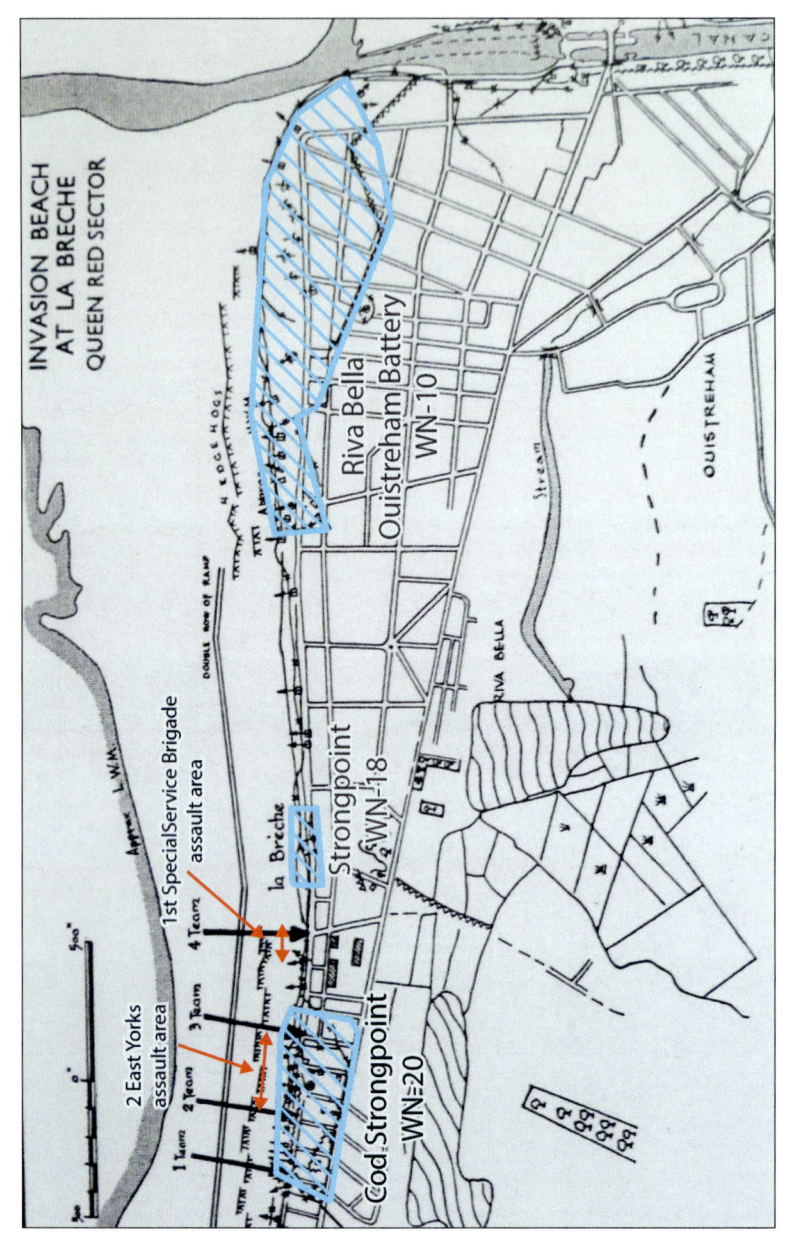

INVASION BEACH
AT LA BRECHE
QUEEN RED SECTOR

Riva Bella
Ouistreham Battery
WN-10

OUISTREHAM

Stream

RIVA BELLA

Strongpoint
WN-18

la Brèche

1st Special Service Brigade
assault area

4 Team

Approx L.W.M.

2 East Yorks
assault area

1 Team

2 Team

3 Team

DOUBLE ROW OF RAMP

Cod Strongpoint
WN-20

4. Queen Red, the target for 2 East Yorks who landed on the beach
at 0725 on D-Day (see Chapter 7)

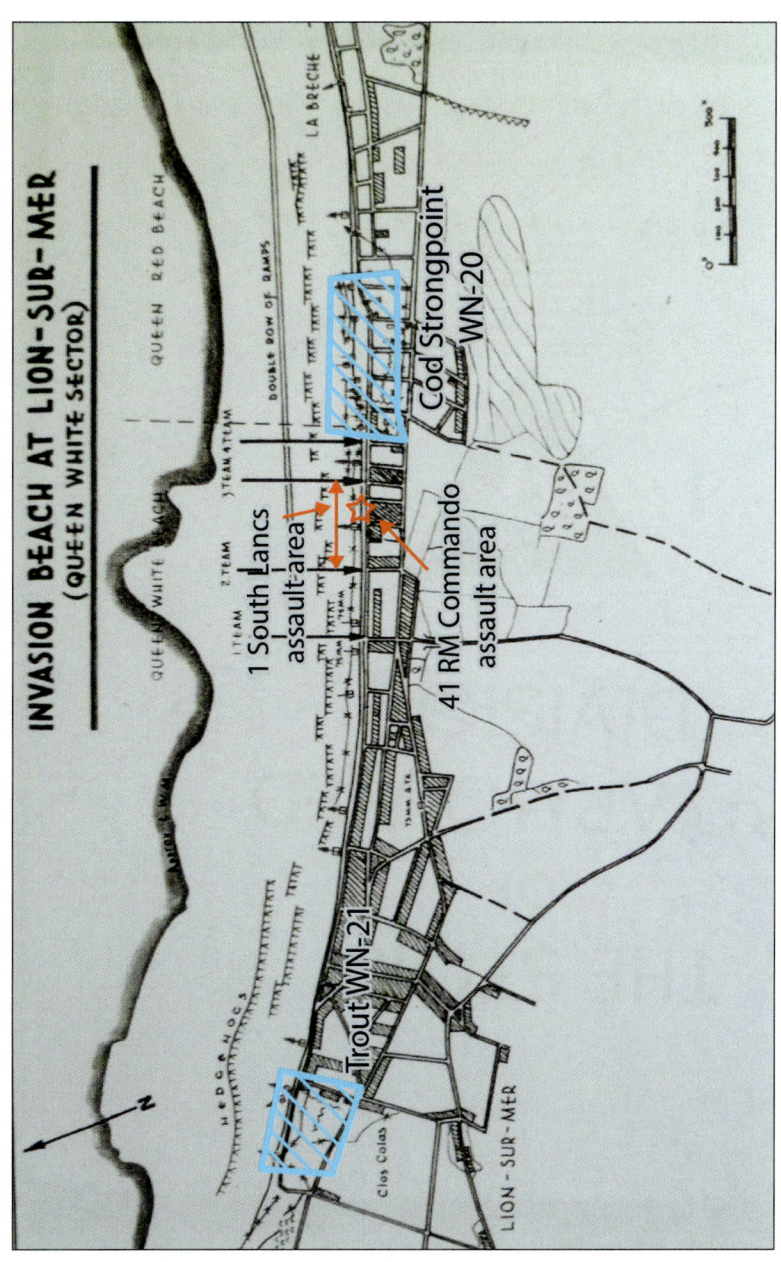

5. Landing on the other main beach, Queen White, were 1 South Lancs (see Chapter 7)

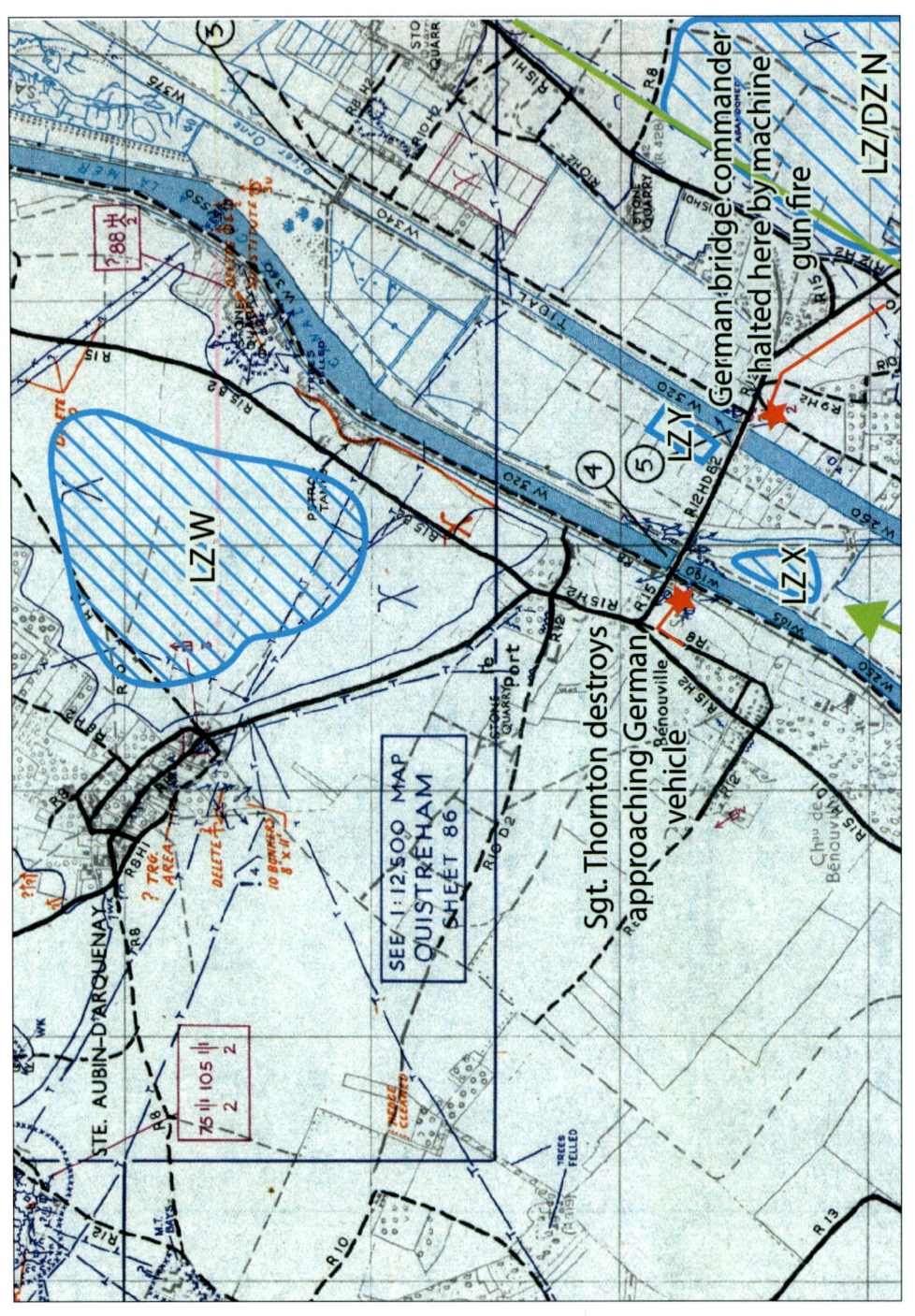

6. The landing area for Operation DEADSTICK, the *coup de main* assault on the bridges over the River Orne and the Caen Canal (see Chapter 6)

Glider flight path
Chalk 91 lands 0016

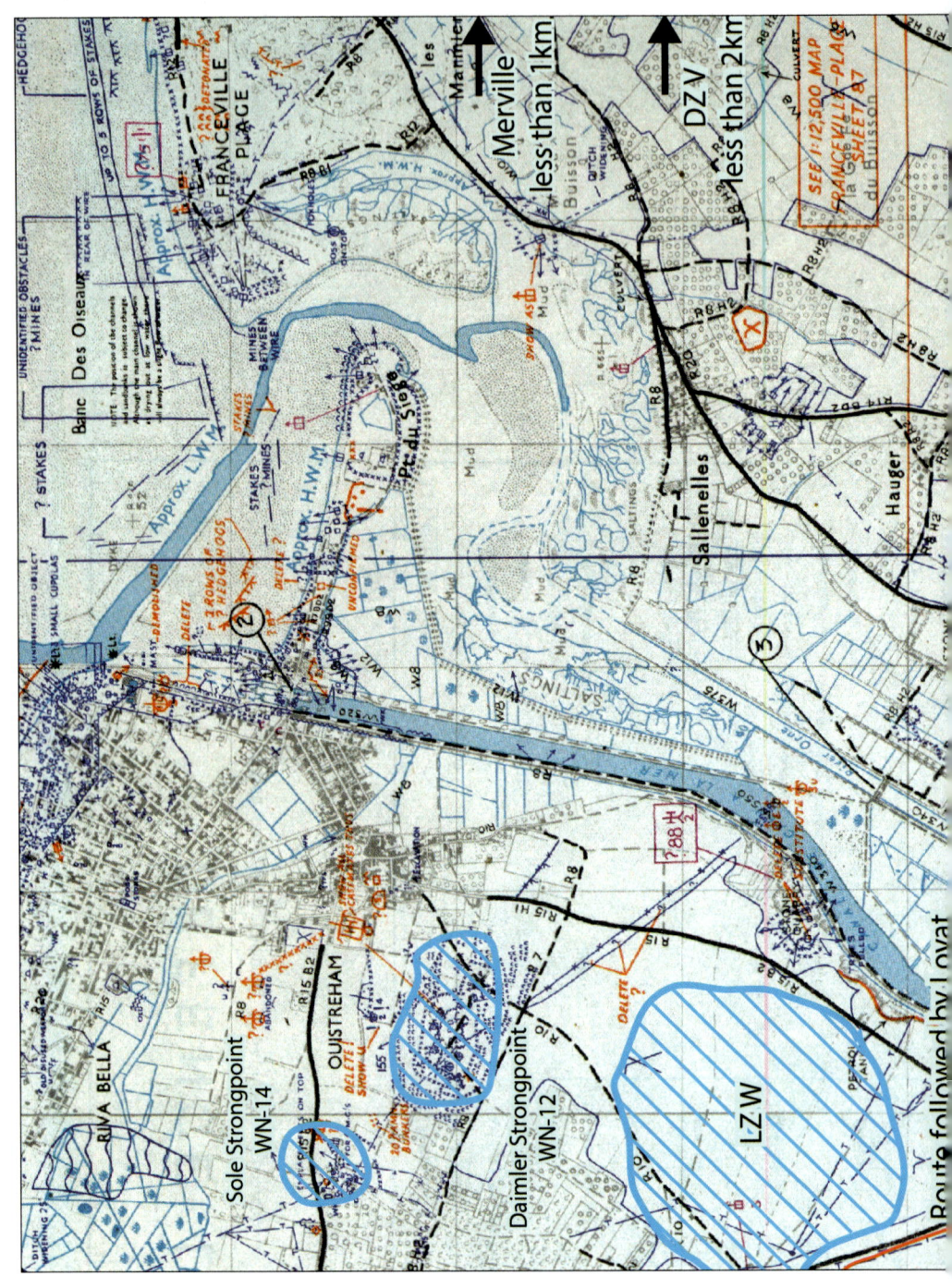

7. The main landing areas for 6 AB Div on the east bank of the River Orne
(see Chapter 6)

Caen Canal and River
Orne bridges

Benouville captured
by 2 Warwicks 2100

LZ N

LZ X

Pont Tournant

le Bas de Ranville

Major-General Gale's HQ
Chateau du Heaume

Lord Lovat's Brigade HQ
farmhouse at le Plein

le Plein

Longuemare

Bréville

Amfréville

LZ/DZ N

Ranville

Ouistreville

Herouvillette

Carrefour de la Madeleine

DZ K
less than 1km

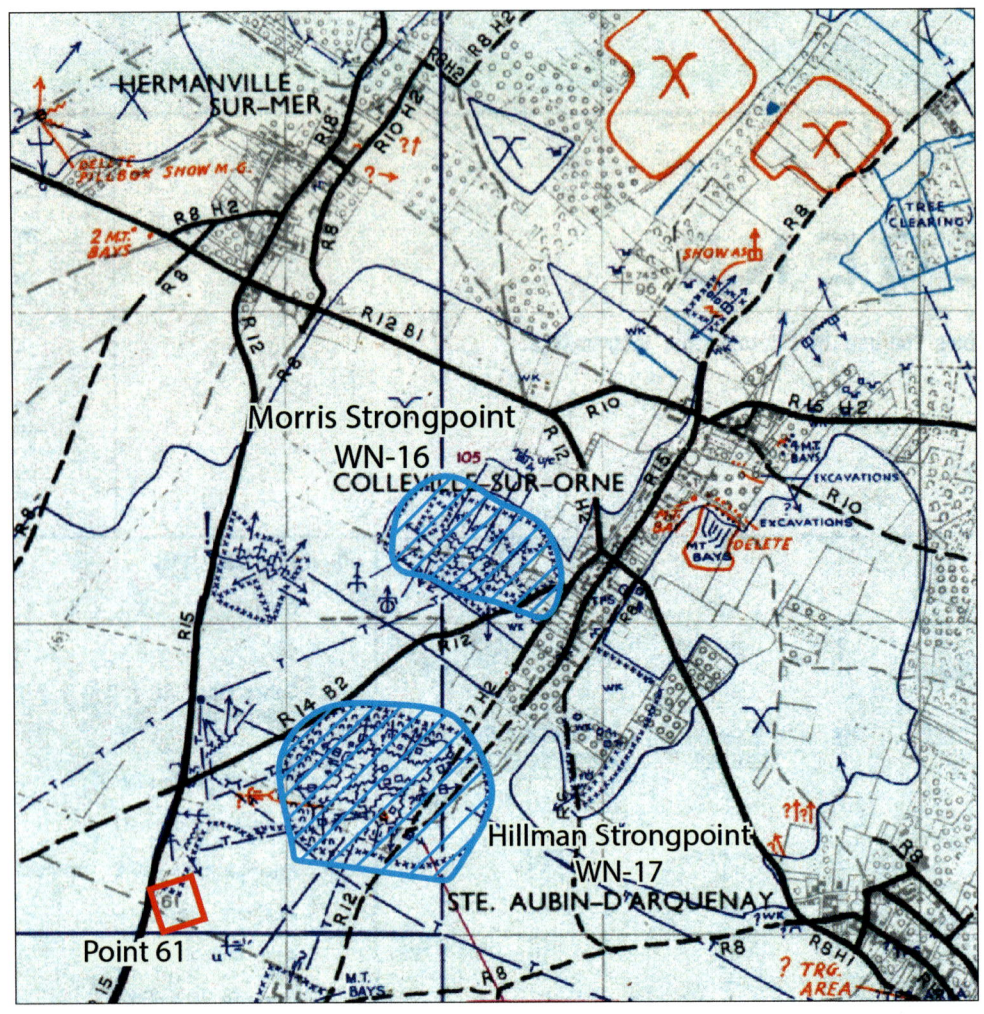

8. The two key German strong-points, MORRIS and HILLMAN, south of the village of Colleville (see Chapter 11)

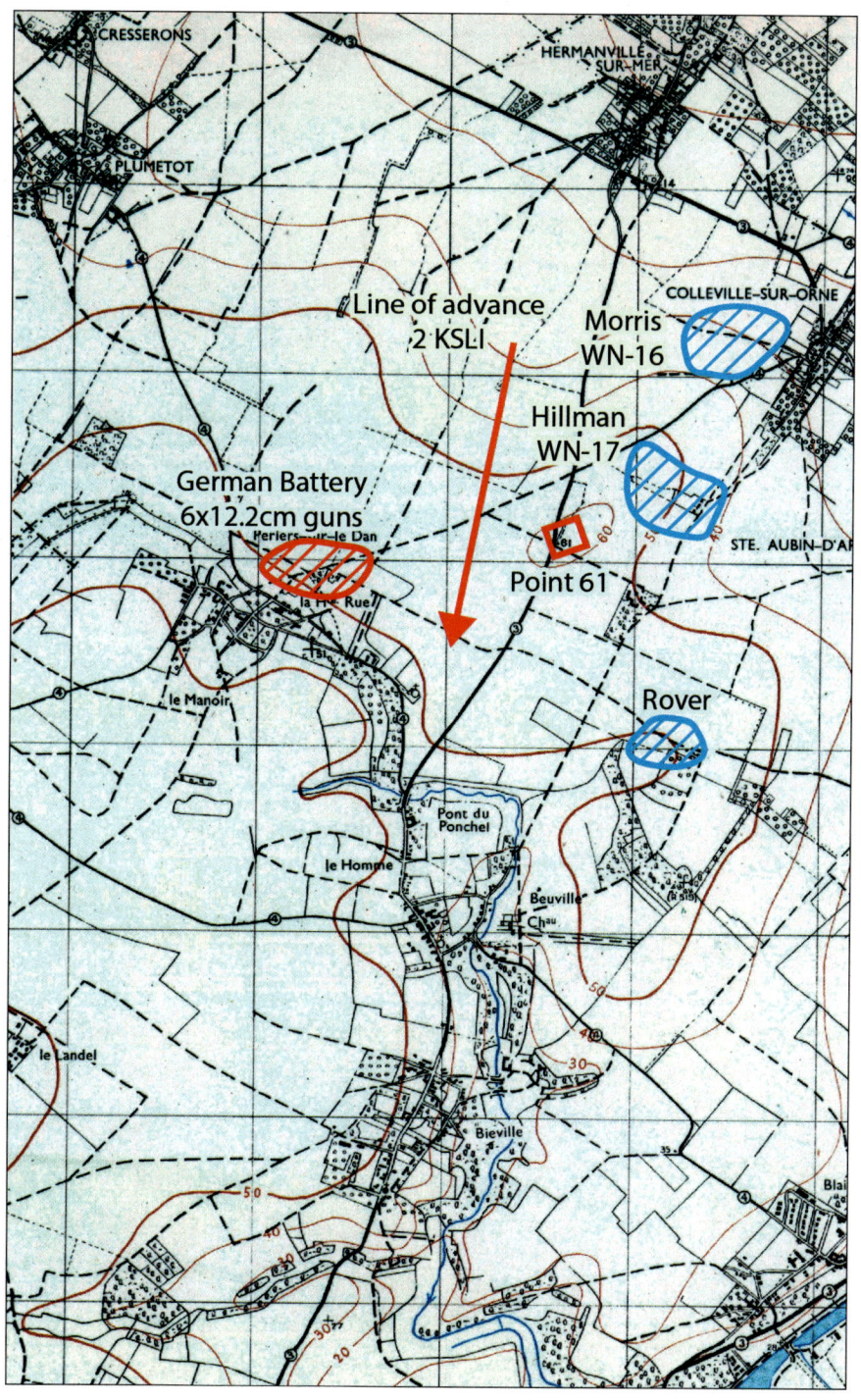

9. The opening of the main German counter-attack on the afternoon of 6, June elements of which succeeded in reaching the coast (see Chapter 11)

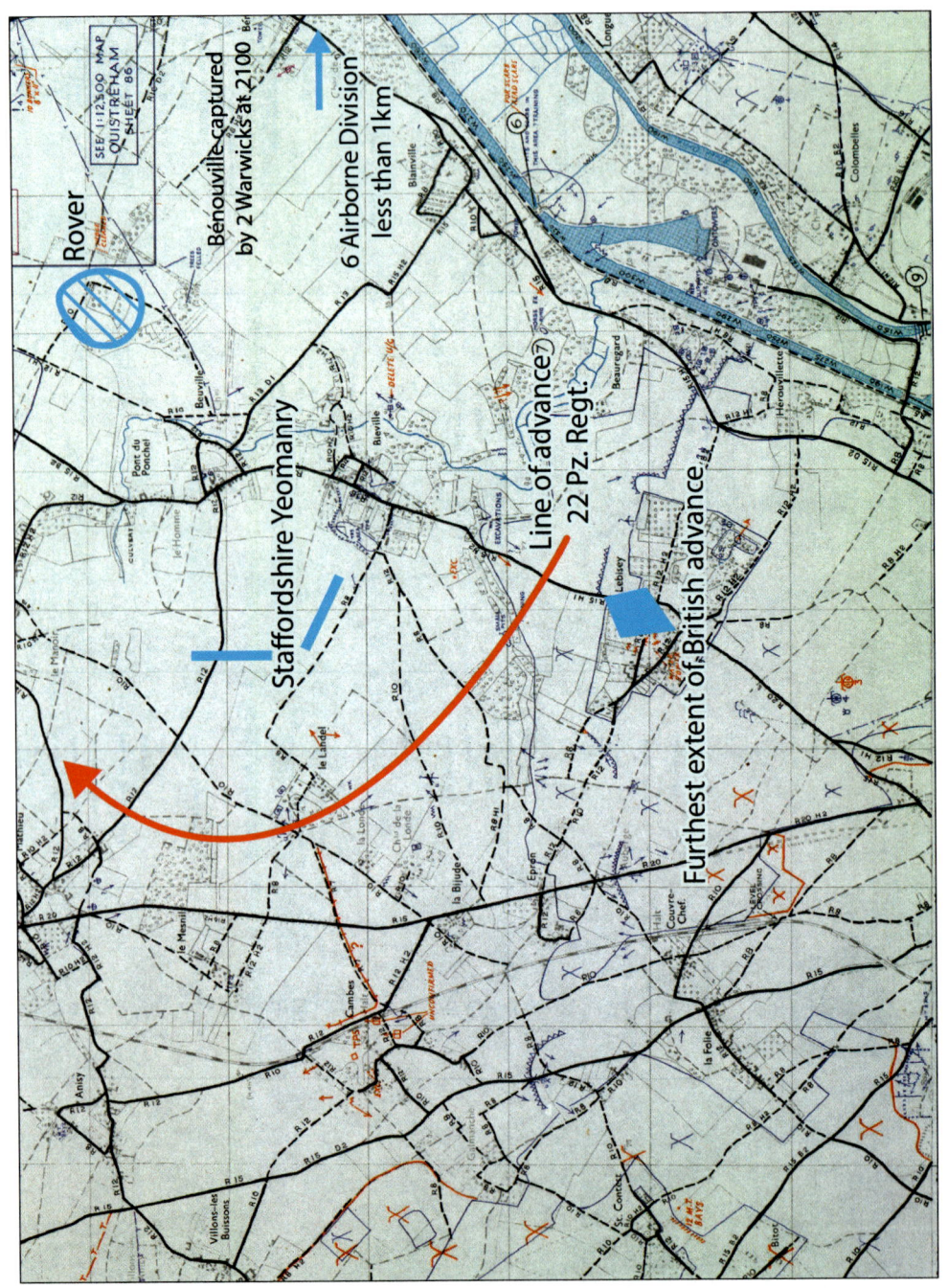

Rover

Bénouville captured by 2 Warwicks at 2100

6 Airborne Division less than 1km

SEE 1:12,500 MAP
OUISTREHAM
SHEET 86

Staffordshire Yeomanry

Line of advance?
22 Pz. Regt.

Furthest extent of British advance

10. The woods and village of Lebisey represented the culmination of the British advance following a fierce engagement with German troops in the late afternoon of D-Day (see Chapter 12)

Two of the Operation DEADSTICK gliders with the Caen Canal bridge in front of them

I had been there before".[18] One of the 2 Ox and Bucks junior officers involved explained their high levels of confidence prior to the attack as being down to the knowledge that they had the best pilots who could land exactly where they wanted.[19] But there was also "our ignorance of the hazards of the whole operation: we had no idea how risky it was because we had no experience of that sort of thing, so you can really say ignorance is bliss". As he recorded later, at one stage the planners even referred to this part of the assault plan as 'The Forlorn Hope'.

Staff Sergeant Jim Wallwork piloting his glider, officially termed as 'Horsa Chalk 91' but nicknamed 'Lady Irene', was the first to land at 0016. Described as "less a landing and more of a controlled crash", one of the narratives describes their target as "a small field south of the eastern end of the Benouville bridge. It resembled an isosceles triangle, the apex being at the perimeter of the bridge defences; one side was the canal bank, the other a small ditch".[20] LZ W was actually about 300 metres long and the glider touched down at a speed of about 80 mph before an arrester parachute deployed. Such was the impact of the landing and the rapid halt that both pilot and co-pilot were ejected through the cockpit windscreen technically making them the first British military personnel in the invasion to land on French soil. As Major Howard later wrote, "the nearness to the bridge astounded everyone, the pilots had indeed exceeded all expectations. The leading glider had crashed through the very wire fence at the exact

18 Ibid.
19 Lieutenant Richard 'Sandy' Smith, cited in Roderick Bailey, *Forgotten Voices of D-Day – A New History of the Normandy Landings* (Ebury Press; London, 2009), pp.114-115.
20 Warhurst, 'Overlord: D-Day 6 June 1944, Book Two', p.192, CAB44/244, TNA.

spot indicated on the model during briefing".[21] The second glider, Chalk 92, which was carrying No.24 Platoon, landed about a minute later fifteen yards to the rear of the first while the third, Chalk 93 carrying No.14 Platoon, landed fifteen yards behind having had to swerve to avoid those in front; all three gliders were smashed on the uneven ground but they had landed within 100 yards of one another.[22]

The garrison on the bridges was thought to consist of about 50 men and the attackers wasted no time with the leading section from the first glider, No.25 Platoon under the command of Lieutenant Den Brotheridge, heading straight across the bridge. His men captured the pillbox after Private Bailey led a group of two other men and put grenades through its slits; the Germans who were supposed to be inside were discovered to the rear where they had been sleeping. As the strongpoint was being disabled the first section was halfway across the bridge; its leader made it across the canal before being shot in the neck by a bullet from an enemy machine gun, dying later from his wounds. He was one of only two to be killed during the attack: Brotheridge was the first member of the Allied invasion force to die as a result of enemy fire but Lance Corporal Fred Greenhalgh, a sapper carried on Chalk 93, drowned in the area of swampy water next to the LZ that had not been marked on the pre-invasion maps, and is considered to have been the first fatality of D-Day. The two following platoons fought to secure the area around the bridge and alongside them were the sappers who found no explosives under the bridge, the same being the case at the Orne river. The bridges also had been prepared for demolition but the charges had not been put in place and were later found in a store by the bridgehead. Once these had been removed, the sappers were to concentrate on laying anti-tank and anti-personnel minefields on the roads approaching the position. It was found that the trenches were to have been booby-trapped with mines but the man responsible for laying them was wounded in the initial stages of the assault and his box of primed charges was found lying next to him.

The attack on the bridge over the River Orne fared even better with the German defenders fleeing and abandoning their equipment. This despite the fact that only one British glider, Chalk 96 carrying No.17 Platoon led by Lieutenant D.B. Fox, landed close to the bridge on LZ Y about 300 metres from the target. A few minutes behind the start of the assault at the canal bridge, it was undamaged despite the field being full not of anti-glider defences but grazing cows. The second glider, Chalk 95 with Lieutenant H.J. Sweeney's No.23 Platoon on board, had insufficient height to reach the bridge and landed about 700 metres to the north. The final one, Chalk 94 carrying Howard's deputy Captain B.C.E. Priday, cast off in the wrong place and came to ground about 13 kilometres from the targets near Varraville and beyond the Dives river. Having captured the river bridge without opposition and with the perimeter only thinly held, Lieutenant Fox's platoon was brought over to form a fighting patrol on the western outskirts of Benouville. By 0030 both bridges were secure and Howard ordered that the coded wireless signal 'Ham and Jam' be transmitted to confirm they were under his control and both intact. As he took out his officer's whistle and repeatedly blasted out the Morse

21 'Report by Major R.J. Howard…', Staff College Camberley 1947 Course, JSCSC.
22 Warhurst, 'Overlord: D-Day 6 June 1944, Book Two', p.192, CAB44/244, TNA.

signal for V to signify 'V for victory' he considered that his company was lucky to have been selected for "what turned out to be a wonderful operation".[23]

Sweeney's platoon holding the river bridge had already dealt with a four-man patrol when the first counter-attack of the invasion followed. At 0115 a German staff car and motorcycle approached from the direction of Ranville and were fired upon by a Bren gun killing the motorcyclist. The car crossed the bridge before its tires were punctured and three prisoners taken, including the badly wounded commander of the bridges, a Major Schmidt, who spoke perfect English and used it to shout that he wanted to be shot as his honour had been lost.[24] There were also a large number of empty wine bottles. It was discovered from the prisoners that the bridge garrison had only numbered about 16 men from 736 Gren based at Merville. Shortly afterwards tanks were heard moving to the north-west of the position. The defending platoon had been given a PIAT (Projector Infantry Anti-Tank) unloaded from the wreckage of the gliders and as the lead vehicle, most likely a lightly armoured French tank or an armoured half-track, approached the bridge it was put out of action by a well-aimed round. As one of those who witnessed the attack recalled:

> We never thought those PIAT bombs would ever do much damage to a proper tank but this flaming tank literally blew up, exploded. The whole thing went up. It was well loaded with ammunition, I don't know what sort of ammunition but within moments of [Sergeant 'Wagger' Thornton] firing there were great spurts of green and orange and yellow as all the ammunition inside was exploding, making a hell of a din. And the other tank behind did a quick revving of engines and disappeared, backed off of the road, and we never heard from them again.[25]

As it 'brewed up' the flames served to illuminate the bridge structure and acted as a marker for the pilots carrying the first main drop of paratroopers. The remaining German vehicles, not knowing the size of the force facing them, withdrew in disorder; as one of those present later wrote, had they realised how few attackers there were they would most likely have overrun the position.[26]

The *coup de main* force had expected reinforcements from 7 Para Bn to arrive within an hour of the initial attack but their drop lacked accuracy and more than one-third landed a mile or more away from DZ N. This also meant there were no machine guns, mortars or wireless sets available throughout the initial period of the operation. With Lieutenant-Colonel R.G. Pine-Coffin, in command of the battalion, leaving his deputy at the previously agreed rendezvous he departed with what men he could reaching the bridges at about 0140. Thirty minutes later, nearly an hour behind schedule, the men of 2 Ox Bucks were ordered to withdraw behind the canal bridge and assume responsibility for the river bridge and the area between the two obstacles. This position they held until the morning of 7/8 June. The attack had proven a tremendous success but the delays

---

23 Major John Howard, cited in Bailey, *Forgotten Voices of D-Day*, p.114.
24 Ibid., p.133.
25 Ibid., Private Denis Edwards, p.134.
26 Edwards, *The Devil's Own Luck – From Pegasus Bridge to The Baltic*, pp.44-45.

encountered by the relief force were commonplace and would prove a standard feature of what followed.

Indeed, the airborne element of the invasion plan was seriously hampered by an inability to concentrate its forces and this prevented all of its objectives from being completed. A total of 27 aircraft carrying the pathfinder sticks took off at 2300 on 5 June from their home bases and the pilots found good visibility with 10/10 cloud at 4,000 feet. The problems began once they reached the DZs with the extra heavy loads that were being carried and the unanticipated issue of moving men who had travelled in cramped positions. Half of those aircraft involved in this initial lift dropped later than scheduled – one required three runs to drop the sticks of Pathfinders it was carrying who were then 14 minutes late reaching their target. Once on the ground the sites were marked with Eureka and green lights which coded the DZ letter and were observed successfully by the approaching aircraft. A critical error, however, came with the two sticks detailed for DZ N who arrived at their target to discover colleagues who were supposed to have been heading for DZ K. The latter had already set up their equipment and sent the incorrect signal to those following them; although this mistake was quickly corrected many aircraft that had followed these signals dropped their paratroopers some two and a half miles off target.[27] For those heading to DZ V they experienced the greatest confusion and this meant that the main body of 3 Para Bde was weakened badly; of the 71 aircraft that had been assigned to this lift, only 17 managed to drop their men inside the target area and approximately 30 were more than 1.5 miles wide. Two sticks even landed in the suburbs of Ouistreham.[28]

Where this failure threatened to have the greatest impact on the operation was in regard to 6 AB Div's other main target. The destruction, or at the very least neutralisation, of the Merville battery, a series of strongpoints situated in a meadow about one mile inland, was potentially key to the entire plan for the assault on the Sword beaches as this was less than four miles away from them and it could bring fire to bear on both Queen White and Red. According to intelligence reports the battery site, the construction of which had begun in 1943, was believed to hold four 155 mm guns; in reality it was armed with four elderly 100 mm light field howitzers. These were the *Feldhaubitze* 14/19(t) which had originally been built for the Austro-Hungarian army in 1914 and later refurbished by the Skoda Works before being seized by the Germans in 1938 following the annexation of Czechoslovakia. These guns had been set aside for coastal defence in 1942 but they still carried great potential to threaten any invading fleet firing 36 pound shells to a maximum range of more than six miles. They were set in casemates, referred to as 'Standard Structure 611', which contained 1330 cubic metres of cement, 63 tons of steel rods and 15.5 tons of structural steel – reinforced concrete about six-and-a-half feet thick with doors made of steel. Rooms had been provided for the gun detachments and additional space for ammunition; off duty personnel were also housed in the shelter and some in the village of Merville. It was believed that spotters were in an observation point on the coast in a known infantry strongpoint on the east bank of the Orne with an additional lookout on the water tower at the northern corner of the village.

27 Warhurst, 'Overlord: D-Day 6 June 1944, Book Two', pp.190-191, CAB44/244, TNA.
28 RAF Narrative, 'Volume III, The Landings in Normandy', pp.96-99, JSCSC.

Only two of the emplacements, Nos.1 and 2, were completed and camouflaged with further protection provided for them from a covering of about 12 feet of earth; construction work was still continuing on the other two casemates. The position was extremely well defended with 15 weapon pits some of which were presumed to contain machine guns, and an inner perimeter wire, about 600 yards out, double width in some places, and about 15 feet thick and five feet high. Around the western half of this inner fence an anti-tank ditch had been dug which was 14 feet wide and beyond the inner perimeter as many as seven rows of mines had been laid. The battery was further surrounded by a mixture of dummy positions and additional machine gun or light anti-aircraft strong points with more concrete shelters in the adjacent orchards and the possibility of one or two anti-tank guns. With an estimated garrison of 180-200, as the official narrative notes "the battery position was a formidable one" and any assault on it would require heavier equipment than could be carried solely by parachutists. Hence the attacking force would need a number of gliders.

This assault was the primary objective for 3 Para Bde, the operational instruction stressing that "no other commitment must jeopardise success in this task".[29] By way of insurance it had been agreed that if the battery were not captured by P-30 minutes – Royal Navy signallers who were assigned to the battalion were supposed to send a signal to HMS *Arethusa* by 0530 – then its neutralization was to become the first priority for naval bombardment support. Once Merville was secured the brigade was to then move on to Le Plein which it was to capture and hold until relieved by the commandos. The commander of 9 Para Bn, Lieutenant-Colonel Terence Otway, was told during an initial briefing by his brigade commander Brigadier Hill that this "one special job" was "a real pukka grade A stinker" and this assessment quickly proved itself to be accurate.[30] Training took place at a specially chosen location near Newbury which was prepared to match the battery site in Normandy. There were nine full rehearsals involving live ammunition, five during daylight and four at night. Timing was an especially critical consideration for this assault and a maximum of four-and-a-half hours were allowed to complete the combined glider-airborne landings followed by the approach march – the nearest landing zones were 2400 yards away – and the completion of the operation. Also included within the plan was the second *coup de main*, three gliders which were fitted with special arrester parachutes and had been earmarked to crash land on top of the gun positions. Reminiscent of the 1940 attack on the Belgian fortress of Eben Emael this carried significant risk and, as was the case with the entire operation, there was a need for meticulous planning and most careful rehearsal. Scheduled for 0430 it was calculated that by this point the obstacles would have been breached and the final assault would have begun.

Whilst the first element of the plan was a success in so much as the reconnaissance and organisation parties landed on time, the main body of the battalion, arriving at 0050, was widely dispersed and only 16 sticks out of 30 landed within a mile of the centre of the DZ. Two hours later the assembled strength was still no more than 150 men and there were no scaling ladders – intended for crossing the anti-tank ditch – no vehicles or other essential stores, and only 20 lengths of Bangalore torpedoes. Armed with what

---

29 Warhurst, 'Overlord: D-Day 6 June 1944, Book Two', p.173, CAB44/244, TNA.
30 James Gleeson and Tom Waldron, *Now It Can Be Told* (London; Paul Elek, 1952), pp.13-14.

they were carrying, one Vickers machine gun and the bare minimum of signalling equipment, Otway decided he could wait no longer and set off for the target. Arriving at the battery they were met by Major George Smith of the reconnaissance party which had, despite the failure of any meaningful equipment to land with him or his men, managed to cut the outer fence, penetrate the minefields to the inner wire, and marked safe routes through by means of the small group scraping their heels in the dust. With a quickly revised plan the much reduced airborne contingent began its assault. As it did so two of the special gliders landed either side of the position, neither having been able to find their exact target. With a bugle sounding the 'charge' the paratroopers moved forward and, after a short but intense fight, the garrison was quickly overcome. The guns, which were destroyed with gammon bombs, were found to be smaller than the intelligence had indicated but the still vital target had been silenced and at 0445 the success signal, a red-green-red series of flares fired by one of the battalion's two-inch mortars was ordered. With a lack of signalling equipment two other pre-arranged signals were also used; a carrier pigeon kept inside the battledress of the battalion signal officer was now released to return back to Britain and at 0500, with aircraft from the Fleet Air Arm due to arrive over the area 30 minutes after dawn, yellow smoke candles were also lit.[31]

One of the series of post-battle reports that were produced described the attack on Merville as "an excellent example of how the handicaps and risks inherent in airborne operations can be overcome by determination, skill and a high standard of training".[32] The battery was neutralised for the critical opening hours of the invasion but elements of the German garrison remained untouched in bunkers unknown to the attacking troops. From these they were able to emerge later and carry on fighting helping make the position untenable. Adding to the confusion once the assault had concluded the Germans began to shell the position from neighbouring Franceville Plage. Three further air raids by the American aircraft, naval gunfire support from the Royal Navy and more raids from the RAF were all eventually needed to complete the job that 9 Para Bn had begun.

There was one other element of the main part of TONGA to be completed, the landing by the main glider force which had been scheduled to arrive at about 0330 carrying the divisional headquarters with Major-General Gale along with additional transport and an anti-tank battery. Some of the gliders carrying the airborne division's jeep transport and other heavy equipment had arrived at LZ N at 0045 but others were scattered generally to the east or south-east. Whilst the pathfinder aircraft had encountered good visibility overcast cloudy conditions, a wind of 10-20 mph, and dust and smoke being blown up by the bombing attacks all restricted visibility and made what few ground signals there were difficult for the tug crews to see.[33] Preparations for the later lifts therefore became a priority task for the airborne sappers of 591st Engineer Squadron, supported by a company from 13 Para Bn, with the plan calling for two-and-a-half strips to be cleared by P-2 hours, initially using explosive 'sausages' to clear any obstacles, before three American airborne bulldozers, scheduled to land with the first glider party, expanded

---

31 RAF Narrative, 'Volume III, The Landings in Normandy', pp.203-208, JSCSC.
32 'Capture of Coastal Bty position at 155755 by 'X' Para Bn 6 Jun 44', Immediate Report No.19, 18 June 1944, CAB106/963, TNA.
33 RAF Narrative, 'Volume III, The Landings in Normandy', pp.96-99, JSCSC.

the site.[34] In reality it was found that many of the obstruction poles had not been put in place – at the Caen Canal the holes had been dug but not filled, at LZ W few of the obstructions exceeded five inches in length – and it proved relatively simple to remove them by hand.[35] The strips that were completed were each 500 yards by 120 yards with a 120 yard funnel at each end but the deteriorating weather and considerable low cloud caused problems. Out of a force of 68 Horsas just 48 landed in the target zone although three of the four larger Hamilcars were amongst them. At the same time as this landing was taking place 13 Para Bn was completing its capture of Ranville, which was held by 0400, making it the first village in France to be fully liberated.

The unofficial history of the role played by airborne forces throughout the Second World War, written by the commander of the Merville action, offered the conclusion that "... the air plan worked, although weather conditions were by no means ideal. All tasks allotted to 6 AB Div were carried out up to time, and such scattering of personnel as there was did not cause failure in any part of the operation of the plan".[36] The official assessment agreed that this element of the operation had generally proven successful. Operation TONGA had involved 264 paratroop aircraft which carried 4512 paratroopers and an additional 1315 containers of equipment. Just seven of these aircraft were lost along with the approximately 200 men and 100 containers they were carrying. For the two parachute brigades that had jumped the final figures for those missing were 30 officers and 628 other ranks although a substantial number of these re-joined during the next few days. The situation was worse in terms of gliders with 98 combinations having been launched of which 74 gliders were successfully released and 22 were lost; for those that landed at night only 52 of them reached the correct LZ. The attrition was particularly acute for the glider pilots, 196 were involved in the operation but only 125 returned unharmed. Although scattered around the drop areas a good amount of equipment was successfully transported, 44 out of 59 jeeps, 55 out of 69 motorcycles, 15 out of 17 six-pounder guns and even a bulldozer which was successfully released over DZ N.

A Horsa glider showing the scars of its landing

34 By P+10 hours they had been extended to 1,000 yards; Warhurst, 'Overlord: D-Day 6 June 1944, Book Two', pp.179, 185, CAB44/244, TNA.

35 Ibid.

36 Otway, *Airborne Forces*, p.182.

By 0600 a divisional headquarters had been established in the Château du Heaume at Le Bas de Ranville, within the perimeter of 12 Para Bn, and wireless sets and stores had been unloaded and defensive slit trenches prepared. An hour later Major General Gale crossed the bridges captured in the *coup de main* to visit 7 Para Bn which was already facing its first substantial counter-attack of the day.

With the arrival of British airborne forces the Germans had received a very clear warning that a major attack was developing. Their confused and hesitant response determined the outcome of the entire landings. Had they engaged the airborne forces in any real strength the plan for the Sword sector would have had to have been changed even more than subsequently proved to be the case. Even so, with their main mechanised and armoured units spread across an area running only as far south as Falaise, the defenders only had a relatively short distance to travel to reach the beaches where the British troops would soon also be arriving. The airborne prologue had, to a large degree, accomplished its objectives but the race was now on to land the invasion force and secure Eisenhower's intent of a lodgement on the Continent.

6

H-Hour – Touch Down

See maps 6 and 7.

As the invasion force neared the coast the preliminary attack on the German defences intensified. 'Bombarding Force D' started its fire plan at 0640 and continued right up until H-Hour which was scheduled for 45 minutes later. It was later estimated that during the first ten minutes of the attack, which took place right across the NEPTUNE area, the naval guns within the two task forces fired more than 2,000 tons of high explosives. For Sword the three heavy batteries south of the Seine estuary at Villerville, Benerville and Holgate, each of which covered the Queen beaches, were the focus for the big naval guns. According to the official account, the bombarding force was successful "to the extent that the enemy return fire was desultory and inaccurate and did not interfere with 'Force S' landings".[1] The British ships had been told they should fire upon these if the fleet was targeted and "periodic treatment" followed; *Ramillies* conducted 11 shoots at Benerville while *Warspite* carried out 20 shoots firing 314 rounds from her main armament on 6/7 June before returning to Portsmouth to replenish with ammunition.

Further along the coast, the intention had been that the heavy batteries at Le Havre and Le Havre Grand Clos would have been disabled from the air prior to the invasion but this did not prove successful. A total of 1056 heavy, medium and fighter bombers targeted what had been assessed to be the ten key coastal batteries forming part of the Atlantic Wall. Between them they dropped 5267 tons of bombs for the loss of 11 aircraft and 70 crewmen before returning back to their bases in Britain; the heavy batteries to the north were left intact. Soon after daylight 1630 Liberators, Fortresses and medium bombers of the 8th and 9th United States Air Forces followed also conducting attacks across the assault zone. Then, 20 minutes before the arrival of the invasion force, fighter and medium bombers focussed on the beach defences while the landing craft were making their final approach; three more missions later in the day were all intended to delay the arrival of enemy troops into the area by creating blockages.[2] For Sword there were eight targets for the initial attack conducted by B-17s and B-24s scheduled to start at 0655 and be finished by 0728 after which there was to be an additional 50 minutes of bombing two pre-determined sets of chokepoints near Caen. All four of the key air missions were subsequently assessed to have had little positive impact, the official record going so far as to describe the first two of them as having been fiascos in large part as a result of the weather and the need to ensure the safety of the Allied troops on

---

1   'Normandy Bombardment Experience (June/September, 1944)', *Gunnery Review*, February 1945, pp.5-6, 8, JSCSC.
2   Warhurst, 'Overlord: D-Day 6 June 1944, Book Two', pp.205-206, CAB44/244, TNA.

the ground.[3] The principal contribution made by this bombing effort was judged to be the demoralisation of the German defenders and the disruption to signals and transport links which slowed the deployment of reserve forces. As the narrative concludes, however, "all the evidence available goes to show that the great bulk of the 2944 tons of bombs on the frontage of the four beaches [on Sword and Juno] almost certainly missed the beaches, chokepoints and headquarters altogether".[4] Neither the regimental headquarters at Bieville nor the battalion headquarters at St Aubin d'Arquenay could be located through the cloud cover and they were not bombed.[5]

This inability for the Allies airpower to have a significant effect was unfortunate as the bombardment plan became increasingly more reliant on air support the further inland the target list went. For example, what was believed to be a major German gun position on the Périers-sur-le-Dan ridge was only scheduled to receive heavy day bombers 30 minutes before the landing and then fighter-bombers for an additional five minutes shortly after the troops came ashore. MORRIS was to be the target of naval gunfire support from the six-inch cruiser *Dragon*, manned by Polish sailors and under the command of the Polish Navy, and this was scheduled from twilight onwards but depended on a FOB to provide details back to the ship. There would be heavy bombers attacking the site for 20 minutes from shortly before H-hour but nothing else beyond that. It is impossible to say what contribution these attacks further inland actually made but as one historian has commented, "guns, sited individually and protected by immense thicknesses of concrete are not good bombing targets". The strategy of drenching the battery sites also depended on a good measure of luck to knock out the command posts and their signal and defensive equipment.[6] Once the invasion began it would quickly be discovered that the results were less than the planners had hoped could be achieved.

Even so the effects were, in many cases, still devastating. The commanding officer of 736 Gren, Colonel Ludwig Krug, who surrendered on 7 June at HILLMAN, described the first few hours of the invasion in his subsequent interrogation:

> After we had been covered by ship's artillery fire for about four hours, tanks drove up and continued to cover [the bunkers]. After about three or four hours everything except one machine gun had been destroyed. I reported that the enemy had penetrated the minefield and that its ships were lying offshore; it was impossible to make out details, there was terrific artillery fire onto my positions ... My guns were knocked out ... one 7.5 cm and two 4.7 cm guns, and an anti-tank gun.[7]

Whilst it was later confirmed that the strongpoints on the beaches and inland had waited until the first waves of craft had touched down before responding, the weight of fire put down on them was huge. Detailed post-landing estimates were produced for the effects achieved along the sectors assaulted by British and Canadian forces by the beach

3   Ibid., p.207.
4   Ibid., p.213.
5   Ibid., p.212.
6   John Terraine, *The Right of the Line – The Royal Air Force in the European War 1939-1945* (Hodder and Stoughton; London, 1985), p.631.
7   'Opposition Encountered...', p.153, DEFE2/490, TNA.

HMS *Ramillies*, the most powerful battleship in 'Bombardment Force D'

drenching fire.[8] The destroyers covering Sword had fired 1636 rounds prior to H-Hour, the lowest total for the three Allied bombarding forces assigned to the different assault sectors but reflective of the much smaller beach area at which they were aiming. For 3 Br Inf Div's beaches they received in total the equivalent of 233.3 tons of ammunition fired from 25-pounder guns, the metric of assessment used in these calculations. It had been calculated prior to D-Day based on previous experiences that a density of 0.3 pounds per square yard of 25-pounder shells was necessary to effectively neutralize beach defences; for Sword the final total was 0.11, the highest for any of the Anglo-Canadian beaches.

Included within this total was a final layer of gunfire provided by artillery rounds fired from some of the assault craft along with five LCT(R) rocket craft. These specially adapted craft were intended to provide a short concentrated, and hopefully devastating, burst of fire onto the fortified German positions at the top end of the beaches. Unable to see their target visually the first three of these vessels fired their salvoes one minute early at 0714, eleven minutes before the scheduled landings, with the remaining two firing their rockets six minutes later. At this point the assault engineers were approximately 1,000 yards out. It was later determined that only two percent of the rockets had fallen short.[9] This was the figure that had been anticipated and a later inspection concluded that the rockets had hit the correct target and to the required depth. Some of the colliding rockets did, however, shower shrapnel over the landing craft approaching the shore, at least one junior officer was killed by a shell splinter. The LCT(R)s were subsequently reloaded and ready for further volleys to be fired by the early afternoon.

8   'Normandy Bombardment Experience', pp.19-20, JSCSC.
9   Pollock, 'Overlord: Plans and Preparations – 1940 to the "Touch Down"', CAB44/242, TNA.

At the vanguard of the first wave of the invasion force were lines of Sherman DD (Duplex Drive) 'swimming' tanks, the only piece of specialised armour to be used on each of the invasion beaches. The driver of the tank, who was responsible for navigating 30 tons of armoured vehicle, sat 11 feet below sea level whilst it was heading towards the shore. A combination of a collapsible canvas screen held up by compressed air and a propeller at the back which provided propulsion, assisted by the tank tracks which revolved while swimming, created a unique weapon of war. It did, however, have two flaws of note. The canvas screen prevented the tank from firing whilst afloat and its fragility meant that the vehicle needed relative calm whilst approaching the beach, something that was not common in the English Channel. A total of 10 armoured units would eventually be trained and equipped with these tanks, half of which were British. Special training sites were required to prepare the crews; initially sea trials were conducted in the Kyles of Bute off Western Scotland and then at Barafundle Bay in South Wales, and finally in a special area at Stokes Bay, beside Gosport. So secret was the project that all those involved had to sign the Official Secrets Act and regular lectures were given to the troops about the need for security. An instructional wing, staffed by Canadians and referred to as 'Fritton Decoy (Lake)', had also been established in Norfolk.[10] It was here, on a large inland lake surrounded by woods which had originally been a duck decoy, where great progress was made in mastering the new vehicles and where the crews also learnt how to use the Davis Submarine Escape Apparatus (DSEA) with which they were equipped in case the DDs sank. One of those who reached the Normandy beaches in a DD later wrote that "a more unseaworthy craft would be hard to imagine!"[11]

For 3 Br Inf Div the unit leading the assault would be 13/18th Royal Hussars (13/18 Hussars), part of 27 Armd Bde. The brigade's operation order noted that they were to immediately look to gain fire superiority on the beach where it was necessary for "the greatest boldness and initiative [to] be displayed by DD Tps who will seize every opportunity to press home the attack".[12] To do this the original plan had apparently called for all of the 40 DD tanks attacking the Sword beaches to fan out into one long line just before they touched down. It was judged that the volume of firepower that they could produce in this formation would be sufficiently immense, with a combination of 17 pounder and 75 mm guns along with two machine guns on each tank, to overcome the German defences. As one of those who had witnessed its effect during a training operation put it:

> ...the tank crews had gained both skill and confidence in their craft ... And they were certain that as they dropped their screens on the waterline and revealed their true identity that the morale effect of a coracle turned into a tank pumping every kind of missile into the beach defences would enable them to accomplish their task.[13]

10 Neave, 'The War Diary of Julius Neave', p.21.
11 Ibid., p.17.
12 'Overlord 27 Armd Bde Operation Order', May 1944, WO171/623, TNA.
13 Neave, 'The War Diary of Julius Neave', p.40.

Leaving their training sites in Scotland on 16 April 1944 with the largely obsolescent Valentines which had been used to that point, the 13/18 Hussars moved southwards to the marshalling areas in southern England.[14] The two squadrons with the DD role, A and B, arrived at Gosport without the specially adapted Sherman versions which had yet to reach them from the production lines; they were given a conversion course in how to use them but were left waiting until the last minute for the replacements.[15] With these having eventually arrived, on 5 June the troops loaded five Sherman DDs in each hold of the LCT(4)s they had been placed with; four of these craft carried each assaulting squadron. The flotilla was commanded by Lieutenant Commander Charles Creighton RNVR who had trained with the regiment throughout its time in the Moray Firth. The tank crews found the LCTs to be particularly unpleasant as they could only see the sky from where they were parked – hence the nickname of 'Altmarks' after the infamous German ship of earlier in the war – and when the engines were running diesel exhaust fumes filled the confined spaces which added to the sea sickness experienced by the men. Such an environment did of course also encourage a sense of wanting to reach dry land and get ashore. During the voyage, as the men used pots of white paint to paint their names on their steel helmets, final instructions were issued.[16] This included orders not to abandon DDs unless they were actually sinking due to the threat that this would pose to shipping. As was the case with all of the regiments within the armoured brigade, there was also an instruction that, once the tanks had entered the concentration area beyond the beaches, one squadron was to be maintained at 30 minutes' notice to repel any counter-attack.

For the Sword sector civil twilight on 6 June 1944 commenced at 0513 and sunrise followed at 0557; low water was at 0500 and high water from 0954 to 1245. It was this data that had been used to set H-Hour at 0725 as, whilst it was impossible to accurately assess the effectiveness of the carefully logged beach obstacles, based on their known sizes any nearer to the high water mark and it was calculated that the majority of them would be either awash or submerged. This would potentially damage or destroy the landing craft before the men and equipment on board them could disembark. This information was also important as it helped produce detailed 'Tidal Curve' and 'Beach Gradient' charts which made it possible to calculate at what point the DD tanks would touch down on their respective beaches. For Queen Red it was 360 yards out with the hull staying down until 280 yards out in what would be approximately four feet of water; for Queen White it was 430 yards and 250 yards for 'Hull Down'.

Launched at about 8,000 yards from the beaches, both DD squadrons were to move forwards in three columns led by a small landing craft or motor launch acting as navigator. About 1,000 yards from the shore they were to then come into line and, as they had trained for, advance in this formation. Conditions on D-Day, however, called for these carefully considered plans to be changed. Julius Neave, was the adjutant of 13/18 Hussars, sat in the gunner's seat of the commanding officer's tank which was nicknamed 'Balaclava'.[17] He was also manning the wireless set over which he heard at about 0630

14 Ibid., pp.30-31.
15 David Fletcher, *Swimming Shermans* (Osprey Publishing; Oxford, 2006), pp.7-14.
16 'A day – and a eulogy – to remember', *Grimsby Telegraph*, 3 October 2013.
17 Neave, 'The War Diary of Julius Neave', p.55.

from Brigadier Eroll Prior Palmer, commanding 27 Armd Bde, the order 'FLOATER 5000' indicating that the tanks were to now be launched at approximately 5,000 yards from the touch down point.[18] There was a Force 5 westerly wind and the seas were much rougher than they had been in training; they had been designed to make four-and-a-half knots in flat calm but were only managing three in the swell. This would prove extremely significant as it had been calculated that the DDs would be able to cover a thousand yards every 10 minutes but this figure was now reduced.[19]

An account of the run in given by one of the Lance Corporals who was commanding a DD provides an idea of what the crews experienced:

> We battled on towards the shore through the rough sea. We were buffeted about unmercifully, plunging into the troughs of the waves and somehow wallowing up again to the crests. The noise continued and by now the shells and rockets were passing over our heads, also, we were aware that we were under fire from the shore. The Germans had woken up to the fact that they were under attack and had brought their own guns into action. It was a struggle to keep the tank on course, but gradually the shoreline became more distinct and before long we could see the line of houses which were our targets. Seasickness was now forgotten. It took over an hour of hard work to reach the beach … As we approached, we felt the tracks meet the shelving sand of the shore, and slowly we began to rise out of the water. We took post to deflate the screen, one man standing to each strut. When the base of the screen was clear of the water, the struts were broken, the air released and the screen collapsed. We leapt into the tank and were ready for action.[20]

It took only minutes before this tank fired its first shot.[21] Neave on one of the other lead DDs described the beach as:

> …a dense mass of smoke on the horizon [which] resolved itself into clumps of burning houses with long sheets of yellow flame resulting from the bombing and naval guns. The noises … were immense, and of every variety and intensity from the rocket ships' barrage and the 25 pounders fired from the LCTs and the bombardments of cruisers, battleships, monitors and the like and medium bombers – and as we drew closer, the crack of rifles and machine-gun fire in a rather desultory manner on the beach itself.[22]

With the divisional plan calling for the assault engineers to land behind the DDs the delay in reaching the beaches was causing problems as the LCTs carrying the next wave

---

18 The other possibility was 'BUNKER' meaning that the tanks were not to be launched at all.

19 'The 13th/18th Royal Hussars (QMO) on D-Day, 1944', *The 13th/18th Royal Hussars' Journal* (Vol. VIII, No.3; April 1951), p.137.

20 Patrick Hennessey, cited in Major Wormald, 'Recollections of the Operations Undertaken by 'A' Squadron of the 13th/18th Royal Hussars (QMO) during the 1944-45 Campaign in Europe', pp.10-11, SLDM.

21 Ibid., Captain P.L.M. Hennessey, 'Some Impressions of June 1944 to April 1945'.

22 Neave, 'The War Diary of Julius Neave', p.58.

Brigadier Prior-Palmer gives instructions to his staff captain

were, in many cases, parallel or on top of the floating armour before it touched down. It had been decided during training to accept the risk of getting the sappers and their specialist equipment onto the beach ahead of the DDs even if it meant potentially ramming and losing the covering fire afforded by them.[23] On the bridge of HMS *Goathland* was Brigadier Prior Palmer – known as 'P.P' – who had taken command of 27 Armd Bde at the end of 1943 arriving direct from a senior role at Sandhurst.[24] Next to him was Eric Bush, who had carried out his first amphibious operation at Gallipoli when he was just 15 years old, and was now in charge of 'S3', the front edge of the naval assault force. He had given the initial order to launch the DDs and now signalled for the LCTs to proceed through the late-running tanks. At least one was rammed sinking about 700 metres from the shore. The commanding officer of the 13/18 Hussars, Lieutenant Colonel Dick Harrap, failed to launch with his tank as a result of an overly complicated plan and a failure to transfer him in time to the LCT. In Neave's view this did not make much real difference as all those involved had their allotted tasks and "there was little or nothing the CO could do to influence the course of events".[25] Nonetheless Harrap would not be able to join up with his command tank until it had reached the first lateral road behind the beaches.

23 Major-General Charles Miller, *The History of the 13th/18th Hussars (Queen Mary's Own) 1922-1947* (Chisman, Bradshaw, Ltd.; London, 1949), p.99.
24 'Obituary – Maj-Gen G.E. Prior-Palmer', *The Times*, August 20, 1977.
25 Harrap was killed along with his driver a few days later; Neave, 'The War Diary of Julius Neave', p.57.

Landing on Queen Red in support of 2nd Battalion, East Yorkshire Regiment (2 East Yorks) was B Squadron led by Major Rugge-Price with twenty of the 75 mm DD tanks. The armoured force was intended to reach the shore approximately 7.5 minutes before the planned H-Hour at around 0718. When the DDs 'touched down' they were to remain submerged with only the turret above the water line "shooting with all their weapons at everything which caught the eye" and destroy any local opposition not already removed by the naval and air bombardments.[26] The assault engineers, covered by the DDs, would land next 2.5 minutes later and move up the beach clearing obstacles in their path. The first wave of the infantry would then follow at 0725. A Squadron, led by Major Wormald who was in command of the same number and type of tanks, was to land to the right of the assault area on Queen White supporting 1 South Lancs. He has provided perhaps the best description of what followed. His tanks launched at 0616 and touched down approximately 67 minutes later. From the launch position approximately opposite the church in Lion-sur-Mer the target beach was about 45 degrees to the port bow.[27] As they launched there was no bombing on the beach and the houses were clearly visible and could be seen from a distance of nearly three miles out. His landing craft, LCT 101, sent its tanks down the ramp in first gear because of the swell and all were launched in just four minutes. They were passed by the LCTs carrying the assault engineers at about H-30 on the port quarter and it was only as a result of rocket fire falling short which forced them to stop their engines allowing the DDs to pass. 'Touch down' on the beach was about 300 yards from the high water mark at which point the LCTs again passed them and were landing before the tanks had been able to deflate their canvas shrouds and commence firing. Another member of the same squadron reckoned that enemy fire began at about 700 yards from the beach targets and up to a distance of 1,000 yards out, closer than had been planned for, he could still pick out the landmarks which allowed him to check the tank was being steered in the right direction.[28]

Of Wormald's 20 tanks only one sank and the remainder approached in four columns "performing well beyond what we thought to be practicable for the apparatus".[29] He saw the leading assault vehicle, which drove down the ramp of an LCT beached a few yards to his left, immediately be hit, "the turret and the contents thereof spun into the air after a violent explosion" and the vehicle 'brewed up'. In an early demonstration of the potentially invaluable role offered by the DD he instructed his gunner to fire on the bunker from where he believed the shot had come and disabled the gun. He then continued with suppressing fire on any defensive position that fired upon the attackers. The DDs had managed to make it to shore and provide armoured support during the critical opening phase of the invasion. Admiral Talbot viewed their use as a great success especially as this was the first time such a weapon had been used and in such difficult conditions. In most cases the enemy guns which the DD tanks knocked out could only have been destroyed by them as the beach strongpoints were completely defiladed from the sea. The naval commander concluded that:

26 Miller, *History of the 13/18th Hussars*, p.98.
27 Wormald, 'Recollections…', pp.6-7, SLDM.
28 Ibid., Captain Denny, 2nd Captain A Squadron, cited in Wormald, 'Recollections…', p.8.
29 Ibid., pp.4-6.

…no one can doubt from these accounts but that the DD tanks justified the time, trouble and training spent on ensuring such a successful and inspiring debut. When the full story is known I believe that the courageous decision to launch these tanks and their gallant swim will be found to have been a decisive factor in the success of the assault.[30]

Out of a total of 40 DD tanks which had been embarked for the Sword assault, 34 of them entered the water and 31 reached the beach. Although a number of these were subsequently swamped by the rising tide – a total of 18 made it beyond the beach – the crews were able to keep firing for some time and carry out their role of providing support to the infantry. In many respects the success enjoyed by this element of the invasion force proved critical in how the operation progressed, certainly in the Sword sector and, more broadly, across the entire NEPTUNE area.

The assault regiment which had approached alongside the DDs was intended to clear beach obstacles and open exits to allow armour and infantry to rapidly move into the country beyond. Working on the Sword beaches and attached to 8 Inf Bde was 5th Assault Regiment, under the command of Lieutenant-Colonel A.D.B. Cocks. At its core were 77th and 79th Assault Squadrons (77 Assault/79 Assault), the first attacking Queen White and the other Queen Red. In addition 629th Field Squadron (629 Field Sqn), 263rd Field Company (263 Field Coy), a detachment from 860th Mechanical Equipment and 22nd Dragoons (22 Dragoons), were all providing specialised assistance.[31] A typical example of how this force was configured was 2 Troop, 77 Assault which was transported to the beach by LCT 1092 commanded by Lieutenant Wigley RNVR. On board this craft were two flail tanks, an armoured plough, and three other vehicles from 79 Armd Div.[32] The latter, unique additions to the assault force, which were referred to as 'Churchill Armoured Vehicle, Royal Engineer' or AVREs, were key to the NEPTUNE plan, as important as the DDs and something the defenders would never previously have encountered. They were intended to give the engineers a platform they could use to reach their intended targets with some chance of survival. A variety of specialist accompaniments, seven in total, could be fitted that would allow each AVRE to assume a different role. These included fascines, strapped on top of the hull, which could be used to bridge small gaps and others with much larger bridging equipment that could span over 30 feet. Another important version included in place of the main gun a "mortar, recoiling spigot" which was known as a 'Petard' and could hurl a 40-pound explosive over 70 metres to its target. Later referred to as the 'flying dustbin' this was used by the assault troops against bunkers and pillboxes.

Along with the AVREs and DDs were the flail tanks, or the Sherman Crabs as they were more commonly known, which were manned by troops of A and C Squadrons,

---

30 Talbot, 'Report by the Naval Commander Force S', 22 July 1944, p.18, NARA.

31 Major-General R.P. Pakenham-Walsh, *History of the Corps of Royal Engineers, Volume IX, 1938-1948* (The Institution of Royal Engineers; Chatham, 1958), p.344.

32 3 Troop succeeded in opening a gap to Road 12 and dropped an assault bridge opposite 'Les Algues'; Captain A. Low, 'Operations in D Day with 2 Troop 77 Assault Squadron', p.1, Cass Papers, IWM. See p.85.

The AVRE Churchill tank with the 290 mm Petard spigot mortar and round

22 Dragoons.[33] The fourth regiment of that name, its predecessor, a yeomanry regiment of Light Dragoons had been disbanded in 1819; following the decision to re-form a number of old cavalry regiments in 1940 it was built around a main body of professional soldiers drawn from 4/7th Royal Dragoon Guards and the 5th Royal Inniskilling Dragoon Guards. In the autumn of 1943 it came under command of 79 Armd Div and was equipped with the new flail tanks to form part of the assault force for the invasion of Europe. Such were the likely numbers of mines that were thought to litter the Normandy beaches that the Crabs were seen as being critical to the entire invasion. Other options had also been trialled but the modified Shermans were assessed as being the most effective at driving a path through minefields on the beaches and those planted further inland. Working alongside them were armoured angle-dozers and bulldozers which completed the equipment to be used during the assault phase of the invasion; their role was to push through the sand dunes and help get the invasion forces off the beaches.[34]

The primary role for the assault regiment was to clear 'lanes' and 'exits' running from the shoreline to beyond the rear of the beach and this mission was critical as speed was the key to securing success in the initial phases and for the later elements of the divisional plan. The quicker the troops and equipment could get into the French countryside behind the beachheads the better their chances of securing the wide-ranging series of objectives that had been given to 3 Br Inf Div. A lane was described as a way that was clear of obstacles or mines running as far as the first lateral road behind the

33 Birt, *XXII Dragoons 1760-1945*, pp.167-176.
34 *The Story of the 79th Armoured Division* (Hamburg, 1945), pp.9-20.

A pre-invasion demonstration of the DD Sherman tank showing the collapsible canvas screen

beaches but which might only be sufficient for infantry to move along and the intention was to clear eight of these. A similar number of exits were planned, these being a lane which had a surface suitable for either tracked or wheeled vehicles and had some form of traffic control on it allowing for movement inland in an orderly fashion. Regimental war diaries provide a fascinating insight into the experiences of the men who carried out this extremely dangerous job. On Queen Red beach 79 Assault along with a mixture of A and C Squadron troops from 22 Dragoons, approximately 10 officers and 169 other ranks, were tasked with establishing lanes 1, 2, 3, 4:

Lane 1 – beached at H-hour. Flails cleared up to low dunes. Log carpet and ches-pale were laid and road clearance began. One Flail knocked out and the other completed clearance to lateral. Bangalore hit side of craft on disembarkation and had to be jettisoned [touched down – 0730; cleared first obstacle – 0800; established first gap to lateral road – 0940];

Lane 2 – landed at H-hour. Both Flails knocked out. Mines were cleared by hand by dismounted crews. Bridge was dropped and later blocked by DD falling off the side of it. The second gap was made by D7 (armoured bulldozer) [touched down – 0725; cleared first obstacle – 0815; established first gap to lateral road – 0940];

Lane 3 – landed at H-hour and Flails began to clear lane to top of beach. They were both knocked out. Bomb release on bridge was hit prematurely and bridge fell. Gap was made with hand placed charges and improved by D7. Bobbin was damaged and had to be jettisoned [touched down – 0725; Flails destroyed];

Lane 4 – landed at H-hour and Flails flailed of beach … one Flail was knocked out. Second Flail continued lane. Bridge was dropped but badly placed. Second lane was started and carpet laid, lane completed. Eventually both lanes made good. Bridge was jettisoned [touched down – 0725; cleared first obstacle – 0730; established first gap to lateral road – 0905].[35]

The sappers found that:

From the water's edge up to the back of the beach is about 250 yards not 400 yards. The first 100 yards is thick with obstacles. First two rows of ramp-type obstacles, every alternate one mined with a 1935 tellermine on top, in four feet of water. Then two or three rows of heavy pit props sunk into the ground, again each alternate one fixed with a tellermine on top. And inland of these, rows of reinforced concrete tetrahedra and steel girder hedgehogs with alternate obstacles wired with shells with German push igniters DZ 35.[36]

This highlights the degree to which the earlier assessments about mines were proved correct although in nothing like the numbers that had been feared. Those that were lifted on the beaches were French anti-tank, Teller, and 'S' mines. The latter were also found in the dunes behind the beach although these generally detonated in the ground not jumping in the air as the engineers had prepared for. The fields further inland of the beaches were all marked with German warning signs which proved largely to be false. Where they were genuine, and on the beaches closer to Ouistreham, there were further Teller, and 'S' mines planted in alternate lines along with Mk V box mines, Picric Pots and Dutch heavy box mines; some of the latter could not be destroyed by flails and had to be tackled by hand. In the case of these larger mines where they had been set amongst crops a method of detonation was to use petrol to set fire to the fields; this had mixed success as some were too damp to light.

Once again with information from the regimental diary, on the second beach, Queen White, the attackers were 77 Assault, supported by the other half of A Squadron 22 Dragoons, a total of 13 officers and 165 other ranks. This group had trained to open four lanes up the beach numbered 5, 6, 7, 8:

Lane 5 – beached on previously chosen exit. Leading Flail disembarked, second Flail was hit by A tk fire and the remainder could not disembark. An explosion occurred on board killing Lieutenant-Colonel Cocks and wounding Lieutenant F.G. Charlton. Total casualties unknown. LCT was ordered back to UK (not landed);

Lane 6 – grounded on top of the DD and, after clearing, beached to the left instead of the right of 4 Troop (Lane 5). Flails cleared tracks, carpet was laid and bridge was dropped on attacked exit which was cleared to lateral. Bobbin hit by mine and A tk fire and was drowned. D7 hit mine (touched down – 0740; cleared first obstacle – 0800; established first gap to lateral road – 0820);

---

35 Ibid., p.103, 104-105.
36 Ibid.

Lane 7 – beach to the right of 1 Troop (Lane 8) instead of to left due to drift whilst LCT lay off. Bangalore was placed in dunes but was blown prematurely by enemy fire. Gap was made and Flails surmounted dunes. One Flail blew tracks on mines but a route was cleared round it. The bridge was dropped right on top of gun position. The bobbin was damaged and jettisoned. D7 was not used (touched down – 0731; cleared first obstacle – 0800/0830; established first gap to lateral road – 0830/0900);

Lane 8 – landed at place previously chosen at H-Hour. Obstacles were six to eight feet high sand dunes. The Flails flailed at the beaches and crossed the dunes. The bangalore was jettisoned. Mines were cleared from the inland roads by Flails and hand clearing teams. One AVRE hit by A tk gun broke track and drowned. Crew dismounted and forced their way into Hermanville killing many enemy (touched down – 0730; cleared first obstacle – 0750; established first gap to lateral road – 0820).[37]

For 2 Troop, 77 Assault, about 1200 yards out from the beach they spotted their marker, villa 'Les Algues', known as 'Sad Sack Villa'; running along its left side was Road No.12, the target they wanted and destined to be one of the main beach exits. Their view was hidden by dust until about 300 yards out when they could once again see the building and they approached looking to touch down as near to it as possible. The congestion even at this very early stage of the attack meant that the men actually came ashore about 80 yards down the beach with 1 Troop on their east side.[38] The troop leader had one of the first tasks as soon as the ramp opened and the Sherman Crabs at the front headed down onto the beach: using his microphone he had to guide them and ensure they were heading in the right direction for the assigned gap as with the flails operating the crew were completely blind to what was going on in front of them.[39]

To help complete the work a second wave of assault engineers, men from 629 Field Sqn, were scheduled to land 20 minutes later. They had trained to clear four zones each 225 yards wide and open up eight exits along the beach for the brigade and its wheeled traffic to move forward. For the landing they were organised into eight teams each which had to clear 112 yards of beach frontage. By H+20 it was hoped that boundaries would have been marked by the assault squadrons who had landed first. For the troop leader his landing craft had an eight mile run to the beaches, a journey which took over an hour, and there was little to do other than watch all that was happening around and try and avoid the sea sickness:

...while approaching the shore, events seemed impersonal, like watching a demonstration; but now they became dramatically close and emphatically personal. Landmarks, which we had been taught to recognise from air photos, loomed through the smoke, but a bit damaged of course; fountains of spray ..., bullets

37 'Opposition Encountered...', pp.104-105, DEFE2/490, TNA.
38 Low, 'Operations in D Day with 2 Troop 77 Assault Squadron', Cass Papers, IWM.
39 Ibid., Major W. Carruthers, 'Gapping on Queen Sector White Beach with 3 Tp 77 Assault Squadron', p.6.

whipped up the water; the noise pressed our eardrums; the smell of explosives and smoke filled our noses; and our eyes taking at a glance the debris, human and material, lying everywhere. Above it all we felt the urge to get ashore and start work.[40]

Each man wore an assault jacket as opposed to the normal web equipment. In this he carried personal kit and rations, demolition packet containing six eight-pound charges, with initiators and fixing wires, shovels, wire cutters, pliers and some additional sling. On top he wore a 'Mae West'. In order to get to work on the mines and shells attached to the obstacles the order was given to remove these jackets and the men plunged into the cold water wading up to their waists to tackle whichever defences they could reach. This particular troop would spend the full day working on the beach, their work eventually being greatly assisted by an armoured bulldozer and an AVRE which smashed the piled obstacles that they had disarmed and stacked together.

For the work done on D-Day on Sword beach the two assault squadrons between them won two DSOs, four MCs, two DCMs, and three MMs – an indication of the bravery they had shown.[41] The vehicle casualties on the beach for this phase of the invasion, not including the LCT which failed to land its cargo, were seven on White – three destroyed, four damaged – and on Red a much higher total of 14 including six Crabs destroyed. For both beaches there were 24 casualties amongst the troops, with Red once again having a much higher share of the total; this was put down to the opposition encountered from the COD strongpoint which also delayed the completion of the lanes and exits. Indeed it was later highlighted that four lanes were cleared on White before the first one had been finished on the neighbouring beach, an even more impressive achievement when the losses suffered by 77 Assault are considered. The most significant statistic, however, must be that relating to how long it took to get off the two Queen beaches. None of the planned eight lanes were completed in the first 30 minutes – it was 50 minutes before the first lane was open – with a total of seven available after 150 minutes. The first tracked vehicles had been able to exit after 75 minutes and the first wheeled exit after four hours.[42]

A reasonable assessment would be that the assault engineers working in the Sword sector had a mixed degree of success. The intention had been to land with the tide lapping the bottom of the ramped stakes which were the rearward of the three types of defences placed by the Germans on the beach (in front of them were stakes and in front of these two rows of steel hedgehogs). The onshore wind had led to a heavy swell and higher than expected tide: obstacles in the sea had been presumed to be in two feet of water but instead they stood in four to six feet. Consequently men were forced to swim in the water in an attempt to remove mines and shells and while they had some success a number drowned; the best that could be done in many cases was to crush the obstacles as opposed to removing them. Fortunately many mines failed to explode and it was found that the defences were having little effect on the landing of craft. Much of the major

---

40 Ibid., Major C.H. Giddings, '629 Fd Sqn in the Assault on Queen Sector Red and White Beaches', pp.7-8.

41 Ibid., Lieutenant I.C. Dickinson, 'Obstacle Clearance with 3 Tp 77 Assault Squadron on Queen Sector White Beach', p.6.

42 'Opposition Encountered…', p.126, DEFE2/490, TNA.

clearance work was, in reality, done later in the day when the tide had begun to go back down and by nightfall all of the obstacles had been cleared. Some of the Crabs lost flails to the mines they were detonating while others were disabled by gunfire coming from the German defenders. In addition to this, the early death of Lieutenant-Colonel Cocks, the commanding officer for all the breaching teams along the divisional front, must also have had some impact on progress.[43] As will be seen later, many of those who followed on to the beaches encountered serious difficulties in getting off them but the breach had been made. It was now time for the main fighting power of 3 Br Inf Div to begin what it had spent nearly a year training for, the invasion of France.

---

43 Talbot, 'Report by the Naval Commander Force S', 22 July 1944, p.20, NARA.

7

H-Hour – Infantry Assault

See maps 3, 4 and 5.

With the DDs and assault engineers established and fighting to clear the beach the infantry now came in behind them. Approaching the beach under this huge weight of gunfire and bombs the lead craft of the assault flotilla sounded off the General Salute, whilst a motor-launch broadcast "rousing tunes" on a gramophone rigged up to the boat's loud-hailer. Landing on a single infantry brigade front meant that there was a great depth to the attack but a much reduced width to that which the Allies were able to produce elsewhere on the NEPTUNE beaches. It was only possible for 8 Inf Bde to put two of its battalions ashore at the outset with the final battalion landing a short time after. Even so on a small beach this would be a lot of men and equipment adding to everything that was already there. The role of the infantry assault brigade was to complete the destruction of the beach defences, notably the COD strongpoint at the division line between the Red and White beaches, and then establish the beachhead up to a depth of about 3.5 miles. To do this it would need to destroy the battery known as DAIMLER and capture the high ground around the village of Périers-sur-le-Dan along with the fortified positions known to be located at grid reference 0777, MORRIS and HILLMAN, both of which threatened the landing area. The brigade would also provide troops to take over the defence of the bridges across the Caen Canal and River Orne which it was hoped 6 AB Div had captured; not less than one rifle company and one squadron of tanks were assigned to relieve the airborne troops, a mission which potentially included the "attack and capture" of these bridges if they were not already held. The two commando units working with the brigade had the additional tasks of destroying the coastal battery at Ouistreham and the fortified TROUT strongpoint.

The first assault waves heading to each beach consisted of ten LCAs covering the length of about 400 yards. The landing tables for the assault brigade had been prepared in a single week by the Royal Marines. The scales employed were for a company to land 103 men, 16 in the headquarters along with a further three platoons of 29 troops. To transport this company was assigned five LCAs each of which was to be loaded with 29 people. The first carried the company commander, part of his headquarters and a Royal Engineer demolition team, the second the Company Sergeant Major, the remainder of the headquarters and a Royal Engineer assault party. Behind them came three further craft each of which carried one platoon of men.[1] The loading process proved more complicated than had been anticipated as attempts were made by Brigade and Battalion staffs to overload craft with more men and materials than they were designed to carry.

---

1   'Notes on 8 Inf Bde During Operation Overlord', D8/2/6, Scarfe Papers, ULSC.

Part of the COD strongpoint as seen from the beach

This was particularly the case with loading Sherman tanks and AVREs onto LCTs; a number of these craft actually sailed with the watertight doors not having been fully closed so tightly packed were they with vehicles on board them. The infantry in the first waves at least had the advantage of having been able to climb into the LCAs whilst they were still slung on the side of the larger vessels. For all subsequent waves the only way to get into the landing craft was to climb down scrambling nets during which there was a chance that they could drop into the sea – with all of the equipment they were carrying this would almost certainly have meant they would drown. Many of the men were also kitted out with the specially designed assault vests worn by the sappers but instead of demolition equipment they carried an anti-tank grenade in a pouch at the back. Long waders had also been issued to the troops to help keep them dry; these "proved exceedingly dangerous, because they filled in the deep water, and made controlled movement of the legs very difficult, encumbered as we were with immensely weighty assault jerkins".[2]

The plan called for each assaulting company to be supported by a demolition team in addition to the sappers that had formed the first wave.[3] For 8 Inf Bde these were drawn from 246th Field Company Royal Engineers (246 Field Coy) and the leading elements were due to land on the beach about 10 minutes after H-Hour directly after the assault had begun.[4] A mixture of regular army and territorials from northern England and Wales under the command of Major Rodney Maude, they were organised into three platoons each of which was placed under the command of an assaulting infantry battalion. In addition to helping the infantry get off the beach there were two other

2   Rylands, '"W" Coy, 2nd Bn. K.S.L.I. in Normandy'.
3   *The Story of the 79th Armoured Division*, pp.45-51.
4   They would play an important role throughout the day but were fortunate to suffer light casualties, three men killed and another six wounded; '246 Field Company Royal Engineers – Company History', Scarfe Papers, ULSC.

critical roles that these assault engineers were tasked to complete. The first involved a small recce group that was to head to the canal lock gates at Ouistreham and make a detailed report on their condition. Another section drawn from 2 and 3 Platoons, under the command of Lieutenant Arthur Heal, were attached to support the 1st Battalion, The Suffolk Regiment (1 Suffolks) and had trained specifically to support the assault on HILLMAN.

The men were loaded into their LCAs and, once lowered into the water, these circled the *Empire Battleaxe* which had transported them across the Channel waiting for all the craft to be lined up in their loading order. It was about 0530 before this small flotilla pulled away heading for the French beaches. As one of those on the run in later wrote:

> God, what a sight, ships and more ships as far as the eye could see, and apart from the LCA, all belching forth fire and smoke. All the landing craft carrying the Third Division had the divisional insignia painted on their funnels, and a tannoy nearby blared out the strains of 'roll out the barrel'. It was a fantastic site, and we must have been united in the thought 'God this will shake them when they catch sight of this lot coming into beach'.[5]

Under the command of Lieutenant-Colonel C.F. Hutchinson 2 East Yorks was heading for Queen Red to land at H+5 and destroy the beach defences before moving inland.[6] Two companies had also travelled on the *Empire Battleaxe* with the remainder of the troops on the HMS *Glenearn*. This arrangement had been put in place to provide contingency, if one of the ships was sunk the other could continue with the assault. Lieutenant H.T. Bone later described the last moments before the men set off for the beaches:

> In the Mess decks we blacked out faces with black Palm Olive cream and listened to the naval orders over the loudhailer. Most of us had taken communion on the Sunday, but the padre had a few words to say to us. Then the actual loading into craft – swinging on davits – the boat lowering and finally 'Away boats'.[7]

On the run in spare gas-capes were used to keep the men dry and gum "was chewed stolidly". In one of the East Yorks' LCAs was A Company Commander, Major C. K. King, known widely in 3 Br Inf Div as 'Banger'. During the voyage across the Channel he read his men famous passages from King Henry V and even on the LCAs was still urging on his "noble English" telling them "The game's afoot". According to the divisional historian, "Major King's action was akin to Wolfe's at Quebec almost 200 years before, and worthy to be remembered with it".[8]

5   Captain Michael Edwards RE, 'Memoirs – Bash on with 246 to Bremen', www.arrse.co.uk.
6   Lt-Col P.R. Nightingale, *The East Yorkshire Regiment (Duke of York's Own) in the War 1939/45* (Mr Pye (Books); East Riding, 1952), pp.177-179.
7   Lieutenant H.T. Bone, cited in Jon E. Lewis, *Eyewitness D-Day* (Robinson Publishing Ltd; London, 1994), p.119.
8   Scarfe, *Assault Division*, pp.61-92.

The first two companies landed at 0725, the next wave thirty minutes later with the battalion headquarters. As they neared the beach the officers knew that, aside from the heavy German guns, there were six or seven machine guns ahead of them each of which could fire about 240 rounds every two minutes firing in bursts of 10 to 20 rounds. It was these that presented the greatest obstacle, one of the first infantrymen ashore later wrote that the beach was like "a bloody skittle alley" with men "being bowled over right left and centre". Another talked of bullets "like raindrops" which could be heard whistling past as the men pushed on to the limited cover provided by the dunes at the back of the beach.[9] One of the LCAs touched down with 33 men on board; by the time the young lieutenant in charge had reached the lateral road there were only 13 left.[10] A sergeant described how his company commander was killed on the beach when he called an orders group and, with his officers formed in a circle, a shell or a mortar round dropped amongst them causing considerable casualties. The result was "after that we'd only some young lieutenants and we'd got to take hold of their hands and take them on with us because they had no idea".[11] Alongside 2 East Yorks there was part of 1 Platoon and all of 2 Platoon from 246 Field Coy with a total of four demolition and two mine clearance teams. This first wave of these engineers found that the heavy gunfire from the naval units and the self-propelled guns on the landing craft had largely neutralised the concrete defences that formed their target. When they landed they therefore dumped their charges and provided support to their respective infantry platoons acting as additional sections.

Also having embarked on the *Empire Battleaxe* on Saturday 3 June at Portsmouth and landing on Queen White was 1 South Lancs under the command of Lieutenant-Colonel Burbury. This unit was amongst those that had also been chosen initially for both the raid on Dieppe and the Sicily landings but on both occasions they had been replaced by the Canadians on political grounds. With an expected casualty rate in excess of 80 percent the men were to go ashore in waves led by A and C companies. Touching down slightly ahead of schedule, initially some good progress was made despite the presence of the COD strongpoint.[12] Some of the light landing craft were buffeted by the current and landed further east than had been planned. Amongst these in A Company was Lieutenant Bill Allen, commanding 9 Platoon, whose LCA was swept much further east than planned as a result of which he and his men came ashore directly opposite COD and he was killed in the subsequent fighting. One of the men in the first wave later recorded how:

I was distinctly surprised to find ourselves moving towards a holiday resort (Hermanville Plage), looking astonishingly like Blackpool, except that instead of the promenade there was a low sea wall, but the gently shelving golden sands were there and a line of seaside villas, though the sands were covered with tripods, with

9   Anonymous private, cited in Lewis, *Eyewitness D-Day*, p.120; Private William Lloyd, cited in Bailey, *Forgotten Voices of D-Day*, p.202.
10 Will Bennett, '50th Anniversary of D-Day: Town gives rousing welcome as veterans return to Sword Beach", *The Independent*, 6 June 1994.
11 Sergeant Arthur Thompson, cited in Bailey, *Forgotten Voices of D-Day*, p.202.
12 'History of the South Lancashire Regiment', pp.400-405, LIM.

mines on top. These towered above us as we made our way between them after landing and were much taller than the photographs had led us to believe.[13]

Working with 1 South Lancs on the right was 3 Platoon and part of 1 Platoon from 246 Field Coy, once again providing four demolition and two mine clearance teams. The first two exits from the beach were made by men from this unit, an NCO from 1 Platoon and the lieutenant who had been ordered to proceed to Ouistreham as quickly as possible to inspect the lock gates. They commandeered a D7 armoured bulldozer and cut out ramps to the first lateral which unblocked the initial congestion on the beach and allowed wheeled vehicles to move forward.[14] This proved to be a critical act as it also meant that those standing in the water could get up onto the beach proper.

The battalion's second wave, consisting of the headquarters and its attached company along with the two remaining infantry companies arrived ten minutes later. There was only a short space of time between these two initial waves but the response they faced was significantly worse. Small arms, mortar and 88 mm gunfire caused immediate casualties. This was in large part because B Company had also landed almost exactly opposite COD which was still being engaged by C Company. The company commander, Major Bob Harrison, was killed almost instantly and his place was taken by a young lieutenant, R.C. Bell-Walker, who personally led the attack against a concrete pillbox that was firing along the beach. One witness described it as:

> … [having been] carried out in classic battle school fashion … He crept round behind it, lobbed a grenade through a gun port and then gave it a burst of Sten-gun fire. He himself was killed instantly by a burst of machine gun fire from strongpoint COD over on our left. He had, however, opened a way through for the rest of the company to get off the beach.[15]

As Mike Edwards, a young captain leading 1 Platoon of 246 Field Coy, moved up the beach at about 0750 he passed his commander Major Maude near the dunes before moving on into a gully. It was here that he saw Lieutenant Colonel Burbury, killed by a sniper as he reached the barbed wire at the edge of the beach and the second-in-command of 1 South Lancs, Major Jack Stone, took charge. The colonel had apparently spent some time thinking about the challenges of leading his men and had had his sister make him a hand flag made in the battalion's colours which he intended to use to identify himself and rally his Regiment. Unfortunately this also made him too conspicuous hence his early targeting by the well-trained German snipers.[16]

One of the most detailed descriptions of the attack on the COD strongpoint is provided by a junior officer from 2nd Battalion, The Middlesex Regiment (2 Middlesex). Not part of the initial assault but still landing at 0745 the first detachment of four officers and nine other ranks landed on Queen White about half a mile to the east of

---

13 Ibid., Jones, 'Wartime Service with the 1st Battalion…'.
14 Sergeant Jack Davies and Lt 'Peter' Pope RE; Michael Edwards, 'Bash on with 246 to Bremen'.
15 Captain (later Major) Arthur Rouse, cited in Jones, 'Wartime Service with the 1st Battalion…', p.21, LIM.
16 Ibid., p.22.

Men from the Beach Group near COD

Lion-sur-Mer. This carrier battalion consisted of three machine gun companies and one mortar: the first men ashore were, however, responsible for controlling traffic through the beach exits but they found an intense battle raging around them:

> COD was located at the junction of two beach areas and extended for 400 metres into Queen Red and 100 metres into Queen White. It actually consisted of 20 separate strongpoints within wire obstacles and interconnecting trenches. The defensive hedgehog comprised a 75 mm gun, two 50 mm anti-tank guns, three 81 mm mortars, a 37 mm gun and five other machine gun posts each in turn equipped with two or three guns.[17]

With the addition of forward observation posts and shelters it was a "formidable defensive area" and covered the whole length of the beach. The delay getting off Queen Red was almost entirely due to the strength of the defence mounted by COD and it would eventually take over three hours before it was fully cleared. To do this men from both the lead assault battalions along with the 13/18 Hussar's DD tanks would all become involved.

The commanding officer of 263 Field Coy, which had been delayed in its landing by 45 minutes due to difficulties in transferring from ship to landing craft, provided a description of the beach by this stage. As they landed from a single LCI, the first waves of LCAs were pulling away to head back and pick up the next group of troops. Beach casualties were also being ferried back on the returning craft, carrying men who had been recovered both from the beach and floating in the sea. As the landing ramp dropped he saw:

---

17 Ibid., Lt K.P. Baxter.

The assault on Queen White

… an absolute inferno, burning tanks, broken down vehicles, and very many dead and wounded lying about in a narrow strip between the sea and the wire at the back of the beach. There were shells, mortars and the occasional bomb falling, and a considerable amount of small arms fire … We were now nearly one and a half hours late, the tide was almost high … Our task of clearing beach obstacles was obviously hopeless, so I organised four sections into parties for clearing beach exits and laying track to try to clear some of the congestion.[18]

It was this last observation which was really important and the inability of the invasion force to get off the beaches was already causing some concerns. It had been anticipated that this could be an issue and steps had been taken to supply specially trained personnel to help. In preparation for the landings about 100 men from 8th Battalion, The Northumberland Fusiliers had been designated as 3rd Reconnaissance Regiment with two specific jobs for the invasion. The first was to act as contact detachments providing a network of communications for the initial assault forces. In addition they also provided

18 Major M. De L'Orme DSO MC, 263rd Field Company, cited in Pakenham-Walsh, *History of the Corps of Royal Engineers*, p.347.

five men who would take responsibility for the control of traffic off the beaches.[19] This small group, a major, a captain and three lieutenants, landed with the first infantry assault waves. The commanding officer, a Major Gill, was soon severely wounded and subsequently amongst the first to be evacuated back to England. The regimental history perhaps rather generously describes the role played as having been very well received. One of the assault engineers noted that there was no sign of these men and his sappers were left to take responsibility for moving vehicles through the gap they had just created.[20]

In reality the congestion on the beaches was one of the greatest challenges impeding progress from the Sword area. What this actually meant was effectively demonstrated in the experience of A Squadron 13/18 Hussars. Having suppressed the beach defences and moved forward, the remaining tanks were forced to wait for the assault engineers to open the exits so they could escape and drive on to their first inshore objective, the village of Hermanville. With no sign of a route to follow – the plan had called for windsocks on poles to be used as markers but these were quickly abandoned as the Germans used them as observation points – its commander therefore dismounted and headed along the beach to his right searching for some form of exit. Reaching a road which led straight off he found that the German anti-tank mines meant to disable it had not been planted and were stacked neatly in a pile. With the beach now under mortar and shellfire at about H+15 he ordered his squadron to follow him. There was not much opposition in the village and the tanks took up defensive positions in the surrounding orchards.[21] In his view the specialist assault vehicles "were not highly successful" and his account makes it clear that it was down to his own efforts that he and his men had passed safely off the beach.[22] It was much the same for B Squadron which had landed on the left and also found no available exits. The squadron had been tasked to work with the 2 East Yorks in attacking two fortified positions, less one troop which had been sent in support of the commandos heading for the Orne bridges, but their progress was delayed.[23] Two tanks were eventually able to call upon an armoured bulldozer to force a passage; the second-in-command then returned to the beach rallying others through the newly opened exit. It was not, however, until 4 Troop came ashore and joined them that they were finally in position to support the infantry.

Across both beaches these same sorts of problems were commonplace. Having struggled to find a gap to drive landing craft on to the beach there were several cases where even with the ramp successfully dropped vehicles could not exit as there was so much traffic in front of them. Other crews found themselves then waiting for the AVREs to clear the suspected minefields.[24] Even when this was completed some vehicles still chose

---

19 'History of the 3rd Reconnaissance Regiment in the Invasion and Subsequent Campaign in North-West Europe 1944-1945', n.d., Scarfe Papers, ULSC; Marshal Ray, 'Vital part of jigsaw in D-Day landings', *Evening Chronicle* (Newcastle-upon-Tyne), 29 May 2004.

20 Major W. Carruthers, 'Gapping on Queen Sector White Beach with 3 Tp 77 Assault Squadron', p.7, Cass Papers, IWM.

21 Wormald, 'Recollections…', pp.6-7, SLDM.

22 Ibid., pp.6-7.

23 The regimental history offers some confusion about this troop, the first which had been rallied off the beach, saying that they "disappeared towards Ouistreham" and all efforts to recall it failed; Miller, *History of the 13/18th Hussars*, p.101.

24 Hennessey, cited in Wormald, 'Recollections…', pp.10-11, SLDM.

to ignore the mine marking signs and lost tracks as a result; in each case they had to be moved aside or towed out adding to the congestion and mounting confusion. For one of the DDs the blockage in front meant that it was pinned down where it had landed, with the front of its tracks just out of the water. Whilst it proved highly effective at firing on the German defenders from this position, the tide was beginning to come in over the driver's hatch and eventually a large wave swamped the engine. The crew kept on firing as long as they could before the vehicle, now stranded 150 yards out, flooded and they were forced to escape using the rubber dinghy and "the map boards as paddles".

Despite this inability to get off the beach quickly the initial lodgement had, however, been achieved but it had come at a considerable cost. One of the official histories records that the German defenders on the Queen beaches were not all prepared to simply surrender and the defence was "grim and fanatical". It noted that:

> The Germans fought the irresistible wave of tanks and men that was flung upon them until it was seen to be engulfing them. Then, firing their useless rifles and shouting, perhaps, their final salute to the *Fuhrer* who had willed their deaths, they ran out into the fire of the tank guns – men thirsty for the privilege of destruction in battle.[25]

Considerable information was gathered by the Army Operational Research Group relating to the landings and these statistics confirmed that it was on the Queen beaches that the greatest number of German weapons remained serviceable during the post-'touch down' phase, a stark indication of the actual degree of success of the pre-landing bombardments. The effects of this failure to neutralise the defenders were best illustrated by the numbers of armoured vehicles that were knocked out at H-Hour: a total of 92 armoured vehicles landed, far more than on any other Anglo-Canadian beach (a total of 369 reached the three sectors), but 14-15 percent were put out of action by enemy gunfire, once again a significantly higher figure.[26] The average across all of the beaches was actually ten percent and the losses for Sword were almost three times higher than the figure at King beach on Gold sector.[27] It was also later calculated that a total of 304 landing craft had been lost or disabled across the five beaches assaulted and of these 50 percent were due to the beach obstacles. From this the total for Sword was 79 craft, more than a third of which were LCAs.[28]

The analysis also produced detailed casualty figures for the initial assault phase. On Queen White the two infantry companies in the first wave suffered 30 percent killed or injured, on Queen Red it was 45 percent. Although high these were well below the figure that had been predicted in advance of the landings – a complicated assessment had considered the amount of fire that could be aimed every two minutes at a wave of advancing infantry crossing a beach 200 yards by 400 yards – which indicated 68

---

25 Birt, *XXII Dragoons 1760-1945*, p.170.

26 'Casualties and Effects of Fire Support on the British Beaches in Normandy', 21 April 1945, p.16, JSCSC.

27 'Opposition Encountered…', p.138, DEFE2/490, TNA.

28 Ibid., 'Operation Neptune – The Normandy Landings, June 1944', Battle Summary No.39 (Vol.1; 1947), p.107, ADM234/366.

A landing craft on the approach to Queen Red with AVREs and DDs on the beach

percent on Queen White and 72 percent on Queen Red.[29] For the first two waves overall the actual figures were 22.5 percent and 28 percent, still by far the highest of any of the Anglo-Canadian beaches. Indeed, of all the British and Canadian beaches assaulted on D-Day, Queen Red was the most deadly with the losses for 2 East Yorks double the average figure for all of the assault battalions across the ten beaches that the these forces attacked on the day. When the losses was considered across the entire day and for all of these same beaches this figure fell to 2.7 percent, a difference of just 0.1 percent with the overall average and lower than the figures for Juno. Added to the percentage level of losses for equipment it can be concluded that the assault was a costly one and resulted in a concentrated burst of devastation as the men from 8 Inf Bde tried to get onto and then off the beaches they were attacking. Finally, the post-landing analysis also recorded that it took 50 minutes to neutralise defences while mopping up had been completed two hours 40 minutes after the landings had begun, figures that were on par with the other Anglo-Canadian beaches.[30] For 3 Br Inf Div, with a plan that relied upon maintaining a high rate of speed and tempo if the advance towards Caen was to succeed, the delays on the beach would have a cascading effect as D-Day moved forward. The impact of these first few minutes would in fact prove to be one of the issues that determined the extent of the division's success and undermined its ability to achieve all of its objectives.

29 'Casualties and Effects of Fire Support...', 21 April 1945, p.13, JSCSC.
30 'Opposition Encountered...', p.126, DEFE2/490, TNA.

8

Morning – 'Break In'

With troops ashore and lines of landing craft moving towards the two already increasingly congested beaches the priority was to make them secure. By 0830, with COD now suppressed sufficiently to allow the men to move forward, Hermanville had been entered by 1 South Lancs who were later acknowledged as having being the first British infantry to press inland.[1] The field used as the initial meeting point – between the chateau and the church – contained a civilian shelter and "half the village seemed to be in it from the glimpses we had when they came up for air, and every so often a wee boy crawled out and wriggled through the long grass until his mother battered a howl and dragged him back below".[2] As more and more infantry arrived on the beach many of them also headed for the same place. Included amongst them were the second wave of 2 Middlesex with three platoons from A Company, one of the machine gun companies, which landed over the course of 90 minutes and split with each platoon supporting one of the infantry battalions.[3] In the divisional plan this village had been identified as the brigade headquarters and was later to become the site of the Corps headquarters. With the rather marshy ground in the area the road running through it was also the only wheeled route inland. As such the crossroads was a critical point to be secured and held by these first British troops. Despite all of the planning and preparation there is no evidence, however, to suggest that this danger had been fully realised: troops and equipment coming off the beach were forced to turn right onto the lateral road making this a potentially significant bottleneck. Nonetheless by midday 1 South Lancs had dug in and consolidated their position.

Elsewhere more armour was arriving, C Squadron 13/18 Hussars was to provide support to 1 Suffolks as they tackled the "German concrete defensive positions south of Colville-sur-Orne", the MORRIS and HILLMAN strongpoints.[4] Heading towards La Breche, by 0755 the LCTs carrying these tanks were only three quarters of a mile from the shore and one of the troop commanders recalled seeing "the outline of houses amidst and behind a confused mass of craft and clouds of smoke". He presumed it had been a popular resort on the Normandy coast but this was no longer the case, "a number of these houses and hotels were already in ruins, some were burning and smouldering,

---

1   They also claimed to have been the first British unit to have brewed tea in France; 'History of the South Lancashire Regiment', p.405, LIM.
2   A British officer walking through the village in the afternoon met a group of civilians who told him that the Germans had been taken completely by surprise and had not mobilised until 0300; Major F.J. Hoadley, 'Experiences with 253 Fd Coy in 3 British Division', Cass Papers, IWM.
3   Lieutenant Commander P.K. Kemp, *The Middlesex Regiment (Duke of Cambridge's Own) 1919-1952* (Aldershot; Gale and Polden Ltd, 1956), pp.80-83.
4   Wormald, 'Recollections…', p.2, SLDM.

Leading companies of 1 South Lancs move inland supported by tanks of 13/18 Hussars

while into others were pouring the machine gun bullets from DD tanks which had apparently landed successfully". The blockage on the beach ahead was making it difficult for the LCTs which came in as close as they could searching for gaps in which to unload their cargoes and then get away again as quickly as possible. The war diary records that C Squadron landed on Queen White at H+45, around 0810, and found that the beach was still not cleared with considerable shelling and mortar fire being encountered. Captain Eric Smith, in charge of 4 Troop, noted that everything was so confused and so much was happening with very little room in which to move; as he wrote later it was like "Piccadilly Circus in the rush-hour".[5] He also noted a number of drowned DD tanks very close to the water's edge along with floating bodies, both British and German. This squadron was acting as the reserve hence its later arrival and the tanks were not fully waterproofed but equipped for what was termed as 'seven-foot wading'. They pulled behind them sledges called 'Porpoises' in which there was a reserve of ammunition presumably to provide them with an extension of their fighting role once they had cleared the beach. It took a further 45 minutes before the tanks were able to pass through one of the marked exits and another ten minutes to reach the initial assembly point where they met up with a company from their infantry partners, the assault brigade's reserve battalion.

---

5   Ibid., Captain E.E. Smith, 'The Assault: 6-23 June 1944 – The Story of C Squadron, 13th/18th Royal Hussars (QMO)'

As was the case with a number of the other infantry battalions 1 Suffolks had travelled across the Channel in a single wave but spread over various landing craft. Two companies and the battalion headquarters were on the LSI *Empire Broadsword* with the other two on *Empire Battleaxe* and these ships reached their lowering position at 0525 and anchored. In addition there was an LCI carrying the battalion headquarters and another with the reserve troops who had been nominated as 'Left out of Battle' (LOB); there was also the alternate brigade headquarters as the battalion commander had been nominated to take over from Brigadier Cass if he was injured. The anti-tank platoon and mortars along with the company carriers were distributed amongst three LCTs. There is some confusion as to what happened next, one source saying it was at 0623 that the twenty-five LCAs began being lowered into the water with another saying it was 30 minutes later. The plan allowed for a two hour run to the beaches with the battalion to land at full strength 55 minutes after the first two. Once ashore 1 Suffolks would then pass through 1 South Lancs and 2 East Yorks heading for the village of Colleville-sur-Orne and, after continuing approximately two miles inland it was to seize MORRIS and HILLMAN.[6] The small flotilla set off in four columns and whilst there was some fire from MORRIS near shore no damage was caused and the battalion touched down only five minutes late at 0825. The men quickly waded the remaining 40 yards ashore and headed for their targets of the 'Funny' house and the 'Tower' and took cover under the lee of the three feet high sand dunes. Only one man was killed on the beach despite two of the LCAs being hit by shellfire immediately after the troops had disembarked.

One of those who landed described the beach as having, "...a background of shattered, smoking seaside houses with naked slats in their roofs. The narrow stretch of sand covered with tanks and men. A pungent, burning and explosive sort of stink. Three wounded men sitting under the lee of the burned-out tank – one of them with a cigarette."[7] The assembly area, which was about 500 yards inland, was a small square wood with a track running diagonally through it. This was reached at about 0930 and found to provide no cover with all the trees having been cut down so a new site was selected a little further inland. D Company went forward first to provide right flank protection; once this was secured the point section from C Company moved along the street past the church to the town hall where it established a defensive position on the first floor overlooking the street. Colleville-sur-Orne was spread along a main road with two parallel roads or tracks on each side and probably 100 buildings in the village. Intelligence reports had indicated it contained German troops; post-invasion it was discovered that aside from a number who were billeted in various houses the officers from HILLMAN had a mess there as did the artillery headquarters located at Point 61. By 1000 the village mayor, Monsieur Lenauld, was sharing a bottle of calvados with the battalion's officers and passing on information about German troop dispositions in the area.[8]

There had been little real opposition and B Company was quickly able to launch its attack on MORRIS. The site had been targeted from the air on at least two occasions

---

6   Colonel W.N. Nicholson, *The Suffolk Regiment 1928 to 1946* (The East Anglian Magazine Ltd.; Ipswich, 1948), pp.87-104.

7   Major Charles Boycott cited in Nicolson, *The Suffolk Regiment*, p.96.

8   Eric Lummis, *1 Suffolk and D-Day* (Privately published, 1989), p.14.

An AVRE with Petard mortar positioned near a beach exit and facing in the direction of Hermanville

during the week prior to the invasion but it was believed that these raids had resulted in little or no damage; in reality one of them had caused many casualties. In addition thirteen American B-17 bombers, each loaded with twelve 500 pound bombs, had been due to hit the strongpoint at 0711 on D-Day but due to the heavy cloud and the risk of hitting British troops only six aircraft dropped a total of 72 bombs. There were, however, additional fire plans and the Suffolks could also call on one battery from 33rd Field Regiment Royal Artillery (33 Field RA), one from 76th Field Regiment Royal Artillery (76 Field RA), C Squadron from 13/18 Hussars and their own mortar platoon. At battalion headquarters the commander of the battery from 76 Field RA coordinated the fire from the artillery units. In addition there was the prospect of naval gun fire support. At Sword two out of the three naval FOB parties landing with their respective assault battalion headquarters at H+20 were quickly disabled either due to casualties or damage to their wireless equipment. For the attack the surviving senior naval officer, Captain Llewellyn, controlled fire from the six-inch cruiser *Dragon*, and the fleet destroyer *Kelvin* which supplied five minutes of high explosive (HE) rounds followed by three minutes of smoke.[9] The information available indicated that the position contained a couple of anti-tank guns and machine guns and was surrounded

9   The subsequent conclusion was that the FOBs had landed too early, and it was recommended that for future assaults these men should land behind the initial wave; 'Normandy Bombardment Experience (June/September, 1944)', p.40, *Gunnery Review* (February 1945), JSCSC.

by barbed wire.[10] Two troops of tanks were to fire more HE rounds along with some anti-personnel (AP) rounds fired at the slits and the corners of the bunkers. A third troop would advance to within 200 yards of the target and provide support for B Company which would attack, breakthrough and consolidate allowing A Company to pass to the far side and prepare for the follow-on assault on HILLMAN. The fourth troop of 13/18 Hussars was tasked with working round the left flank and clearing Colleville-sur-Orne which commanded one of the main roads inland. Once the attack began it was quickly found that the Germans had withdrawn and both the village and the strongpoint had been secured by 1130, the latter with around 40-50 prisoners who surrendered under a white flag. With this part of the plan completed preparations for the attack on the next strongpoint started immediately and A Company moved up through the village.

With large numbers of landing craft approaching the beaches the groups of Royal Navy Beach Commandos which controlled their arrival and departure were playing an increasingly key role. Sword was designated as '101st Beach Sub-Area' with 5th Battalion, The King's Regiment (5 Kings) providing the 'Beach Group' and working with F(Fox) and R(Roger) RN Beach Commandos led by Captain William Leggatt RN.[11] The plan called for F Beach Commando, which was the most experienced having seen action before during the Italian campaign, to land first followed by R1 and the two reserve forces, R2 and R3. Each group landed with the assault troops and consisted of seven officers and 48 ratings split into four parties headed by an Assistant Beachmaster. Presumably working with the previously mentioned 3rd Reconnaissance Regiment, once the landing craft had discharged their loads, Army Beach Groups then took responsibility for the cargoes whilst small Royal Air Force beach units handled all of their service's needs.

Casualties were disproportionately high amongst these commando groups with three of the four parties suffering casualties almost immediately they landed. Acting Lieutenant-Commander Teddy Gueritz, the Principal Beachmaster of F Beach Commando, found himself taking over the role of Deputy Naval Officer in Command. He had landed about thirty minutes after the first wave, at about 0755, "wearing a blue painted helmet [which designated his role] and red scarf while armed with only a large blackthorn walking stick". Gueritz has described what he found when he landed:

> A number of armoured vehicles were standing halfway up the beach, some firing; flail tanks were operating to explode beach mines; beach exits were jammed with vehicles impeded by the soft sand and mine explosions. The sharpest impression, as always, was created by the sight of bodies scattered on the beach from the water's edge. One of these turned out to be my immediate superior, Commander Rowley Nicholl, who was deputy naval officer in charge of the Sword Assault Area; not dead but severely wounded, having insisted upon accompanying the leading Beach Parties. We had been right to expect casualties among the early landings of the

---

10 Smith, 'The Assault: 6-23 June 1944 – The Story of C Squadron...', pp.8-10, SLDM.
11 'Combined Operations Pilotage and the Beach Organisation', Ministry of Defence, 30 January 2006; David Lee, *Beachhead Assault – The Story of the Royal Naval Commandos in World War II* (Greenhill Books, London; 2004), pp.181-194.

Naval Beach Parties, and each of the first reconnaissance parties suffered losses. A little later a Beachmaster was killed when a mine exploded. As I stopped to talk to Commander Nicholl, Colonel [D.V.H.] Board [the Beach Group Commander] went on. We did not see him again until we found his body in the evening, only a short distance along the beach lying beside his dead escort.[12]

Gueritz remained on the beach for another 19 days before being seriously injured; just 24 years of age at the time, he was later credited with having played a leading role in helping get 3 Br Inf Div of the Queen beaches on D-Day.[13]

As the attack continued to develop pace, at 0840 further along the beach on Queen Red the main body of 1st Special Service Brigade landed under the command of Lord Lovat. He is often described as one of the Second World War's legendary figures despite the fact that he saw less than six days of action and was badly injured in the days following the landing near Breville, probably by a stray British artillery round.[14] Known by his men as 'Mad Lovat', in 1940 he had volunteered to join the commandos immediately following their establishment. Two years later, as a Lieutenant-Colonel and now the commanding officer of 4 Commando, he had led his men in the raid on Dieppe and their attack upon a German gun battery which was one of the few positives to emerge from the ill-fated venture. As he wrote later in his memoir, for D-Day the commandos "had been assigned a formidable task".[15] Along with 6 AB Div their main role was to hold the left flank of the Allied assault, Lovat's brigade of four commandos landing on the western most beaches and then moving inland to join forces with the two airborne glider and parachute brigades that had been dropped overnight. Landing first No.4 (RM) Commando (4 Cdo) was given the role of destroying the battery and garrison at Ouistreham; touching down 30 minutes later the remainder of the brigade was to move through enemy defences and provide the reinforcements for the airborne division. The distance from the landing beach to the River Orne was 4.5 miles and from there to the village of Le Plein a further 1.5 miles and they were expected to cover this whilst also fighting.

With only the advance brigade headquarters accompanying them, 4 Cdo had sailed independently from Southampton in the LSI *Princess Astrid*, a former Belgian ferry, and the LSI *Maid of Orleans*, and deployed on 14 LCA which arrived on schedule at H+30 at La Breche. They used steel landing-craft which moved in the water more slowly than the traditional LCA but provided a good deal more protection; one troop amongst them went in singing 'Jerusalem'. With an initial strength of 500 men and commanded by Lieutenant-Colonel Peter Young DSO, MC, fully integrated with the British force was *1er Bataillon de Fusiliers Marins Commandos* (B.F.M.C.), 177 French troops under

12 Ibid., p.185.
13 He would go on to finish his naval career as a rear-admiral; 'Obituary – Rear-Admiral Teddy Gueritz', *Daily Telegraph*, 7 January 2009; 'Obituary – Rear-Admiral Edward Gueritz', *The Independent*, 4 February 2009.
14 'Obituary – Captain Arnold Wheeldon', *Daily Telegraph*, 20 November 2012; 'Obituary – Lord Lovat', *The Times*, 17 March 1995.
15 Lovat, *March Past*, p.293; additional information on the D-Day role played by the commando forces on Sword can be found in 'Normandie 6 juin 1944', *Historica* (No.75; avril-juin 2003), pp.119, 131, 133, 135.

Lovat's commandos on board the LCIs approaching Queen Red

About 0845, men from 8 Inf Bde landing on Queen Red

Commandant Philippe Kieffer and the only French ground-based contingent to take part in the D-Day landings. Kieffer, who had been born in Haiti, was serving as a reserve officer aboard the battleship *Courbet* when the German invasion of France began and, following the surrender, he immediately joined the Free French and later raised the first commando unit. Having travelled in a separate convoy, 'S6', aboard two LSIs which had sailed from Warsash, his marines now formed the first wave in the assault on France. Heading for the barbed wire which was breached with cutting pliers Kieffer was wounded, but he was quickly bandaged up and retained command; 40 of his troops were either killed or wounded during this initial assault. Nonetheless they now took the lead along with 4 Cdo's C Troop and secured the main coast road followed by the rest of the commando. Reaching their target, Ouistreham, one of the two French troops, Troop 1, suffered heavy losses in front of the casino strongpoint which it reached at about 1000 and only after severe fighting was the position taken about 30 minutes later. The British troops moved towards their objective, the Riva-Bella strongpoint, which they found did not contain any 155 mm guns. At 0958 a *Luftlotte III* intelligence officer recorded that enemy tanks had broken through at Riva-Bella and St Aubin and were heading for Caen while the bulk of forces were believed to be assembling in front of the Orne estuary.[16] This was one of the very few messages received from the German defenders throughout this entire phase of the battle for Sword.

The main body of the commando brigade headquarters along with No.6 (RM) Commando (6 Cdo) landed at 0840 to hear that the bridges on the east bank of the Orne had been captured intact. They had made their run in to the landing beaches in two groups, a deliberate decision by Lovat who did not want all of his forces to land at the same time. The first group, which consisted of 12 craft carrying over 1,000 commandos, was followed about thirty minutes later by eight more. The senior naval officer for this convoy, 'S9', was Lieutenant Commander Rupert Curtis RNVR and his job was to guide the marines to the middle of a strip of beach only 800 yards wide. He directed the first wave of the main body aiming at the landmarks of the lighthouse at Ouistreham to the left and the old château at Hermanville to the right. Lord Lovat later wrote what happened next as the captain of LCI(S) 519, the 105 feet long flat-bottomed landing craft:

> …gunned his engines and bumped over the shallows. 'Stand by with the ramps!' Four able seamen sprang to the gangways. 'Lower away there,' and the brows ran sweetly down at a steep angle. The command craft had a comfortable landing. On these occasions the senior officer, stepping cautiously (rather than attempting a headlong dive), is first off the boat. Surprisingly, it is as safe a place as any. The water was knee-deep when Piper Bill Millin, struck up 'Blue Bonnets', keeping the pipes going as he played the commandos off the beach. It was not a place to hang about in … The eruption of 1200 men covered the sand in record time.[17]

---

16 'Field Headquarters, Gruppe Ic (intelligence), 6 June 1944', Wilmot Papers, LH15/15/32, LHCMA.

17 Bill Millin was 21 years old, the only one wearing a kilt and, with his role on Sword beach, he became the only piper to play in action during D-Day. He did, however, recall the tune slightly differently stating that it was 'Road to the Isles' and it seems he played a medley which also included

The famous picture of Bill Millin coming ashore also shows the congestion of
DD tanks on the beach

As the commandos came ashore armour-piercing rounds hit both landing craft
carrying the brigade headquarters but failed to detonate the 4,000 gallons of high
octane petrol carried by the vessels. The senior naval officer and the brigade commander
both later wrote that had HE or incendiary ammunition been used most of the headquarters group would almost certainly have been lost.[18] As Lieutenant Commander
Curtis put it: "At the end of the day I estimated that half of the brigade might not
have got ashore but for the fact that the Germans used solid shot on us which was
really meant for tanks". The war diary records that progress was slow as the advance to
the airborne troops began, a result of the marshy conditions of the ground and enemy
mortar fire. Even so the forming up point was reached an hour after landing by which
time both No.3 and No.45 RM Commandos (3 Cdo/45 Cdo) had also landed and
caught up with their colleagues.

According to the 8 Inf Bde war diary, all opposition on the landing areas aside from
the occasional fire of snipers, had been overcome by 0810; this was later recorded as

'Highland Laddie'; Lovat, *March Past*, p.310. 'Lovat said: "There you are, it's two Scotsmen leaving
the greatest invasion in history"'; 'Piper's tunes of D-Day glory', The (Glasgow) Herald, 17 January
2001.

18   Rupert Curtis, 'D-Day – We Landed the Commandos', 9107-238, National Army Museum (hereafter 'NAM'), p.7; Lovat, *March Past*, p.310.

being the point at which the defenders' ability to bring aimed fire to bear on the beaches effectively ended although this was not actually the case.[19] Another statement that could perhaps also be challenged was that by 0943, only eighteen minutes later than planned, the whole of the Sword assault brigade was on shore. In reality intense fighting was still raging across the assault area. A Company had been isolated from the rest of 1 South Lancs on landing and would take the remainder of the day before it returned and took over defences on the left flank. For the men of this company there was a battle within a battle as they moved towards the TROUT strongpoint. The lead landing craft in the company's centre, at the vanguard of the assaulting forces and amongst the first to land on the beach back at H-Hour, could see no sign of the DD tanks that should have been ahead of them.[20] The first thing that could be seen when they touched down was the road leading from the beach but it was "literally choked with coils of barbed wire, perhaps as much as 12 feet in height"; whilst Lieutenant Eddie Jones, commanding No.8 Platoon, was thinking about how to tackle this with wet Bangalore torpedoes, an AVRE ploughed through it and then lost its tracks. By this stage shells were already falling on the roofs of the nearest buildings and the men were moved off toward a large house immediately on the left of the beach. The exit had a broad grass verge which, on closer inspection, was found to contain a number of well camouflaged dugouts each filled with German soldiers. The lateral road was about hundred yards ahead of them running behind houses facing the sea and parallel to the beach. This headed west towards Lion-sur-Mer, a distance of about half a mile, and the men moved along it encountering no German troops but a number of French civilians "many who seemed too stunned to comprehend what was happening".[21] On reaching TROUT they found it cleared of civilians and occupied and strongly defended by German troops. The buildings had been converted into blockhouses and some of the streets completely barricaded with barbed wire practically up to roof level and 20-30 feet deep.

Heading for the same target was No.41 (RM) Commando (41 Cdo), part of 4th Special Services Commando Brigade, which landed on the far right of Sword beach meaning that there were commandos on both flanks. The war diary recorded at 0825:

> Coastline now perfectly visible and Troop Commanders were able to identify their beach from previous study of aerial photographs during the briefing. The beach appeared a bit of a shambles. It was littered with dead and wounded and burnt out tanks and with Sherman Crabs flailing through wire and mines, Bulldozers clearing gaps etc. the beach was quite obviously still under fire as mortar bombs and shells were crashing down fairly plentifully. It appeared however that Red Beach was getting a better share of the fire than White.[22]

The six LCIs carrying the commandos touched down at 0845 about 300 yards from the planned landing point, coming ashore on Queen Red and not Queen White, just shortly after the main commando force began its assault further down the beach. Led

---

19 'Opposition Encountered …', p.108, DEFE2/490, TNA.
20 Jones, 'Wartime Service with the 1st Battalion…', p.25, LIM.
21 Ibid., p.28.
22 'War Diary – 41 RM Commando', June 1944, ADM202/103, TNA.

An AVRE of 79 Armd Div near Lane 2 on Queen Red

by Lieutenant-Colonel T.M. Gray it was divided into two forces, the first of these, containing P and Y Troop, had the initial objective of neutralising TROUT. The others, B and X Troop, were to attack the château in the south-west of Lion-sur-Mer which was thought to be being used as a German staff headquarters. Once both forces had completed their missions they were then to move further right with the ultimate aim of meeting with No.48 (RM) Commando (48 Cdo) which had landed at Juno and was hopefully moving in the direction of Langrune. This would complete the link up of the Allied invasion along this section of the coastal strip. Getting off the beaches proved extremely costly and both the commanders of Y and B Troop were killed before they had managed to reach the sand dunes. On the approach to TROUT sniper and mortar fire continued and the commandos were unable to call in fire support as the FOB had been wounded and their wireless sets had been damaged on the beach. Y Troop, supported by three Centaurs of 2nd Armoured (Royal Marine) Support Regiment, moved forward first to attack the strongpoint. The German defenders in turn remained dormant waiting for the attackers to approach; they opened fire almost at point-blank range of about 100 yards and destroyed all three armoured vehicles.

Initially part of this same attack were the remnants of A Company 1 South Lancs, along with No.1 Platoon 2 Middlesex, but having failed to make much progress at TROUT, they were diverted to attack a large farmhouse further inland which was being used to target the British troops. A cluster of mortar bombs led to further casualties and the surviving men withdrew after they were ordered to re-join the remainder of the battalion back at Hermanville where they dug in and spent a quiet night.[23] It had been a long day for the assault battalion fighting on the beaches with the battle for COD and the support given to the attack on TROUT followed by the capture and consolidation of Hermanville and local patrolling. Although the regimental account describes them as "surprisingly light", this had led to heavy casualties with a total of 18 men having died, five of whom were officers – it was noted that the officer casualties were disproportionately high – with another 89 wounded and 19 missing. Contact with 2 East Yorks had not been established until 1100 but the two lead assault battalions had succeeded in expanding the opening provided by the engineers and specialist armour. Behind them a great deal would depend upon the follow-up or intermediate force which would have the responsibility for building upon the initial success and driving on to achieve the divisional objectives.

23 Jones, 'Wartime Service with the 1st Battalion…', pp.27-30, LIM.

9

Morning – Consolidation

Whilst General Eisenhower's primary goal had been to secure a lodgement on the French coast, 3 Br Inf Div had more expansive aims and these would depend almost entirely on the next phase of the battle. Following the initial assault 185 Inf Bde was to land at H+2 with infantry from the 2nd Battalion, Royal Warwickshire Regiment (2 Warwicks) and 1st Battalion, Royal Norfolk Regiment (1 Norfolks). They would then move quickly off the beaches before concentrating just north of Hermanville in a wooded area and on each side of the main road running out of the village. These two battalions would wait and allow 2 KSLI, landing next, to pass through the line where it would join with the Staffordshire Yeomanry (Staffs Yeomanry) to form a mobile force supported by elements of 17 Field Battery RA (17 Field RA) and two Forward Observation Officers (FOOs) from 33 Field RA. Once assembled it was to strike out past the villages of Beauville and Bieville and occupy the high ground above Lebisey before, if the situation was favourable, pushing into Caen and capturing the crossings over the River Orne. With this done a covering force, based around a company of infantry and a squadron of tanks, was to be sent an additional seven to eight miles south to occupy the high ground astride the main Caen-Falaise road. The Warwicks were to move cross-country on the west of the main axis, the main road between Hermanville and Caen, with the Norfolks on the east; the plan warned that these routes were liable to be changed depending on the situation on the flanks. If 2 KSLI were unable to follow the potentially key approach route through Lebisey the two other battalions were to carry out the operation against Caen. Having provided covering fire during the run into the shore, 7 Field Regiment RA (7 Field RA) would then deploy to the south-west of the Hermanville crossroads before moving up to the Périers-sur-le-Dan ridge and on to the valley north of Lebisey. If the plan had worked it would move on to the racecourse in Caen to support the city's defence. It was a hugely ambitious task and would depend on a huge range of factors, not all of which were in the control of the brigade commander.

The command ship was HMS *Dacres* which embarked from Newhaven on the morning of 5 June. On setting sail one of those on the bridge recorded that "the weather did not look at all auspicious – a fairly large sea was running, whipped up by a cold wind, while the sun only occasionally managed to break through the clouds".[1] Also on the bridge was Brigadier K.P. Smith – or Pearce Smith as he is titled in some texts – commanding 185 Inf Bde. He had enjoyed a long career which spanned from serving as a young infantry officer in the trenches of the First World War through to his current senior appointment. In between he had fought in North Russia against the Bolsheviks, in Ireland during the

---

1 Lieutenant-Colonel N.P.H. Tapp, 'Regimental Commander's Account on 'D-Day' and 'D plus One', Regimental History N.W. Europe 1944/45, 7 Field Regiment RA, Scarfe Papers, ULSC.

rebellion, and had served in both India and West Africa. In 1939 he was back in Ulster and went on to command an infantry brigade during the siege of Malta. It was from here that he went to Scotland to take charge of 185 Inf Bde, aged 45 and with 28 years of military service behind him. As his own autobiography accepts this final move was a disappointing one, the result of his having been effectively dismissed by Monty from his Malta command and confirmation that he was viewed as an officer who had little recent experience in battle.[2] Here therefore was an infantry commander who was not apparently considered to be amongst the most capable of senior British officers.

For the most important battle of his career he decided that the brigade would advance with one battalion up – 2 KSLI – and the other two in reserve. As it was expected that within two hours of the start of the landings the bridgehead would have been secured, the brigadier planned for the rifle companies of all of the battalions to land in one wave of LCIs together with small supporting headquarters for each. This landing would be made entirely on foot with all of the vehicles scheduled to land a further two hours later and join the men in the assembly area or, if the troops had already left, to follow them up. Also aboard *Dacres* was Lieutenant-Colonel N.P.H. Tapp commanding 7 Field RA.[3] His regiment started firing on the Queen beaches at 0655 at a range of just over 10,000 yards and continued for the next 30 minutes with 90 rounds for each of the 72 guns.[4] Five minutes later 33 Field RA who were 400 yards behind and to port also opened fire on their principal target, an enemy strongpoint behind the beach.[5] Colonel Tapp later recorded that the entire process went much better than had been the case on any of the exercises that had been conducted in Scotland. The guns had kept the right range and communications between the various vessels had worked far better than had been hoped. By 0725, as the first elements of the invasion were reaching the beaches, all firing ceased and the guns were emptied in preparation for themselves being transferred ashore. During this losses were limited, something which was put down to the coxswains who ran the LCTs ashore at top speed, albeit about 400 yards further west than had been planned.

The plan, as it had been given to 1 Norfolks, seems to have been slightly different to the brigadier's intentions. They were to pass through the assault brigade, cross an anti-tank obstacle, push on to some high ground overlooking Caen and then if possible capture the town itself. As the battalion history described this was, "an ambitious plan, but by no means an impossible one if all our intelligence was correct. The intervening country was chiefly standing crops, and was good tank-going except for a few woods here and there".[6] The battalion was split between three landing craft with the commander and vital staff

2   Brigadier Kenneth Pearce Smith, *Adventures of an Ancient Warrior in Peace War and Revolution* (Stones Printers; Milford-on-Sea, 1984), p.94.

3   Tapp highlights in his account that "the main object was to seize the crossings over the River Orne – nothing was to interfere with this"; Tapp, 'Regimental Commander's Account on 'D-Day' and 'D plus One', Scarfe Papers, ULSC.

4   'Obituary of John Talbot – Artillery commander who saw off an SS Panzer Division attack in Normandy', *The Daily Telegraph*, 14 July 2009.

5   '33 Field Regiment Royal Artillery – 6 June 1944 to 8 May 1945', June 1945, p.3, Scarfe Papers, ULSC.

6   *The History of the 1st Battalion The Royal Norfolk Regiment, During the World War, 1939-45* (Jarrold and Sons Limited; Norwich, 1947), p.20.

A carrier from 2 KSLI on the road to Hermanville

distributed to offer some contingency. A number of accounts once again praised the Royal Navy for having taken the men to the exact spot on the beach called for by their operation orders and praised them for the dry landing. The troops in D Company were carried to the beaches by LCI 126 commanded by Lieutenant E.W. Moore RNVR; this particular landing craft was badly damaged as it beached disabling the port-side ramp and forcing all of the troops down the one side. From the beach the men proceeded to the battalion assembly area which they reached at about 1050 whilst the LCI, having also taken a hit to the bridge, returned back to Newhaven. The infantry had been given folding bicycles as part of their assault equipment, it being thought that this would allow them to get inland more quickly. Company Sergeant Major T.G. Catlin of C Company described them as "not the familiar heavy type of bicycle but a lightweight model with wing nuts so they could be folded – I must say not the easiest of machines to ride in full battle order (many a sore backside)".[7] The vast majority of these were in fact dropped on landing and not recovered. Because the men had typically been up to their armpits in water during the rehearsal landings they had also been issued with the waterproof 'overtrousers' which covered everything up to the neck. It was believed that the nearer a soldier was to the sea the greater the chance of being shelled and once they had landed there followed "a short comic interlude while everybody tried to doff this gear while

7   John Lincoln, *Thank God and the Infantry: From D-Day to VE-Day with the 1st Battalion, the Royal Norfolk Regiment* (Sutton Printing; Trowbridge, 1999), p.18.

balancing on one leg". Nonetheless there were no casualties on the beach despite the battalion history referring to what it termed "the scrum to get to the beach exits, struggling to avoid the usual bunching, and finally trying to find out where you were and make sure you are heading in the right direction for the right RV".[8]

Within 2 KSLI, under the command of the highly respected Col Jack Maurice, there were four rifle companies. In each the commanding officer was a regular who had been with the battalion for some years; even so of these only Major A.F. Slatter, who had won a DCM shortly before Dunkirk, had seen active service. This battalion had in fact experienced considerable reorganisation following its return to Britain as it had been realised then that, after such a long absence overseas, many of the officers and men had been "out of touch with the conception of a modern mobile battle".[9] The plan called for it to be 'phased in' with a staggered landing of men and equipment and four parties subdivided by different days and tides on which each was due to land. With the requirement to bring all the rifle troops ashore first it meant that they would potentially be waiting a minimum of two hours for their transport; at best they would be able to move from the initial assault area at around noon. In light of this Colonel Maurice's plan called for the battalion, when it was assembled, to initially use the tanks of the Staffs Yeomanry as transport although only if the shelling was not too heavy otherwise it was thought that this would increase casualties and waste time. The advance was to proceed on a two company front, W Company on the right and X on the left of the road, with Z and Y behind them. They would be followed by the support company and the other detachments as required. 7 Field RA would provide the artillery support with a battery commander landing alongside Colonel Maurice; the FOOs from 17/43 Battery were only scheduled to join the battalion at the assembly area as they were first supporting the assault brigades during the landings.

The first rifle companies from 2 KSLI were supposed to land at H+120 but the initial LCI touched down early at 1010 and heavily laden men waded in four to five feet of water on to the beach at La Breche. As had been the case earlier they were greatly aided by ropes which had been carried ashore by the naval crews of the landing craft. Casualties were few despite the beach being under fire and the assembly area was quickly found. One of these landing craft, which had carried in X Company, was hit by shellfire just after the men disembarked and sank on the beach. Each man carried a sandbag labelled with their name which contained a gas mask, cardigan and other items which would be needed later and these were dumped in the assembly area, the orchards immediately north of Hermanville; nearly all of them were recovered the next day. In the assembly area, which they also reached at about 1050, men warmed themselves with self-heating tins of cocoa and were pleased to discard the first of their maps which covered an area they had now already cleared. As one of them later noted, however, this pause also marked the point at which any similarity to the exercises they had conducted ceased and from then on "the operation became a rather impromptu affair".[10] This of course was the real problem, a great deal of the plan for 185 Inf Bde required that the landings progressed according to schedule and that the various components should all be able to

8   *History of the 1st Battalion The Royal Norfolk*, p.20.
9   Radcliffe, *History of the 2nd Battalion, the King's Shropshire Light Infantry.*
10 Rylands, '"W" Coy, 2nd Bn. K.S.L.I. in Normandy'.

meet at the assembly area so they could form up and move on quickly to the next in the long series of objectives that had been given to them.

For the final battalion, 2 Warwicks commanded by the 38 year old Lieutenant-Colonel Hugh Herdon, there were also four rifle companies along with support and headquarters companies, and the separate battalion headquarters.[11] It had approached the Normandy shore in three LCIs and arrived exactly on time at 0955 and, for A Company, the target was the beach in front of Lion-sur-Mer and a 'gable-ended house' which, on the run in, could be seen to have survived the intense bombardment. The landing craft carrying C Company hit a mine on the beach as it grounded whilst the third LCI was hit by shellfire three times and then had both its landing ramps shot away by mortar fire; it was steered alongside a previously abandoned landing craft over which the men scrambled and then onto the beach. From here they moved to their initial assembly area which was about half-a-mile south of Hermanville and, at around 1100, they started digging in around the cemetery.[12] Accurate German sniper fire from the church bell tower and machine gun fire from positions to the west led to several casualties amongst both companies before the order to withdraw was given. Setting off on a fast march shortly after midday all the companies and the battalion headquarters were reassembled in the village for the first time since they had left England.[13] The regimental history referred to the "sense of oddity" which persisted throughout the battalion about a battle which did not seem what had been expected. This was only increased with the news that the brigade plan has been changed, "for all the world like one of those big exercises in which the participating units moved from point to point without learning whether there was any pattern to events".[14] For 2 Warwicks they were now ordered to advance along an axis Colleville-sur-Orne – Benouville – Blainville following the river road to Caen that ran on the west bank of the Orne. This line of advance meant that the battalion would be available both to provide support to the airborne troops on the opposite bank whilst also still potentially moving forward towards the city.[15]

Just 30 minutes before the divisional commander on *Largs* moved in close to the shoreline in readiness to land on the beach, at 0900 Smith had made the decision to go ashore. At a distance of 2,000 yards the command party moved with him from the *Dacres* and were transferred to a small craft which made the run in without any issue. Tapp, who was with this group, was struck by the "already almost unbelievable congestion" one result of which was that the guns and armoured vehicles of 33 Field RA and 76 Field RA were unable to get off the beach and were firing from the water's edge. Enemy shells were either hitting the houses on the beachfront or were passing over into the sea but there were various burning British vehicles and casualties. The group moved rapidly ashore and collected themselves on a small side street off the first lateral. From there it

---

11 He was killed the following day in the attack on Lebisey and is one of five Lieutenant-Colonels buried in La Delivrande War Cemetery including Harrapp from 13/18 Hussars and Maurice from the KSLI.

12 H.C. Illing, 'No Better Soldier, 1939-1945' (Privately published, n.d.) pp.14-15.

13 Ibid.

14 Marcus Cunliffe, *History of the Royal Warwickshire Regiment 1919-1955* (William Clowes and Sons Ltd; London, 1956), pp.79-81.

15 'War Diary – June 1944', WO171/1387, TNA.

Commandos moving in file on
the road from Colleville

was a further 70 yards to the second lateral where they orientated themselves; the road was blocked with tanks from the 13/18 Hussars so the group turned west and walked along to the first crossroads which was a further 200 yards away. From here it was an additional 500 yards inland towards an orchard which had been identified during the planning phase as the location to hold the initial brigade order group. On the way Smith managed to get lost and it was not until 1000 that this meeting began and he issued his first orders; it had taken the command group about an hour to travel less than half-a-mile. It would take another hour before the main brigade headquarters was established. At this stage Hermanville was still not fully secure with the assault brigade struggling to capture the ridge to its south and establish a defensive position to the east of the main road. This meant that the artillery from 33 Field RA and 76 Field RA was not available to provide support to 185 Inf Bde's planned advance.

Whilst this confusion was going on, the decisions being made by the Staffs Yeomanry commander were to prove of vital significance to how D-Day was decided for the Allies. Colonel Eadie had initially been commissioned into the regiment in March 1924 and when he had mobilised in September 1939 at the war's outbreak he had progressed to become second-in-command. After a period spent by the unit in Palestine there had been service in the North African campaign for which he was awarded the DSO. This was followed by an appointment as Commanding Officer in October 1942 and attendance on the Senior Officers course.[16] The plan for the invasion, which would be taking

---

16 He would be awarded a bar to his DSO for his leadership during the Normandy campaign; he was

place just three days before his birthday, had the regiment acting as part of the follow-up force landing directly behind the assault armour of 13/18 Hussars on the most easterly beach where they would act as the left flank of the whole operation and, potentially, provide support to 185 Inf Bde. The commanding officers were: A Squadron, Major M.A. Spencer-Nairn; B Squadron, Major George Turner MC, 33 years old and, in civilian life, a Works Superintendent in Birmingham; C Squadron, Major Patrick Griffin MC, 25 years old, who would later receive a bar to his MC and post-war would be appointed as the regiment's second-in-command. The recce role was provided by light 'Honey' tanks which moved forward looking for enemy troops and strongpoints. As the tanks landed at about 1030 the state of the tide meant that they were almost entirely dry as they reached the shore. The post-war history notes that "they had to stand by for a short while before landing, and tank crews were able to take the opportunity of picking out various landmarks shown on the photographs to thoroughly orientate themselves before being committed to the battle".[17]

There had been a failure on the beach to open the exit earmarked for the regiment and the area chosen for assembling the tanks was discovered to be in the centre of a minefield. The war diary recorded "a terrible jam on the beach where no organization appeared to be operating and no marked exits were to be seen" as a result of which the majority of the tanks remained stationary for the first hour.[18] Even then with traffic control "non-existent" on the only available routes "vehicles remained head to tail for long periods". It therefore took some time before the regiment was able to reach its initial assembly point at the crossroads in Hermanville although they did so without having encountered any significant enemy fire.[19] B Squadron was assigned the role of protecting the right flank with the regimental headquarters positioned on the road from Hermanville to Caen whilst A Squadron provided the reserve. As the tanks came off in twos and threes and formed up they engaged enemy guns overlooking the village of Beauville.[20] At this stage B Squadron was also engaged by an 88 mm gun which had allowed C Squadron to pass through; in an early demonstration of the power of this weapon, before it was silenced five British tanks were destroyed along with the medical half-track and all of its supplies. From here the remainder moved down into the town where they encountered further gunfire. In terms of the divisional plan the continuing delay was critical, by noon the Staffs Yeomanry had only managed to get one-and-a-half squadrons ashore and assembled and a large minefield had been discovered which crossed the planned axis of advance.

---

replaced as the unit's commander at the end of July by his second-in-command Charles Farquhar; 'Officers Record Book', D1300/3/10, SYA.

17 Major D.F. Underhill, *Queen's Own Royal Regiment, The Staffordshire Yeomanry: An account of the operations of the Regiment during World War II 1939-1945* (Staffordshire Yeomanry Museum, 2000), p.25.

18 Staffs Yeomanry War Diary, vol.54, SYA.

19 C Squadron's unit diary also recorded "the beach was very crowded and Squadron was held up badly"; Lieutenant-Commander P.K. Kemp, *The Staffordshire Yeomanry (QQRR) in the First and Second World Wars* (Gale and Polden; Aldershot, 1950).

20 'Tuesday June 6th – D-Day, Diary of C Squadron of the Yeomanry covering D Day and the Invasion of Germany 1944-45', D1300/4/7/1-2, SYA.

A mixture of sappers and armour on the road to Colleville

It was at this stage that the first doubts emerged about the plan and what could be achieved. The war diary records that at 1115 Brigadier Smith and Colonel Maurice passed the assembly area on folding bicycles. More than an hour before the brigade commander had already reportedly warned during his senior officer group that there would have to be a delay until the armoured unit had formed up; as Tapp later wrote "they [the Staffs Yeomanry] were obviously going to be late, as the beach exits were blocked and in addition this was the first time [they] had landed their whole Regiment". The gunners were at last beginning to come off the beach with the first gun and carrier leading at 1130 and moving past Hermanville to deploy in the open fields to the south and just in front of 1 South Lancs who were still at this stage the lead infantry. Within 30 minutes Tapp's entire regiment with all of its vehicles was finally fully deployed. By this stage the order had, however, already been given changing the brigade plan of advance. The men of 2 KSLI were to advance by the main road on foot, with the tanks to join them as soon as possible, heading towards Périers-sur-le-Dan in the direction of Point 61, and 2 Warwicks would now follow an entirely different route to that which they had anticipated. Fifteen minutes later Smith received information that enemy tanks were north of Caen, there was fire coming from the ridge in front of him and the Canadians on his flank were being heavily engaged by the German defenders.[21] The situation appeared to be threatening to unravel.

There had been concerns throughout the planning stage about the potential impact of the small beach on the speed of the landings and these now seemed well placed. The diary kept by a senior naval officer on HMS *Goathland* provides an interesting review of progress recording messages received on board ship from the beach signal station which had been established at 0900. The first, sent just six minutes later, advised that two exits had been secured on White beach but within quarter of an hour congestion was reported, and this message was repeated twice in the next 40 minutes. By 1027 vehicles on the right edge of the beach were reported as being so congested that they could not move.[22] Three minutes later, with the tide coming in, the beaches were now nowhere more than 25 yards wide and in some places this was down to just 10 yards.[23] An intelligence officer who landed at approximately 1045 had found it surprisingly difficult on the run in to identify any of the landmarks along the beach despite his having had the opportunity to study the target in some detail using the material that had been supplied to him well in advance of the regular troops.[24] He could only make out the lighthouse at Ouistreham and the low cliffs to the west of Lion-sur-Mer. By the point that he arrived there were no visible beach obstacles as the incoming tide had covered them all with the water being much higher up the beach than he had expected and the congestion of men and equipment "considerable". He also noticed a complete lack of any exit markers from the beach and no barrage balloons protecting the landing craft; these had been cut adrift once it had become clear that the Germans were using them as markers for their mortar fire. He described enemy action as "not intense, but irritating, being confined to an occasional shell and one salvo of incendiary rockets. Snipers were also active at the extremes of the beach".

Aside from the challenges of terrain perhaps the greatest issue in getting men and equipment off the beach was the apparent lack of contingency in command. A good example of this was experienced by 22 Dragoons who by 1000, with their primary mission completed, had rallied at a point between two villas in which the gardens had been heavily fortified. These remaining Sherman Crabs now began to open up the lateral roads which still contained a great deal of barbed wire and numerous mines. There were two of these and the distance between them was about 75 yards with the ground immediately inland from the second in most places soft, liable to flooding and not considered safe for tanks which had to keep to the main roads for the first three quarters of a mile. They would continue this work until about 1500, the first two hours of which were described as a "most challenging" consolidation role, but without any direction. One of the regiment's officers, a Captain Wheway, set out on foot to find the Royal Engineer commander who was tasked to coordinate this phase of the assault; he could only find a single surviving subaltern officer who reported that he was now the senior member of

---

21 'Notes on 3 British Division during the Opening Phases of Operation Overlord', p.9, D8/2/3, ULSC.

22 Talbot, 'Report by the Naval Commander Force S', 22 July 1944, p.24, NARA.

23 *The History of the Corps of the King's Shropshire Light Infantry*, p.230.

24 Captain T.L. Clark, 'Personal Impressions of D Day in 101 Beach Sub Area Queen Sector', pp.16-17, Cass Papers, IWM.

his squadron and the casualties to his men and the machines they needed to use were so great that no further beach clearance could be attempted.[25] It had come down to the initiative of individual tank commanders to open up more exits and clear mines wherever possible.

The blockages on the beach only became worse as the final reserve element, 9 Inf Bde, also began its landings around 1000. It was designed to be mobile and had been specifically told that it must be prepared to carry out a variety of tasks with orders to concentrate initially in and around Hermanville where it was to be at the disposal of the divisional commander. The lead troops, 2nd Battalion, The Lincolnshire Regiment (2 Lincolns) supported by tanks from the East Riding Yeomanry was to first establish a concentration area near Cresserons. Here it would be joined by 1st Battalion, King's Own Scottish Borderers (1 KOSB) before pushing out and establishing contact with 8 Canadian Infantry Brigade which had landed at Juno. The final battalion, the 2nd Battalion, The Royal Ulster Rifles (2 RUR), was to seek out and make contact with the nearest unit of 8 Inf Bde whilst also following the same line of advance as had been taken by 185 Inf Bde heading for the areas designated on the bogus maps as 'Marigold' and 'Lupin'. These were to the north-west of Caen and behind the anticipated position of their sister brigade from where they would be in a position, if required, to assist with the attack on the city. Indeed, the operation order as it was issued to the brigade was explicit that the division intended to capture Caen and it had a potential role to play.[26] Holding these positions they could also provide flank protection and prevent any German counter-attack.

Again speed was clearly recognised as being central to the reserve brigade's role with there being specific instruction that all troops should endeavour to keep forward routes clear and safeguard the flow of traffic from the beaches. There was also guidance that transport must disperse into fields if necessary and tanks should proceed across country. Unfortunately there proved little opportunity to implement these instructions to the full as the brigade's role in D-Day was seriously curtailed. Its commander Brigadier Jim Cunningham was badly wounded very shortly after the landings when six mortar bombs landed on and around his armoured vehicle. With both arms broken and shrapnel in his back and legs he was evacuated the following day.[27] Immediately 9 Inf Bde had landed his deputy Colonel Dennis Orr having been sent to the Caen Canal bridge to assess the situation and some confusion followed in the absence of any senior leadership. With this any chance the brigade may have had in supporting the advance on Caen was removed.

The impact of Cunningham's loss was perhaps best illustrated by the experience of 2 RUR who got ashore in relatively good order but then struggled to take any real part in the battle. The Ulsters were the only British regiment to have both its regular battalions involved in OVERLORD with 1st Battalion (1 RUR) landing by glider as part of the support lift for 6 AB Div that arrived on the early evening of D-Day. Reaching France before them 2 RUR had been the first element of the reserve brigade to land, slightly west of Ouistreham, transported in LCI 973 which they had embarked on two days before. While some of the infantry, notably 1 Norfolks, had landed dry, it was an entirely

25 Birt, *XXII Dragoons 1760-1945*, pp.172-173.
26 '9 Br Inf Bde – Operation Order No.1, Operation Overlord', 21 May 1944, WO171/616, TNA.
27 'The Memoirs of Brigadier J.C. Cunningham', Docs 10909, IWM.

different experience for the Ulsters with most of the men landing in at least four feet of water. For a battalion in which many of the Rifleman were small in size, a life-line ashore was needed from the steps of the LCI so that the men would be able to reach the beach. One of those waiting to go ashore was carrying his kit, his Bren gun and his folding bicycle and reckoned he was almost twice his normal weight: hence his decision to leave the latter behind, as many of those British troops who landed in Normandy on 6 June had also done.[28] Despite being part of the reserve brigade, the landing was still "very difficult and uncomfortable" as enemy shells continued to hit the beach and several men were wounded but none of their injuries were fatal.[29] The assembly area for the battalion was at Lion-sur-Mer and it was there they headed next, the site having been inspected by a small group who had landed an hour earlier in order to conduct a reconnaissance. From here they were ordered to occupy the high ground at a point slightly north-east of Périers-sur-le-Dan where they dug in for the night. Men and equipment were landed throughout the day with the last, the carriers for the mortar platoon, not arriving until late afternoon. The next day, having recovered many of the discarded 'infamous bicycles' 2 RUR set off in the direction of Caen but with revised orders to now instead capture the village of Cambes, about six miles inland; they eventually secured the woods next to the village two days later and remained there for another three weeks. Cunningham's injury had led to the battalion losing its commander, Lieutenant-Colonel I.C. Harris, to temporarily replace him albeit for a short period of time, but enough to disrupt its progress.

According to the writers of the Ulsters' history, "the loss of the brigade commander was a severe blow as his enthusiasm and charm during approximately two years with the brigade had made him particularly popular with all ranks of the battalion".[30] Although Cunningham made specific reference in his memoirs to the impact of his injury and the potential delay it caused to progress, interestingly his headquarters war diary makes no similar reference despite the fact that it was both forced to move and had little clear command.[31] At the same time the impact of the congestion on this brigade was all too obvious. The beach signal station had reported at 1105 that on Queen Red soft sand and wrecked vehicles were leading to congestion and had forced the effective closure of the beach which it was estimated would take two hours to clear. Nearly 50 minutes later slight congestion was still being reported on White while Red was now under fire although the disembarkation of vehicles there was said to have improved and was proceeding "satisfactorily". The result was that nearly an hour later two of the approaching groups carrying elements of 9 Inf Bde were held out at sea due to the continuing congestion; they did not proceed ashore until 1550, about three hours behind schedule.[32]

At the same time as the infantrymen of 3 Br Inf Div were struggling to move forward the battle to protect the invasion's flank had intensified. Having completed the initial landing phase of their operation the airborne force to the east of the Orne estuary had

28 David Orr and David Truesdale, 'The Rifles Are There' – 1st and 2nd Battalions the Royal Ulster Rifles in the Second World War (Pen and Sword; Barnsley, 2013), pp.33-36.
29 'History – 2nd Battalion the Royal Ulster Rifles…'.
30 Ibid.
31 'War Diary – HQ 9 Inf Bde', June 1944, WO171/616, TNA.
32 Talbot, 'Report by the Naval Commander Force S', 22 July 1944, p.24, NARA.

No.4 Commando heads for Ouistreham with the support of armour from
27 Armd Bde

numerous additional missions to complete as D-Day developed. For 3 Para Bde it was
able to complete the destruction of three bridges over the Dives river, the two at Bures
were destroyed at about 0930 and the larger bridge at Troarn at about 1500, and this
ensured that any German movement in the area would be severely hampered. With so
many paratroopers remaining scattered across the landing areas it was recognised by
the various British commanders, however, that there were insufficient forces to prevent
the enemy repairing the bridges. The battery at Merville, whilst its main guns were out
of action, could also potentially be reoccupied. Throughout the morning determined
attacks had meanwhile continued on 12 Para's positions holding the perimeter around
Le Bas de Ranville to the south of the divisional headquarters. These initially came from
the direction of Longueval and Ste Honaire and enemy patrols were repulsed at about
0800; a more determined attack from Hérouvillette which began at about 1005 was
repulsed 30 minutes later with three German self-propelled guns knocked out by the
anti-tank guns from 4 Airlanding Anti-tank Battery. The men of 7 Para Bn also faced
determined opposition with eight organised counter-attacks throughout the day which
were all beaten off. The official narrative's description of their defence recorded that:

> The enemy showed little initiative and repeated the same tactics time after time,
> suffering severely in the process. All the while he persisted with his infiltration
> methods using snipers, small parties and, occasionally, armoured cars. The para-
> troopers countered this infiltration by sending out small patrols to break up the

enemy parties. The snipers, also, were made to pay heavily for their unintelligent work. A PIAT was used against a number of them in the church tower at Le Port and 12 bodies were found there.[33]

The scattering of the airborne forces had seriously diluted their fighting power but they were hanging on and relief was on its way. D-Day in the Sword sector was moving towards its decisive point.

---

33 RAF Narrative, 'Volume III, The Landings in Normandy', p.217, JSCSC.

10

Afternoon – Exploitation

With the leading elements of the British invasion force having left their transport craft several hours before, the invasion was in many respects going as well as could have been hoped. The troops had landed on and then managed to get off the beaches but at a much slower pace than had been hoped. Two of the units involved in the initial assault landings were still fighting hard and would continue to do so for several more hours. B Squadron of 13/18 Hussars was providing support for 2 East Yorks in attacking the SOLE strongpoint. This had continued to act as the observation point for mortar fire onto the beach, indeed most accounts highlight it as having provided the most effective German response. The attackers had only been able to make slow movement towards it in large part because the naval FOB could not be found and this limited the amount of support that could be brought to bear. SOLE eventually fell at around 1545 with about 40 prisoners taken and the infantry moved forward for its attack on DAIMLER supported by the guns of 76 Field RA and the Hussars' tanks. With this objective captured there was a further advance to St Aubin d'Arquenay which they found to be empty of Germans and in ruins and they formed a defensive position. Having eventually been relieved by 1 KOSB the exhausted troops withdrew to a cornfield west of Hermanville where they stayed for the night. A total of five officers and 60 other ranks had been killed with a further four officers and 37 other ranks wounded. In a single 24 hour period the battalion's casualties roughly equated to one quarter of the strength it had at the beginning of the assault which, as has been highlighted, represented the highest losses on any of the British or Canadian beaches.[1]

Another key moment involved the airborne troops. The decision had been taken during the refinement of the plan to commit these relatively lightly armed forces to seize and hold Sword's flanking position until such a time as they could be relieved by the commandos and they were now facing considerable pressure. During the continuing counter-attacks in the Ranville area there were several points where the planner's decisions looked to have been too ambitious. It was reported at 1300 that a platoon of enemy soldiers dressed in airborne smocks and red berets had penetrated part of the position and self-propelled guns had reached a point about 500 yards south of the bridge over the Orne. Men from 12 Para Bn came to the assistance of their colleagues in 7 Para Bn and by 1400 all the ground that had been lost was regained. The situation for 5 Para Bde was also becoming increasingly critical with determined attempts at infiltration by German infantry and supporting guns approaching to 500 yards to the south of the Pont de Tournant. The defending force's position changed dramatically when at 1353 the lead

---

1 Nightingale, *The East Yorkshire Regiment (Duke of York's Own)*, pp.177-179.

The village of St Aubin d'Arquenay being cleared by commandos and tanks of
13/18 Hussars

commando elements crossed the bridges, the forward troops being immediately diverted
to provide support and no further significant enemy attack was made that day.[2]

Contact had actually been made with 6 AB Div's perimeter at 1230. Although this
seemed to have been unknown to 2 East Yorks St Aubin d'Arquenay was an objective
for Lovat's men and had been initially assaulted by 6 Cdo. During this attack an Italian
manned battery was found behind the eastern end of the village; this was "sorted out
with no great difficulty" and the guns spiked. The commando brigade headquarters led
by the Brigadier passed through shortly afterwards and encountered poor quality troops
as it moved up the main street with Lovat narrowly avoiding a sniper's round. A platoon
level counter-attack was in turn disrupted, in part by the appearance of a DD tank from
13/18 Hussars, the prisoners turning out to be Russians who had been press-ganged
into service.[3] After clearing the village the commandos moved on with scouts advancing
through fields containing flowering crops of red poppies before reaching Benouville
which also showed clear evidence of a fierce fight between the airborne troops and its
German defenders. The main body of the commandos had covered a distance of nearly
five miles in less than four hours in order to reach the bridges.[4] The initial objective had

2   '6 Airborne Divisional Troops', Staff College Camberley 1947 Course, JSCSC.
3   Lovat, *March Past*, pp.317, 319-321.
4   Following slightly behind 3 Cdo crossed three hours later. For a full account of the fighting around
      the bridges see Lloyd Clark, *Orne Bridgehead* (Sutton Publishing; Stroud, 2004), pp.151-163.

been secured and 6 Cdo's cycle troop continued on to capture Le Plein as 45 Cdo moved on towards Merville and Franceville Plage.

Whilst the German land-based response at the key bridges appeared to have been halted there was one other notable attack during the afternoon when two German gunboats came up the Caen Canal and one of them engaged the troops on the bank. Corporal Claude Godbold, who was now in command of No.24 Platoon, 2 Ox Bucks, waited until the boat was within 50 yards and opened fire with the platoon PIAT. The boat and its crew were captured; the second boat was forced to withdraw heading in the direction of Caen. Despite the bridges appearing to be firmly held a key decision was taken. Although his men had managed to achieve the link up needed to safeguard the division's flanks, the continuing German pressure and anxieties about progress being made back on the Sword beaches led to Lovat abandoning the original plan for his commandos. Instead of pushing on he took the decision to consolidate his forces and hold the high ground near the bridges establishing his headquarters in a house at the north end of the village of Le Plein.[5]

At the opposite end of the Sword area by about 1310 the situation for 41 Cdo was worse with heavy mortar fire coming from the château along with destructive fire from at least one self-propelled gun; this quickly developed into a full counter-attack from 716 Inf Div with around 60 German infantry, in addition to the increasingly accurate supporting fire that was being put down by elements from 1716 Arty Regt.[6] The commandos were forced to fall back on to a defensive line east of their objective unable to complete the capture of TROUT. Here they remained until the two battalions of 9 Inf Bde eventually arrived later in the afternoon to provide support after they had freed themselves from the delay on the beaches. There was, however, to be no link up between Lion-sur-Mer and Langrune, which 48 Cdo had successfully reached, and there was nine kilometres of beach including the village of Luc-sur-Mer which remained in German hands. Amongst Lovat's main body of commandos and the naval crews who had transported them to Sword there were a total of 49 killed and 27 wounded. For 41 Cdo approximately 140 had been killed, wounded or missing, seven of whom were officers, out of an initial strength of about 450 men. The men of the Special Service Brigades had provided an invaluable addition to the fighting power of 3 Br Inf Div but their success had come at great cost.

Sword was the scene of the first observations to be sent back to the OVERLORD headquarters in southern England detailing the weather on the beaches: at 1500 Double British Summer Time, more than seven hours after the troops had begun to land, it was recorded as being mainly sunny, with a north-westerly wind at Force 4, small amounts of broken cumulus cloud about 4,000 feet, good visibility and a temperature of 59 degree Fahrenheit (15 degrees Centigrade).[7] At about the same time the German coastal guns at Le Havre had, however, opened fire on the invasion fleet and the decision had been taken to move two columns of LCTs out of firing range. This meant that whilst the

5   'War Diary – No.1 Special Service Brigade HQ, June 1944', WO218/59, TNA.
6   One source describes this as the only substantial counter-attack made that day by the division, men from 10th Battery 1716 Arty Regt and 3rd Battalion 736 Gren; Ken Ford, *Sword Beach* (Sutton Publishing; Stroud, 2004), pp.65-66.
7   'D-Day: The Role of the Met Office', The Met Office (1995).

reserve infantry landed on time it was about 75 minutes before their armoured support could join them.[8] Landing at Lion-sur-Mer shortly after 1400 a driver in the East Riding Yeomanry, working with 9 Inf Bde as the divisional armoured reserve, recorded that "the beach was littered with various tanks and other vehicles, burning or broken down and there was obviously still a lot of shelling and there was an aircraft bombing".[9] This gives some indication as to the seriousness of the delays still being experienced: the Yeomanry had been scheduled to land shortly after noon. As they landed a wireless operator in one of A Squadron's tanks saw six JU88s make a low-level bombing raid on the landing craft scoring hits but losing three or four shot down. By about 1420 the regiment had moved to its initial assembly area where they removed waterproofing attachments and made the tanks ready for combat although at this stage they had yet to receive any orders. Here they waited in part hampered by the bombing of the infantry brigade headquarters which had wounded Brigadier Cunningham and left several other personnel dead or wounded. These casualties and a lack of communications meant that the Yeomanry effectively sat for several hours being shelled and did little to support the divisional objectives being secured. By 1500, with the final remnants of opposition at the beachhead now having largely died down, the remaining tanks of 22 Dragoons moved from their work on the laterals to help establish a more secure assembly area for the East Riding Yeomanry. Of the 26 Sherman Crab tanks that had landed along the beach around H-Hour only 11 still remained operational; five tanks were beyond repair and the remainder more or less seriously damaged. Of the crews nine men had been killed, eight wounded, and a further 25 were missing.[10]

Whilst the situation on the beaches and on the flanks was significant it was not where the now critical actions were poised to take place. For 3 Br Inf Div the outcome of D-Day would actually be determined across its central position. The progress made by 185 Inf Bde remained slow and there had been a prolonged wait at the assembly area at Hermanville. Having deployed 2 KSLI on foot Smith finally ordered the rest of his troops to move at 1300 and the mobile column headed off with the supporting troops behind. At the vanguard of the advance at 1315 X Company of 2 KSLI came under fire as it moved up the slope from a machine gun post on the right-hand side of the road and hidden in the corn on top of the Périers ridge. In an appendix to the war diary the author records that to tackle this threat "we then spread out with two platoons advancing rather like a row of beaters through the crops, and from time to time we would despatch a small post of Boche and then on again". It was at this point that the unit suffered its first casualty when a private stepped on a mine. The battalion commander played a key role in keeping the advance going, it being noted that "it was wonderfully heartening at this critical moment to see Colonel Maurice walking unconcernedly at the centre of the road, playing as usual with the chin-strap of his helmet. Everyone followed his example,

---

8   According to the semi-official history offloading commenced at approximately 1414 and the tanks came ashore mostly on their own tracks; Mace, *Forrard: The Story of the East Riding Yeomanry*, p.120.

9   Jack Farrell, 'We landed at Luc-sur-Mer', 25 May 2005, *BBC People's War*; according to the regimental history the tanks actually landed at Lion-sur-Mer.

10 Birt, *XXII Dragoons 1760-1945*, pp.172-173.

moving steadily forward under the enemy fire".[11] In W Company No.9 Platoon had taken the lead with the men, who it was later said feared mines more than anything, strung out along the road in a single file advancing on both sides. The entire company was now ordered to outflank this position and deploying into the cornfields they reached the peak of the ridge where they stumbled into Germans – parachutists armed with machine guns – who they captured by 1400. Despite having advanced uphill and in the open none of the attacking platoon was injured and the advance now continued over the crest and downhill towards Périers-sur-le-Dan. In the village much of the opposition was coming from the church and this was silenced and the men continued along a lane leading south which returned the company to the main line of advance and the road to Caen. This was re-joined just beyond the village of Le Homme which had been captured at 1400 by X Company.

At 1425 Colonel Maurice ordered Z Company to attack the battalion's main objective, the enemy gun battery near Périers-sur-le-Dan. Tapp confirmed that there were six German 12.2cm guns firing across the main axis of the advance throughout the afternoon.[12] According to the KSLI regimental history, "…this battery had the whole of the main road down the south side of the slope under observation and [they] were firing over open sights, thereby preventing either the tanks or the vehicles of the support company, which had started to arrive, from going forward".[13] The target had clearly also been missed by the RAF and, with it surrounded by barbed wire and in a well-defended site, it was a struggle for the infantry lacking in any artillery support due to an absence of FOOs. They were able to drive the gunners from the emplacements but only as far as weapon slits where they used heavy machine guns to push their attackers back and then returned to their guns and once more opened fire on the road. This sequence was repeated several times and was only broken when a captured Polish deserter revealed a way through the wire. Attacking from behind the battery the gunners were finally driven off and pursued into the woods. The guns meanwhile were blown up by a badly wounded Royal Engineer before the remaining troops, about 30 men, consolidated their position. The company commanding officer, Major Wheelock, was subsequently awarded the MC for leading this action.

At about the same time as the battery was being attacked, X Company, which had moved down the ridge from Le Homme, was now held up by heavy and accurate sniping from the north end of Beauville, a series of "strong stone buildings, interspersed with wall orchards – a paradise for determined marksmen fighting a delaying action". By this stage in the battle the company had already lost 15-20 men, the diary noting that snipers in the village's houses had "picked off all section commanders of the leading platoon".[14] Remembered later by the Company Sergeant Major as "22 or 23 [years old], junior NCOs, very capable, intelligent, able to adapt themselves

---

11 *The History of the Corps of the King's Shropshire Light Infantry*), p.230; Rylands, '"W" Coy, 2nd Bn. K.S.L.I. in Normandy'.

12 Demonstrating that memory could become confused he also believed that the battery was not silenced until 2100 by an infantry assault from a detached company of 2 KSLI.

13 Radcliffe, *History of the 2nd Battalion, the King's Shropshire Light Infantry.*

14 Rylands, '"W" Coy, 2nd Bn. K.S.L.I. in Normandy'.

to situations" their loss was felt keenly.[15] The decision was therefore taken at about 1450 for W Company, which was next in the line, and Y Company to both bypass this village and an hour later they reached the forward edges of Bieville. The deputy commander for the first of these companies later wrote that "once again we were strung out, with little power of manoeuvre, along the axis. There was, however, no very obvious alternative".[16] His men focussed on mopping up the area around the village's château whilst the other company continued moving forward. In the attack the experienced Major Slatter and one of his junior officers were both wounded and evacuated. The post-battle report highlighted that the advance into the centre of Bieville was slowed down as "the civilians refused to evacuate themselves, and at that early stage we were too soft-hearted to shell their homes … which might have facilitated our advance considerably".[17] The troops moved forward with two companies up, the now arrived X going round the back of the street on the east side of the village and W on the west. The château was finally cleared with the assistance of a few Shermans; this was actually the site of a German headquarters but it was found to be almost deserted with the lunch meal still on the tables.[18]

At the same time as the men were tackling the German battery a much more intense battle was also underway nearby one which would largely confirm that Caen would not be captured on D-Day. About 1300 Brigadier Smith and his staff had moved in the direction of Colleville where he intended to establish his tactical headquarters. By the time he had arrived about an hour later it was "a scene of incredible confusion" a result of the continuing failure to suppress HILLMAN.[19] Less than half a mile behind the village on the right-hand side of the road this position dominated the high ground and had an uninterrupted view of the beaches and the Allied line of advance. Surrounded by fields of corn, which at that time of year were about 18 inches high, the best approach for the attackers was through the village and then, providing it had not been covered by a machine gun, along a sunken track with high hedges on both sides. From here it would be possible to breach the barbed wire at the northwest corner of the position and launch the attack. The strongpoint was thought to be a battalion command post but it was actually the headquarters for 736 Gren, the right-hand regiment of 716 Inf Div. Adjacent to it at Point 61, near the crossroads for the Hermanville-Bieville road, there was also the headquarters for the first section of 1716 Arty Regt.

In the lead for the attack was A Company, 1 Suffolks, which had been reinforced with the breaching section from 246 Field Coy, all the men involved having practised the assault a number of times before. At the assembly area small packs and respirators were removed to allow the attackers to move more freely but as they formed up there was no evidence of any aerial bombardment of the target; six B-17s had been tasked to attack prior to the troops landing but none of them were able to see the strongpoint due to the cloud cover. A direct hit from a mortar on his LCA had also killed the FOB who had

15 'John Roberts', Interview by Peter John, 3 November 1999, http://warchronicle.com/ksli/soldier-stories_wwii/roberts.htm.

16 Rylands, '"W" Coy, 2nd Bn. K.S.L.I. in Normandy'.

17 Ibid.

18 Roberts, Interview.

19 Tapp, 'Regimental Commander's Account on 'D-Day' and 'D plus One', Scarfe Papers, ULSC.

been tasked to support this element of the brigade plan along with the rest of his party meaning that there could be no naval gunfire support. Further hampering the attack that was about the follow, photographic reconnaissance had neither revealed the depth of the concrete shelters nor the presence of steel cupolas. The road along which it was planned for the Suffolks to advance was also only about eight feet wide. Nonetheless at 1300 the battalion commander gave the code word for the fire support – 'Grab'- and ten minutes later a troop of tanks, two field batteries and the company's own two-inch mortars started to provide smoke and covering fire.

Initially relying upon the same plan as for MORRIS it quickly became obvious that it would not be so easy this time; a much greater depth of mines and barbed wire presented a barrier that the armour could not cross and attempts to create a gap by hand proved equally unsuccessful as the concealed Germans continually changed their positions.[20] Were it not for the sunken path with its steep banking, which had also not been identified before, it could have proven even more difficult to approach the position. The attackers were able to use this and reached within 100 yards before breaching the initial two belts of wire using Bangalore torpedoes. They then cleared a track through the minefield all the while under heavy fire; following the white tapes that had been laid to mark the boundaries of the gap No.8 Section managed to move forward but came under immediate fire from one of the steel cupolas, which was only 30 yards from the inner perimeter wire, killing the section commander. At this stage the platoon commander, Lieutenant J. Powell, came forward bringing with him a PIAT team as a message was sent back to the company to say that the men were pinned down. Captain R.G. Ryley also moved forward but machine gun fire once more held up the advance and he was one of only four to make it through the gap. This small group were only able to move forward about 200 yards with the ground providing some limited cover but it was clear that there would be no further advance without much stronger assistance. Powell was sent back but could only return with three other men and found that two of those he had left were now badly wounded – both would die of their injuries – and Ryley shortly afterwards was also killed whilst returning for more assistance. With the young lieutenant now in command of the company a stalemate had been reached and a new plan was required.

One of the senior brigade commanders who arrived at Colleville at 1400 described the scene he found:

> Small attacks insufficiently supported by artillery were going in [against HILLMAN] – the supporting tanks of the 13/18 Hussars being fired upon by guns in the strongpoint, and two tanks which had advanced off the track had blown themselves up on mines thus successfully blocking the track. There were dead men and burning motorcycles in the street – a horrible sight for my first close view of war since Dunkirk's beaches. [1 Norfolks] were blocked by [1 Suffolks] and were waiting in the orchards and gardens beside the road. [2 Warwicks] were close up behind them on the roads leading to the village blocked by tanks and vehicles of [8 Inf Bde] Group. There was, of course, the steady rattle of sniper fire – this again was more probably caused by British troops shooting at houses from opposite sides.

20 Smith, 'The Assault: 6-23 June 1944 – The Story of C Squadron…', pp.8-10, SLDM.

At moments there were queer periods of unreality, I remember the sun shining brightly on the gardens, and orchards, and except for the frightful traffic jam, which blocked all roads, we might have been out for a picnic.[21]

With the confusion, first at Colleville and then now at HILLMAN, it appears to have taken Smith some time to determine an alternative course of action despite the clear plan that had been previously agreed and the emphasis that had been given to maintaining the operation's speed and tempo.

At this stage two Sherman Crabs and remainder of the 13/18 Hussars troop were called forward. The flails did not arrive until after the gap had been opened by the sappers who had by then cleared the mines by hand; according to one of the assault engineers the issue was that these tanks could only travel at one-half mile an hour.[22] The battalion commander for the Suffolks, Lieutenant-Colonel Dick Goodwin, later concluded it should have been obvious at this point that it would not be possible to capture the position until such time as tanks could get inside the wire and allow the infantry some greater freedom of movement. The defenders' anti-tank gun had no underground access passage and any movement towards it by the HILLMAN garrison was soon stopped by fire from the British troops. With this small advantage it was decided that the tanks could be moved forward and Arthur Heal, commanding the sappers, was tasked with widening the gap so as to allow the Shermans to get up the lane. Along with two other Royal Engineers he crawled flat on his stomach towards the strongpoint. Despite some suspicion that the minefield was a dummy, as one of the Suffolks later wrote, Heal was quick to find a mine which he started to examine. He had made himself familiar with all types of German mines likely to be found during the landings "but here was one that he could not identify. With some trepidation he pulled it out and examined it more closely; he was relieved to find it was an obsolete British Mk III mine captured at Dunkirk".[23] The mines were spread in four rows at about five yard intervals. The tank squadron leader agreed to move his tanks forward even though Heal's method of clearance, using gelignite charges to blow a row of mines, meant that he could only create a gap five yards wide. One of the underground shelters was also neutralised by a demolition team using a beehive charge which killed all of the occupants whilst Private 'Tich' Hunter, suddenly stood up from the cover of a bomb crater and slowly but determinedly walked towards the cupola, firing his Bren gun from the hip; for this he was awarded a DCM.[24]

It took Heal ten minutes to clear the gap and then the tanks passed through taking another 20 minutes to clear the site. After a brief bombardment two platoons from the company, supported by two more from a different company, moved into the perimeter before fanning out from the gap and using grenades and small arms to take control. Captain Smith commanding No.4 Troop later wrote that:

> …the tank commanders had a great time winkling the Germans out of their trenches by throwing grenades into them from their turrets at the same time the

21 Tapp, 'Regimental Commander's Account on 'D-Day' and 'D plus One', Scarfe Papers, ULSC.
22 Arthur Heal, 'Landing in Normandy', n.d., LHCMA.
23 Lummis, *1 Suffolk and D-Day*, p.21.
24 Heal, 'Landing in Normandy'.

tanks drove for the far side at full speed, to cut off any retreating Germans. The squadron leader's tank [Major Sir Delaval Cotter] amidst all this suddenly almost disappeared from view in a flash. I wondered what on earth had happened and learned later on that he had run over a very large Officers' Latrine which collapsed under the weight of the tank!

The consequences of the delay at HILLMAN were, however, hugely significant. The Norfolks had been forced to wait until about noon before they eventually received orders to advance along the pre-planned route and moved away from near Périers-sur-le-Dan towards its first objective. The regimental record describes the countryside through which they advanced as consisting mainly of small cultivated fields separated by large ditches and numerous small orchards. The roads were very narrow and the ground, which was low-lying, was often rather soft. At 1500 Brigadier Smith had ordered the battalion to make a wide detour to the east of HILLMAN and advance towards Bieville. The wide flanking move was carried out by the Norfolks' two leading companies but it went badly as the first, A Company under the command of Major Eric Cooper-Key, was fired upon by two German machine guns from the strongpoint.[25] There had already been some casualties during the move from the initial assembly area after British tanks had fired on the men mistaking them for enemy troops trying to escape. Eventually, with the remainder of the battalion moving even further round the left flank, A and B Companies were able to disengage and re-join them. Together they captured a feature, referred to during the planning phase as ROVER, which was dominated by a single building and soon to become known as 'Norfolk House'. The enforced left flank move had cost one officer and 13 other men killed with several others wounded; the battalion's casualties for the day were twenty men dead – another officer died of his wounds the following day – and many more injured.[26]

The greatest impact caused by the HILLMAN delay was that the British forces were nowhere near the positions they would have been required to hold if they were to mount an attack on Caen. They were also potentially exposed in the event of a German counter-attack and this is what now followed. Fortunately a second potentially decisive series of actions, perhaps the most important of the entire day, had been taken by Colonel Eadie with the Staffs Yeomanry. He had apparently decided prior to landing that Point 61, the high ground of the Périers-sur-le-Dan ridge which overlooked the beaches, could prove critical and determined to move his C Squadron there at the earliest opportunity. When Patrick Griffin arrived at the high ground, he and the tanks under his command found it to be free of any German forces. They engaged a number of distant guns and transports until accurate shelling in response forced them to find cover until orders were received to support 2 KSLI in clearing Bieville and Beauville. With this successfully completed the attacking force pressed on towards Lebisey Wood which had been one of the armoured

---

25 By the war's end this officer was one of only two in the entire division to have survived and remaining in command of the company which he had led on D-Day. He was awarded an MC and mentioned in dispatches for his part in the campaign; 'Lieutenant-Colonel Eric Cooper-Key', *The Times*, 23 March 2011.

26 *The History of the 1st Battalion The Royal Norfolk Regiment*, p.42; Lincoln, *Thank God and the Infantry*, p.27.

regiment's main objectives. There are no precise timings available about this brief spell of events but after the action at Beauville the squadron headquarters took up position to the west of Bieville with No.4 Troop on the west of the road. At this stage 2 KSLI had one company still at Périers-sur-le-Dan and another at Bieville with a third pushing forward reaching the outskirts of Lebisey at 1730. The Staffs Yeomanry diary specifically records that Lieutenants Knight and Winterhalder had managed to cross the anti-tank ditch allowing their tanks to move into the woods; it was recorded that "No.1 Troop found very few enemy in Lebisey", indeed there were "only a few very frightened and disorganised infantry". [27] There is some question about when this initial attack went in; officially it was recorded as starting at 2114 but a handwritten note reads "No, it was at 1615!", in reality it was likely somewhere in between.

The note may in fact have referred to the first sighting of German tanks with about 20 of them being seen to be approaching from the west towards the British right flank. Guns from 41 Battery, 20th Anti-tank Regiment along with 2 KSLI's six pounder guns and the Staffs Yeomanry all lining the southern face of the Périers-sur-le-Dan ridge now combined to drive off the developing counter-attack. [28] The infantry had been aware even before the landing that 21 Pz Div had moved up into the Caen area "so we were on our guard, and it was no surprise we had this attack on out right-hand side". [29] The German tanks were initially engaged at around 1630 at the western edge of the anti-tank ditch and, after two had been destroyed, the remainder moved west into the woods near Le Landel taking advantage of the dip in the road running along the slight valley that ran from Bieville. Two troops of A Squadron Staffs Yeomanry engaged the Panzers as they emerged from cover moving in the direction of the ridge destroying at least four more.

This German counter-attack had in fact been developing since 0400 when an alert had first been issued to 21 Pz Div by Army Group B and some of its tanks had moved in the direction of the Orne estuary, initially along the eastern bank of the river. Two hours later Seventh Army Command was formally asked by 84 Corps for permission to use the tanks. [30] At 1000 this was rejected although it was agreed that 12 SS Panzer Division could be moved up but permission would still be required for its actual use. With an absence of any orders from higher command at 0630 Feuchtinger is reported to have directed his division to attack the airborne troops. [31] At 1000 he received his first operational order from 84 Corps, only having been placed under them the previous hour, to stop this move and turn west to support the forces protecting Caen which were rapidly disintegrating. For the armoured element, 22 Pz Regt, this meant a sudden change in direction with one battle group later crossing the river at Colombelles and another using one of the bridges in the city.

27 'Tuesday June 6th – D-Day, Diary of C Squadron of the Yeomanry covering D Day and the Invasion of Germany 1944-45', D1300/4/7/1-2, SYA.

28 Paul Carrell, *Invasion – They're Coming!* (George G. Harrap & Co. Ltd.; London, 1994) [Trans: E. Osers], pp.99-102.

29 Roberts, Interview.

30 Wilmot (handwritten notes), n.d., LH15/15/32, LHCMA.

31 Ibid., 'Special Interrogation Report – Genlt Edgar Feuchtinger, Comd 21 Pz Div', LH15/15/146/1.

At 1415 von Rundstedt had sent a personal request to OKW warning that, "no time may be lost in throwing the enemy out. It may be too late tomorrow for what, added to the advantage of cloudy weather, is still possible today".[32] Hitler's block on the use of the Panzers was only finally removed fifteen minutes later but according to an influential post-war assessment, the result of examining captured German documents, whilst this "played its part in preventing the concerted counter-attack" it was important to play down "the inflated importance" the decision had attracted subsequently.[33] It was certainly the case that the Seventh Army telephone log included a note at 1620 that "strong enemy forces at point of breakthrough but no special fear". At the same time it was reported that 21 Pz Div was providing reinforcements and elements had taken up positions to the north of Caen where they expected contact with the enemy to follow shortly. The tone of the message was, however, positive with surprise that the Allied airborne troops had been landed without support from the sea and a conclusion that operations to the east of the Orne were of a diversionary nature. Despite Allied airpower having destroyed large numbers of German vehicles as they approached the battle area, at this stage 21 Pz Div was reported to still have between 90-100 effective tanks along with the two battalions of infantry. Colonel Hermann von Oppeln-Bronikowski, commanding 22 Pz Regt, had the 25 tanks of I Company and his headquarters, established in the area between Lebisey and Bieville by about 1430 in readiness for moving towards Lion-sur-Mer. The Panzer commander was told by General Marcks, directing the 84 Corps response from this forward position, that "the future of Germany may very well rest on your shoulders. If you don't push the British back to the sea, we've lost the war".[34] The combined 35 tanks of the other two companies had meanwhile headed further west and reached the foot of the Périers-sur-le-Dan ridge about an hour later.

In terms of what happened next according to Feuchtinger's account the "excellent" Allied anti-tank guns on the high ground at Point 61 opened fire on his tanks from a range of about 2,000 metres and quickly destroyed eleven of them.[35] As has been noted, the German account was likely incorrect when apportioning credit solely to the gunners. As his C Squadron had been drawn to Lebisey Wood in the mid-afternoon Eadie appears to have concluded that his forces were thinly spread and potentially vulnerable in the face of a counter-attack. As a result he was granted permission to move A Squadron forward so that they might link up with the tanks of C Squadron at a position west of Bieville. As a history of the regiment's action on D-Day, written the following year whilst its author was stationed in Germany, described it:

---

32 The daily report provides von Rundstedt's estimate of the situation which ends: "enemy's intention is doubtless to cut off the Cotentin Peninsula locally in order to win the important harbour of Cherbourg and secure a springboard for further operations. In spite of the strongest commitment against a relatively narrow area it is probably to be assumed that this assault is only the precursor of further invasion attacks"; 'AL1636/1, Commander-in-Chief West's War Diary, June 1944: 6 June 1944', EDS Notes, CAB146/337, TNA.

33 Ibid., R. Wheatley, 'EDS Comments', May 1960, CAB101/308; 'Special Comment – Movement of Panzer Reserves on D-Day', 27 May 1960.

34 'Normandie 6 juin 1944', *Historica* (No.75; avril-juin 2003).

35 'Special Interrogation Report – Genlt Edgar Feuchtinger, Comd 21 Pz Div', LH15/15/146/1, LHCMA.

Soon after this particular move, an enemy attack was launched on C Squadron, and Sergeant Billings in his 17 pounder Sherman, knocked out at least one enemy tank before being hit himself. The tank caught fire and the crew baled out, but after seeing that the fire was not serious, Billings and his crew extinguished the flames, remounted and carried on. The enemy armour, finding that they were unable to make any impression on the C Squadron position, moved across towards the right flank of A Squadron, and the high ground where B Squadron was safely in position. Sergeant Joyce of A Squadron was moving his 75 mm Sherman into very good cover on the right of his squadron overlooking an open piece of ground between two wooded areas, when he was amazed to find some enemy tanks moving in line ahead across his front at a range of only 600 yards. He allowed the armour to come well into the open and fired on the last tank, scoring a direct hit with the first shot. He then traversed down the line of tanks, knocking out two with three shots and finally finished off the fourth tank, leaving them all burning wrecks. Two others, which had escaped his devastating fire, immediately came under fire from B Squadron, who dealt with them adequately.[36]

Eadie's determination to cling to the ridge line had proven decisive. Once C Squadron had moved forward in support of 2 KSLI, B Squadron had been ordered to take up battle positions in its place with the tanks positioned to the south-west "in case an outflanking attack by enemy armour should develop".[37] Added to this A Squadron, despite having been detached by Smith to move against HILLMAN, was only about one mile away. The colonel's perception had ensured a strong blocking force was exactly in the right place just when a moment of potential crisis arrived. Between the tanks and the anti-tank guns the German attack had been largely blunted.

Unfortunately across the brigade there was far less evidence of similar strong military leadership. In fact the entire divisional offensive had been unhinged by a lack of decisive action from the brigade commander in the face of an unexpectedly strong fortified position. Both the Norfolks and Warwicks had been intended to form part of the advance towards Caen and their absence from the initial contact at Lebisey probably proved critical.[38] At around 1600 General Crocker had made his first appearance at the brigade headquarters at which point he urged Smith to release the Warwicks, once again in line with the original plan. According to Tapp, his brigadier had been unwilling to do this until he knew the village of St Aubin d'Arquenay had been cleared; Crocker reassured him that this had been completed some hours before and only then were the Warwicks ordered to advance on Benouville and Blainville. What this meant at Lebisey, the decisive point if there was to be any attack on Caen, was that the small company strength force from 2 KSLI and the troops of tanks from the Shropshire's 13/18 Hussars had entered the wood lacking any meaningful support. and had been forced to retire to the Bieville-Beauville area. By 1730 infantry from Y Company had reached the outskirts of Lebisey but it was 30 minutes before the battalion's commanding officer was able to make contact with them. By this stage there were heavy casualties including Major

36 Underhill, *Queen's Own Royal Regiment, The Staffordshire Yeomanry*, p.26.
37 Staffs Yeomanry War Diary, Vol.54, SYA.
38 Underhill, *Queen's Own Royal Regiment, The Staffordshire Yeomanry*, pp.25-26.

P.C. Steel, leading the company, who was killed by machine gun fire. The remainder of the troops were pinned down and there was a clear danger of being encircled. As dusk began to fall, Colonel Maurice, who was awarded a DSO for his leadership on the day, therefore took the decision that the advance could go no further and withdrew the men shortly after dark. The main effort had culminated and the British had not done as well as they had hoped.

11

Evening – Culmination

See maps 8 and 9.

Across the British sector 'The Longest Day' was drawing to a close but, aside from Caen, there still remained several objectives that needed to be captured or suppressed. B Squadron of 13/18 Hussars, which had landed on the left just after H-Hour and had helped with the capture of SOLE, was still fighting at 1900. The attack on a heavy gun emplacement less than a mile further north – DAIMLER – was variously reported both as having encountered little effective opposition and strong resistance which took an hour to bring under control. What was certain is that by this stage of the day, while the supporting infantry of 2 East Yorks had been reduced to little more than a company in strength, this armoured squadron had only eight tanks remaining and little ammunition and this was the last contribution either would make.[1] A rough assessment at the day's end was that 13/18 Hussars overall had lost about 50 percent of its tank strength although many of these were only temporary casualties and the vehicles were soon repaired. The losses were listed as, 14 tanks in A Squadron, ten in B Squadron, seven in C Squadron, and one in the regimental headquarters. In terms of casualties the final tally was one officer and 15 other ranks killed and another officer and 18 other ranks wounded.[2] The squadrons and supporting infantry battalions had spent the day fighting separate actions with only minimal direction and control from the headquarters. Captain Smith and the remnants of his No.4 Troop, C Squadron, wrote later that having witnessed the capture of the HILLMAN at 1930 he was sent to take up turret down positions behind the Périers-sur-le-Dan ridge in order to observe and repel the expected German counter-attacks. He was surprised that nothing happened and after four hours he finally with-drew back to a small orchard north of Colleville and received fresh ammunition and fuel before laagering for the night.[3] The following day the squadron initially took up defensive positions at MORRIS and remained there until late in the afternoon still expecting a counter-attack to be launched. They actually did little other than fire a few rounds from their 75 mm gun at the town's church spire which was being used by a sniper. In the early evening of 7 June they were moved to the west banks of the River Orne to provide support to 6 AB Div in and around Benouville.

At HILLMAN the success signal was finally given at about 2000 with about 50 prisoners taken; the position was supposed to have been captured around noon and it was

---

1   Neave, 'The War Diary of Julius Neave', pp.46-47; Miller, *History of the 13/18th Hussars*, p.100.
2   Neave, 'The War Diary of Julius Neave', p.48.
3   The regimental history says that they concentrated in an orchard on the southern outskirts of Hermanville where they remained for the night; Smith, 'The Assault: 6-23 June 1944 – The Story of C Squadron…', p.11, SLDM; Miller, *History of the 13/18th Hussars*, pp.103-104.

only the next morning at 0645 that Colonel Krug emerged from his deep shelter to surrender with three of his officers and 70 other ranks.[4] One witness commented that a great deal of credit needed to be given to him "despite his very unimpressive appearance when seen in captivity [as he], was able to conjure up some spirited opposition".[5] With the position secure B and D Companies of 1 Suffolks were immediately sent just forward on the right and left respectively to consolidate. The remainder of A Company withdrew behind the position having lost two officers and four other ranks killed and eight men wounded during the attack. For D Company the battle was not yet quite over as, in advancing to their position, they found a small farmhouse called Beauvais about 300 yards ahead of them and when a platoon was sent in to secure it, after a short engagement the garrison of two officers and 48 other ranks surrendered, their packs and equipment being laid out neatly in threes ready for surrender.[6] HILLMAN retained its important strategic position only this time for British troops who were pointing their firepower away from the shoreline; during the following weeks various field artillery units were dug in around it and according to one account "[they] never seemed to stop firing, day or night".[7] As for Arthur Heal, he would be decorated for bravery and take command of a sapper platoon the following day.

By the day's end 185 Inf Bde was spread across a considerable area. The Norfolks were on high ground east of Bieville and the brigade headquarters remained on the northern edge of Colleville with the artillery just south of the village. While others might have been easing down 2 Warwicks was encountering meaningful resistance at Benouville; this was the first since the troops had landed, a 'German Mobile Delaying Force' armed with machine guns and anti-tank weapons, the regimental history referring to "scattered yet unpleasantly accurate small-arms fire".[8] The battalion commander was forced to produce a 'hasty plan' of attack which was scheduled to start at around 1830 and be led by A Company. At 1900 Brigadier Smith moved again this time to a position a few hundred yards south of Benouville looking out from a crest above the village with Tapp alongside him where he could observe the infantry assault. Concerns were starting to grow about the loss of daylight and 90 minutes later it had still not begun.

It was at about this stage, at 2100, that the glider lift in support of 6 AB Div came in overhead and some of them landed amongst the infantry, causing casualties amongst the troops already on the ground. It also provided cover for the village to be rushed and it was quickly occupied. This fourth phase of the airborne plan, Operation MALLARD, was widely observed by the men of 3 Br Inf Div and it is clear that it had a huge positive impact on morale. The two massed glider landings were intended to provide critical reinforcements for the airborne forces and included 6 AB Div's main fighting strength, its airlanding brigade. This comprised 1 RUR, 2 Ox Bucks less the company that had conducted the *coup de main*, and 12th Battalion, The Devonshire Regiment, a company of which would arrive by air and the remainder later by sea. In addition there

4 B. Lawson, 'The Assault on Hillman', n.d., Lummis 6/6, LHCMA.
5 Neave, 'The War Diary of Julius Neave', p.47.
6 'The History of the Suffolk Regiment – D-Day to VE Day by Members of the Regiment' (Privately published, n.d); Lummis, *1 Suffolk and D-Day*, p.24.
7 Michael Edwards, 'Bash on with 246 to Bremen'.
8 'War Diary – June 1944', WO171/1387, TNA.

was the armoured recce regiment, light artillery and medical personnel. The division was supported by the Tetrarch, the only British tank able to be carried by the heavier Hamilcar gliders. According to the commander of the Armoured Recce Regiment these were "obsolete" and not to "be looked upon as tanks [but as] mobile machine guns, with sufficient protection against small arms fire".[9] There were two landing zones both of which had been cleared by advance parties and had radar beacons and ground markings set up on them. Once again LZ N would receive the bulk of the force and the landings were a great success with 142 gliders, including 30 Hamilcars with their heavy equipment, arriving over a period of 32 minutes, the last one at 2123. The official narrative noted an unexpected problem which affected this landing; abandoned parachutes from the earlier drops were blowing across the LZ some of which wound around the tracks of the light tanks that had been carried in the Hamilcars and in the space of just five minutes 11 of them were immobilised.[10] In addition a new landing zone was also used, LZ W, which lay between Ouistreham, the Caen Canal and Benouville, and approximately 106 gliders landed safely there from 2052 and continuing for the next 28 minutes. Despite conditions being excellent there was considerable bunching at this LZ leading at one stage to six gliders landing abreast; nonetheless it was viewed as a great success and would have a considerable influence on planning for later wartime airborne operations.

Whilst the gliders had provided a considerable distraction in the Benouville action the Warwicks still had to deal with "those ever cunning snipers" who "remained to harass and kill, and ... had to be hunted out and despatched before the way was clear for us to get on".[11] The remainder of the battalion less D Company now moved on as dusk settled towards the final link on the axis, the village of Blainville, supported by some remaining armour. Two of these tanks were knocked out almost at once and, as one of them was carrying the FOO, there was no opportunity to call in artillery support. On the outskirts of the village, following another "brisk little attack" against some houses which led to the capture of a few German prisoners, the battalion halted at around midnight and dug in for the night. Despite continuing German attacks throughout the evening and mounting casualties the airborne troops had continued to hold positions near the bridges until 2115 when the lead elements of D Company 2 Warwicks finally approached having fought their way through Le Port. It was not until 0100 of D+1 that the relief was completed and, after 21 hours of continuous fighting, 6 AB Div moved back across the bridges to the east bank of the Orne. Casualties for the day for 2 Warwicks were four killed and thirty-five wounded; by the end of July of 1001 men who had landed in Normandy more than 700 had either been killed or wounded.[12]

A firm base had also been established by 2 KSLI just forward of Bieville with three companies holding the southern outskirts and the headquarters on the northern edge. The anti-tank feature, referred to as 'Port', was only 200 yards to the south of the orchard at the edge of the village. On a forward slope and covering a square of less than 100

---

9   Lieutenant-Colonel R.G. de C. Stewart (Commander 6 Airborne Div Armd Recce Regt), 'Summing Up of the Lessons Learnt', Staff College Camberley 1947 Course, JSCSC.
10   Ibid., RAF Narrative, 'Volume III, The Landings in Normandy', p.102.
11   Illing, 'No Better Soldier, 1939-1945', p.16.
12   Steve Evans, 'Three in line, but Ted was the only one to survive', *Coventry Evening Telegraph*, 5 June 2004.

yards, this orchard became the consolidation point for both W and Y Companies with Z Company to the rear. It possessed a stout hedge, interspersed with trees on all sides except the front and had covered approaches into it from the enemy side. The men of the KSLI hoped that this would make it "practically tank-proof" as they had no anti-tank weapons and the Shermans had withdrawn; the best they could rely on were forward patrolling platoons and strings of grenades at crucial points along with the support of a FOO from 7 Field RA who promised "to arrange rough treatment in an emergency for the ground in front of us".[13] There was still sufficient concern about the potential for a counter-attack in this area that an order had been given for half of all the available ammunition for field artillery regiments to be held in reserve.[14] Throughout the day 2 KSLI had lost 113 all ranks killed and wounded.

The intermediate brigade's war diary includes a fascinating two-page summary of events during the day in which it offers a rationale for Smith's decision-making and the conclusions he had reached.[15] With his three infantry battalions ashore by around 1100 and in their assembly areas, he was said to have been mindful that congestion on the beach was delaying the armour, Colleville had yet to be cleared and the two German strongpoints were reported to still be held forcefully. His nerve had been further shaken at 1215 when he received the word of enemy troops north of Caen and an artillery position on the ridge at Périers. The diary noted that the situation at 1430 revealed "no battalion at this time had yet got any support weapons with them owing to the congestion on the beaches". Despite this assertion being underlined this was not the case as there was a good deal of armour moving forward by this stage; the artillery position had also been widely referenced in the pre-invasion intelligence reports and it is improbable that he would not have known in advance about the threat it posed. The entry also includes details about the failed assault at Lebisey stating that the commander of 2 KSLI had taken his decision not to continue the attack at about 1800 when he had managed to establish communications once more with his forward company. This had confirmed to him that there were heavy casualties, the company commander had been killed, and the troops were unable to penetrate the wood because of its thickness and concealed enemy firing positions. As a result "the CO considered that to commit his two available companies (already considerably depleted by casualties) into this extensive and obscure objective and without a firm base behind him would be running the risk of defeat in detail". Smith apparently agreed with this not unfair assessment and the withdrawal was confirmed. The report described this as a disappointing decision but the result of delays encountered by the Norfolk and Warwick battalions owing to the opposition they encountered during their advance. The conclusion was that "the advance of seven miles, mostly across country, and against considerable opposition, considering also the delays experienced in getting up its supporting arms and its tank regiment from the beach was an extremely creditable performance" with the brigade's troops having "fought most gallantly under very difficult circumstances". In many respects this was reasonable but there was little reference made to the lack of urgency in command which had seemed to exist at various stages throughout the day.

---

13 Rylands, '"W" Coy, 2nd Bn. K.S.L.I. in Normandy'.
14 'RA 3 Br Inf Div Operation Order No.1', 15 May 1944, WO171/414, TNA.
15 Ibid., 'War Diary – HQ 185 Brigade', June 1944, WO171/702.

The three brigadiers from 3 Br Inf Div back together on the beach at La Breche in 1954; (L-R) Copper Cass, Jim Cunningham, K.P. Smith

With the assault brigade exhausted and in defensive positions near the beachhead the evening of D-Day found 9 Inf Bde more or less scattered across the Sword area with 1 KOSB on the left flank at St Aubin, 2 RUR near Périers and the Lincolns still in Cresserons. Despite tanks from the East Riding's C Squadron having finally moving inland at 1920 there was little indication of any aggressive intent on their part. Even entreaties by Brigadier Prior Palmer to move forward had little effect.[16] And so it continued until at 2245 when the Yeomanry reached its final position for the day just south of Colleville where it drew up its forces in close laager and bedded down for the night. The history notes that there were as yet no supplies ashore but "fortunately no replenishment was needed as none of the tanks had moved far or been heavily engaged".[17] The absence of orders had proved critical and this reserve regiment of tanks appears to have neither participated in the engagement with 21 Pz Div nor made itself available for any drive on Caen.

With the fighting elements of the division having virtually concluded their efforts, patrols were established across the divisional area. For the whole of I Corps the challenge on D-Day was a simple 'V' garnering the response 'For Victory'; it was changed for the following day to 'Handle' with a reply of 'With Care'. Back on the beach activity had, if anything, increased as the afternoon wore on. At 0800 the first units of the REME had landed along with their commander and some of the Beach Recovery Section. It would take more than five hours for the build-up of this group to be completed, its tasks

16 Mace, *Forrard: The Story of the East Riding Yeomanry*, pp.124-125.
17 Ibid., p.126.

being to keep the beach exits clear as far as the first lateral, the recovery of drowned vehicles and the clearance of any disabled vehicles on the beach that could be moved. A number of DD tanks were lying well below high watermark and it was feared they could be struck by incoming landing craft so once the tide receded it was considered a priority to remove these. Men of this section performed another vital role as they used the only Scammel truck – which had carried ashore an armoured bulldozer – with its trailer now unhitched to drag carriers and six pounders which could not negotiate the steep bank on the right of the beach. Once the tide started to recede the other priority became disabled landing craft, those that had beached and were unable to pull off back into the sea. Further recovery work became much easier and all obstructing or damaged tanks and vehicles were pulled to the rear of the beach. This meant that the later waves of landing craft had no risk from obstruction and not one report was received of a craft being damaged.[18]

At 2250 orders were given to the invasion fleet to lay smoke in and around the anchorage area in anticipation of a dusk air attack from the *Luftwaffe* within the Sword beach sector. This raid commenced approximately 30 minutes later, immediately prior to the arrival of the third and last wave of airborne troops which formed part of the airlanding brigade. Operation ROB ROY I involved 50 Dakotas but as they flew over the Eastern Naval Task Force they were mistaken for German aircraft, even though they were flying at only 1,000 feet and at a slow speed. The aircraft that were fired upon were in fact part of the first of the series of re-supply missions that commenced on the evening of 6 June and were intended to provide food, ammunition, medical stores and petrol to the airborne forces east of the Orne. Despite repeated signals to ceasefire some shore-based light anti-aircraft continued to target these transports and were joined by a few merchant ships and LSTs.[19] As a result of the ground fire five aircraft were lost and another 14 damaged. With the remaining aircraft having taken evasive action they were no longer in the correct flight path when they reached DZ N and the supplies they carried were scattered over a wide area. Out of 116 tons of supplies less than a quarter reached the airborne forces, with the majority falling to 3 Br Inf Div.[20]

Throughout the early hours of the morning and the entire length of D-Day there had been a considerable air effort on-going with a total of 11,590 aircraft flying 14,764 sorties – of these 5510 belonged to the RAF and flew 5656 sorties; losses throughout the day amounted to 113 aircraft, or less than one percent of those involved, mostly as a result of German flak. In response the *Luftwaffe* only managed to fly 319 sorties throughout the initial 24-hour period of the invasion.[21] One Spitfire squadron was assigned to give dedicated support in and around the Sword area while the RAF's heavy and medium bombers attacked a total of 11 targets in and around the beach. They were also available to conduct air spotting on seven of the sites which allowed additional naval gunfire support to be provided. At 0930 a further ten minute air raid

18 'REME History', pp.1-3, Scarfe Papers, ULSC.
19 'Operation Neptune…', Battle Summary No.39, p.105, ADM234/366, TNA.
20 RAF Narrative, 'Volume III, The Landings in Normandy', p.103, JSCSC.
21 John Terraine, *The Right of the Line – The Royal Air Force in the European War 1939-1945* (Hodder and Stoughton; London, 1985), p.632.

was conducted near Caen by Allied bombers in an attempt to create chokepoints. The continued cloud cover once again made accuracy impossible and nearly all of the aircraft involved were unable to attack their targets and instead returned to base with their bombs.[22] By early afternoon, with concerns mounting about the failure of offensive air action to delay enemy movement into the area, it was decided to make a further attempt to destroy the two bridges over the River Orne in the centre of Caen. Six squadrons of Liberators attacked and at 1330 56 aircraft dropped almost 156 (US) tons of bombs; it was subsequently learned that the two bridges were not damaged. The final mission of the day, conducted in the early evening, involved one final attempt being made by the heavy day bombers to stop movement the critical city. Although evidence suggested that it was slowed down but not stopped, there was even some suggestion that much of the damage achieved came as a result of raids by the tactical air forces employed throughout the first day of the invasion. The way in which airpower was used over Caen remains a controversial subject with one noted historian having described it as a 'war crime'.[23] Leaflets had been dropped during the first raid of the day warning the civilian population of the imminent danger of bombing and urging them to evacuate. This was not always possible and the people of the city would ultimately pay a huge price for their liberation; it was later calculated that 73 percent of Caen had been destroyed prior to its eventual capture in July with estimates of casualties ranging up to 5800 people.[24]

For the German defenders it had been a catastrophic day. At 1830 a situation report confirmed that Allied forces had established bridgeheads and were advancing along both sides of the Caen Canal north of Blainville as a result of which there was a gradual withdrawal of German troops. About the same time the first battle assessments were being submitted to the Seventh Army's headquarters including a situation report from 716 Inf Div. This stressed that the landings had taken place at the ebb tide which meant most of the beach obstacles were visible and that the attackers had also bypassed and infiltrated strong armoured units supported by infantry and cyclists which then attacked from the rear. With the help of special bombs and bombardments which had eliminated the minefields all of the preparations of the previous years had been largely negated. Another important source is the telephone log for the Seventh Army headquarters.[25] At midnight von Rundstedt's Chief of Staff, Lieutenant General Günther Blumentritt, met with Feuchtinger and Richter at which point it was confirmed that communications had been cut with the infantry division's various command posts and it was not known how many were still holding out. Nonetheless Blumentritt ordered that "the counter-attack of 7 June must reach the coast without fail, since the strongpoint defenders expect it of us".

The opportunity had, however, been lost during the afternoon when Eadie's tanks had fought and largely defeated the German armoured reserve. Despite the brief violent

---

22 Ibid., p.216.

23 Antony Beevor's claims were widely dismissed; Ian Johnston, 'Allies bombing on D-Day 'close to war crime', claims historian', *Daily Telegraph*, 24 May 2009.

24 Hugh Clout, 'Destruction and revival: The example of Calvados and Caen, 1940-1965', *Landscape Research* (Vol.24, No.2; July 1999), pp.117-140.

25 'Telephone Log – German Seventh Army Headquarters', LH15/15/33, LHCMA.

encounter at Point 61 elements from 22 Pz Regt had managed to push through and reached the coast at about 1900. Further west the armoured cars and infantry of I Battalion, 192 Pz Gren also pressed on towards the coast and at about 2000 the surviving elements of 21 Pz Div's mechanised infantry reached the sea between Lion-sur-Mer and Luc-sur-Mer. With the subsequent airborne reinforcement passing over them and a sharp attack from British tanks near Douvres, they turned back and consolidated about a kilometre north of Epron. At this stage in the battle about 25 percent of the defenders' divisional strength had gone. In Feuchtinger's assessment 716 Inf Div had been "completely decimated" and he never saw it in action again. As one post-war assessment put it, "without air and naval support, and with less than 80, mostly immobile guns, the Caen Division was supposed to defeat the initial assault on a stretch of coast about 18 miles wide. All considered, the division put up a good fight".[26] Another assessment concludes that whilst it was practically destroyed there was virtually nothing that could have been done in the face of the full weight of the British attack.[27]

For the Allies it was a different story. On D-Day a total of 28,845 troops were transported across the Queen White and Red beaches; over the assault beaches and jumping or landing from the air, eight divisions had been delivered to Normandy on D-Day. Five more would follow on the next day with there being 21 divisions in France by D+12 and 39 within three months. On that first day 2603 vehicles landed on the Sword beaches along with 1,000 tons of stores. Over the following twelve days a further 16,300 men were landed and by mid-July, D+34, just short of 60,000 tons of stores had been landed and 7677 vehicles.[28] Such was the concern that existed, Eisenhower had kept a brief hand-written note in his pocket which provided a simple explanation to the media explaining why NEPTUNE had failed. Prior to the landings the expectation had been the casualties could be as high as 30 percent but Churchill's predictions and the fears of many senior British officers were thankfully proven wrong.[29] For Sword the actual total losses for D-Day was estimated as being 630 men, 594 of them during the assault phase. The total losses for the ten Anglo-Canadian beaches running across Gold, Juno and Sword was estimated as 1848; Sword had cost over a third of all the casualties.[30] When this was considered across the whole of the landings – with 300 casualties on Utah and 3000 on Omaha – it was just over 12 percent of the 5148 casualties recorded by the official account, costly but not catastrophic.[31] The attack on the Sword sector had been an outstanding success in many respects, the British forces had punched a breach five miles

26 'The German Defences in the Courseulles-St. Aubin Area of the Normandy Coast – Information from German Sources', Historical Section (G.S.) Army Headquarters Ottawa, Report No.41, p.19, CAB146/482, TNA.

27 Marc Hansen, 'The German commanders on D-Day' in John Buckley (ed.) *The Normandy Campaign 1944: Sixty Years On* (Routledge; London, 2006), p.43.

28 'Appendix D: Total Stores Landed', D8/2/7, Scarfe Papers, ULSC.

29 F.H. Hinsley (ed.), *British Intelligence in the Second World War – Its Influence on Strategy and Operations: Vol 3/Pt II* (HMSO; London, 1988), p.131.

30 'Opposition Encountered...', pp.128-129, DEFE2/490, TNA.

31 This same report lists the total number who landed on the five D-Day beaches as 133,300: Sword, 28,800; Juno, 24,000; Gold, 25,000; Omaha, 34,200; Utah, 21,300; 'Comparison of British and American Areas in Normandy in terms of Fire Support and its Effect', Army Operational Research Group, Report No.292, 14 August 1945, p.6, CAB106/1033, TNA.

deep by four miles wide in the German defences. At the same time they had, however, also categorically failed to get anywhere near capturing the key city of Caen. The reasons for this significant failure in the original plan remain an enduring controversy.

12

'Caen Controversy'

See Map 10.

It is difficult to know what to make of the events of 6 June 1944 in and around the Sword sector of the NEPTUNE operation. There is no shortage of information confirming that Caen had been determined as being a key objective. The Cabinet Office prepared account begins its chapter on the role played by 3 Br Inf Div by highlighting that "the intention was to land on Queen White and Red beaches in conjunction with Naval Force 'S' … and capture Caen and a bridgehead south of the River Orne at that place".[1] This text was drawn from the operation order and emphasises where the focus was thought to lie during the final planning phase. The actual order given to the division's artillery explicitly stated that the British assault forces intended to capture Caen and "a bridgehead south of the River Orne at that place". This confirmed that 185 Inf Bde, on securing the city, was to then send forward a covering force based on a company of infantry and a squadron of tanks which was to occupy the high ground near Vimont "with the task of denying the enemy reconnaissance of the area SE of Caen" objectives that were repeated in various other documents relating to the landings.[2] At the individual unit level the same was also the case, the history of 20th Anti-Tank Regiment, which played such an important role in the defence north of Lebisey, also recorded that "…185 Brigade…were to push south towards a town with code name 'Poland' which was to be captured with the aid of various armoured units landing under command".[3]

Reflecting afterwards on the battle this intent quickly changed. According to the KSLI regimental history, "although the battalion had not captured Caen, we had never expected to, and the other two battalions, having become involved in the beachhead area, there was no way to support us at Lebisey".[4] It went on to note that "in war no operation goes exactly according to plan, and the invasion of Normandy was no exception. This time the bad weather was the culprit. It had rather assisted at first by producing the element of surprise, but now [once the invasion was underway] it became a serious handicap to the follow-up troops who were landing on the beach".[5] The war diary for 185 Inf Bde revealed a sense of achievement in the fighting throughout June:

> We had nearly bounced the enemy back into Caen on D-Day, but having not
> succeeded in what would have been a very remarkable event in the face of the

1 Warhurst, 'Overlord: D-Day 6 June 1944, Book Two', CAB44/244, TNA.
2 Ibid., 'RA 3 Br Inf Div Operation Order No.1', 15 May 1944, WO171/414.
3 History of 20 Anti-tank Regiment, p.17, Scarfe Papers, ULSC.
4 Radcliffe, *History of the 2nd Battalion, the King's Shropshire Light Infantry*.
5 *The History of the Corps of the King's Shropshire Light Infantry*, p.230.

opposition from one infantry division and one Panzer division (the pride of the German armoured formations in the West) we were forced to sit down and 'take it' … behind a wall of mines and very positive patrolling.[6]

The official history adopted a slightly different tone reaching the conclusion that all three of the British divisions within I Corps "had made a good start" but each had subsequently developed too slowly to accomplish their "perhaps over-ambitious" main objectives.[7] This was put down to a combination of factors in part physical – with an unexpected high tide which had led to congestion on the shore delaying the advance inland – and also in part down to the strength of the German response at certain points not least of which was the intervention of 21 Pz Div. Added to this there was also the question of speed with it being emphasised that the distances to be covered meant that progress needed to be as rapid as possible "and at times there was little evidence of the urgency which would have to characterise operations if they were to succeed fully". There was, however, also a specific reference elsewhere within this same account to the role played by the Suffolks, the light casualties they experienced during the entire day and the consequences of "the failure to take Hillman [which] was to cost another battalion dearly".[8] Major Ellis nevertheless remained generally sympathetic and concluded that for the attackers to have fought their way inland "for an average depth of four to six miles on most of a twenty-four mile front, was surely a notable feat of arms".

A number of themes emerge from the day's events that could warrant additional investigation in determining why the British assault culminated where it did. Perhaps key to these would be how the battle was conducted, not in terms of the fighting spirit shown by individual units but the manner in which the senior commanders sought to prosecute the plan they had spent some months developing. The reality is that for many of the British troops the afternoon of D-Day was spent being almost entirely responsive according to one junior officer at the time, "reacting to every threat, real or imagined, instead of concentrating our strength against vital ground which would force the enemy to react to our moves".[9] His post-war critique went on to note that "this was all the more surprising because, in all our briefings, we had been urged to 'bash on regardless', bypassing opposition until we reached Caen and even 'staking claims' beyond". In his autobiography Brigadier Smith confirmed that the essence of success for the entire plan was speed and that the men under his command had to be prepared to move forward as quickly as they could using the flanks to pass through Caen "and establish fortified roadblocks on the other side of the ancient city".[10] 'It would be unfair to be too critical of the infantry who were following the direction given to them by their NCOS and junior officers who, in turn, looked to their company and battalion commanders; this smaller group also looked upwards at the brigade commanders who, for all intents and purposes, were leading the way.

---

6   Ibid., 'War Diary – HQ 185 Brigade', June 1944, WO171/702.
7   Ellis, *Victory in the West – Volume I, The Battle of Normandy*, pp.212-213.
8   Ibid., p.202.
9   Robin Dunn, *Sword and Wig – Memoirs of a Lord Justice* (Quiller Press; London, 1993), p.62.
10   Smith, *Adventures of an Ancient Warrior*, p.103.

There was also a real disparity in terms of the distribution of the objectives given to individual battalions and how they responded to them which in part connects with the lack of tempo shown in some cases. 1 Suffolks were required to overcome two known strongpoints within two hours of landing; on the day, whilst they came ashore pretty much on time, they had only reached the second of them, HILLMAN, an hour after they were supposed to have already captured it. They would then spend the rest of the day trying to restore momentum to the plan they had been given. For 1 Lincolns, admittedly landing in a reserve role, they finished the day almost where they had began; the same could in fact be said about almost the whole of 9 Inf Bde which was supposed to have raced down the right flank to help force the attack on the Caen but found itself distracted and apparently disinterested. Some of the infantry companies appeared to be loaded with objectives particularly the men of the assault battalions who fought throughout the day. Others, once they landed, found that there was a lack of clear direction whilst Smith's decision, apparently with Rennie's support, to change the plan meant that some units would find themselves with little to do other than hold ground.

As with all battles the 'fog of war' also had a significant part to play in exacerbating delays and friction. With only limited numbers of FOBs and FOOs their loss had a disproportionate effect as there seemed to be little effective alternate or contingency to coordinate air and maritime support. Due to the restrictions on bringing combat power ashore naval gunfire and close air support had been anticipated to play a potentially crucial role helping overcome resistance as it was encountered. Without this 3 Br Inf Div was increasingly reliant on its own ability to push through any blockages using its armour and artillery. Communications problems throughout the day, particularly with the smaller sets, only served to exacerbate such problems. Whilst there were a large number of these they were spread across a small area and because they had been readied several days before the invasion fleet sailed some had come slightly off net. As an example, prior to the assault on HILLMAN the FOO had some problems using his 18 set to communicate with his gunners back near the beach.[11] With the congestion on the beachhead it was not always possible to get the tanks and guns to where they were most needed as quickly as required to maintain speed and tempo. This meant that at key points, notably some of the strongpoints but also further inshore where the division's troops were at their most extended, there was considerable risk. The German failure to organise their response in a timely fashion meant that the Allies escaped the consequences of this failure and what could potentially been a very different outcome. The actions of the Staffs Yeomanry and 2 KSLI proved to be the critical difference helping ensure both that the high-ground at Point 61 was captured and held and that there was a sufficiently strong defensive screen to blunt the one significant counter-attack made during the afternoon.

There was also a question of the degree to which the men had been adequately trained. Wilmot's criticisms are well known but other contemporary observers also had their concerns. Lord Lovat was damning in his assessment of the performance of 3 Br Inf Div arguing that "in spite of the good record under Monty, [it] proved sticky throughout the landing. They had become muscle-bound mentally and physically, after four years' training in the United Kingdom". To emphasise his point he provided an example of a Monsieur Lefevre, a Resistance leader who had walked from Ouistreham and cut cables

---

11 Lummis, *1 Suffolk and D-Day*, p.17.

which connected to beach flame-throwers. In so doing he believed "he did more than the 8th Brigade, 3rd Division, who landed to our immediate front. A poor showing in the last rehearsal was faithfully repeated on the battlefield".[12] According to a company sergeant major in KSLI they had only conducted a limited amount of training for street-fighting and house-clearing, in Brighton when they were down in the J-camps, "there were terraces of houses which had been taken over, and I think we had two or three sets of training".[13]

There was, perhaps, a more general malaise particularly for a plan which relied on maintaining speed. James Hargest was a New Zealand brigadier who had fought in North African before being captured by the Italians. Having escaped and made it back to Britain he was an observer to the D-Day landings accompanying 'G Force' assaulting Gold beach. His comments were, however, equally as true to the men who landed at Sword.[14] He noted that the casualties amongst officers was particularly high, something he put down in part to the terrain which allowed snipers to get in really close to the attackers and to the carrying of map boards which glinted in the sun and marked them out. He also felt that there was a problem with the troops in so much as they were "only urged forward by the personal example of their officers". He was also worried about the degree to which the soldiers lost confidence once the officers were removed; this in turn led them to bunch together which was a fatal weakness. For the attacking force by far the greatest threat came from machine guns and mortars on the beaches and snipers once they were inland; there were only limited encounters with heavy guns and German armour and the tanks. This kind of close infantry fighting is some of the most challenging for troops lacking in leadership and the attrition rate amongst junior officers was just high enough to act as another brake on progress.

The degree to which the plan was changed before the landings has also been highlighted as having undermined its ability to secure the ambitious objectives.[15] Aside from settling on a single brigade front, something that the terrain made largely inevitable, the decision to break up the armour to work more closely with the infantry has been criticised for having reduced its ability to concentrate the division's fighting power. There are also questions about why the original COSSAC plan of using airborne forces to capture Caen was altered so that 6 AB Div would in fact provide flank protection. This was a role that seemed to be something of a waste of their training and capabilities. Although the paratroopers and glider-borne infantry secured the high ground to the east of the River Orne there was a lack in depth to the defensive positions and this would eventually undermine the ability to use the Sword beaches for bringing in supplies and equipment. During the 17 days from 14-30 June they were shelled and mortared 19 times with a total of about 200 rounds hitting and resulting in considerable tonnage losses.[16] Ouistreham and the Caen Canal were also attacked, the lighthouse at the former, which was being used as an

12 Lovat, *March Past*, p.313.
13 Roberts, Interview.
14 'Reports on the Normandy campaign 1944 June 6-July 10, by Brigadier James Hargest, New Zealand Army Observer with 30th Corps', 1951, CAB106/1060, TNA.
15 Robin Dunn, 'A Disastrous Change of Plan: Why Caen was not Captured on D-Day 6th June 1944', *Royal Artillery Journal* (March 1995), pp.33-35.
16 'Opposition Encountered...', pp.147-148, DEFE2/490, TNA.

Observation Post, was hit several times on 21 June largely destroying the upper floors. On 30 June the decision was taken to close the three eastern beaches – including Roger Green – and they were not used again other than as a decoy and shelling continued until the first week of August. Whilst such criticisms only consider some of the facts, indeed they generally avoid the challenges presented by terrain and the availability of critical enablers such as landing craft and transport aircraft, they do serve to highlight how the plan was, in many respects, an uncertain one.

For each of these themes a linkage can be seen to exist with Brigadier Smith and his role and performance on D-Day. In a number of areas he made critical mistakes and undermined the ability of the troops he commanded to push forward and engage the enemy; his calculation of risk seems to have been skewed towards a defensive mind-set when the operational plan for the division relied upon speed and rapid movement. According to the official history air reconnaissance had confirmed German armoured movements throughout the morning and at 1100 Dempsey had asked that air attacks be made on troop movements to the south and south-east of the city. Quite rightly Smith was not prepared to send unsupported infantry into what he termed "a tank trap" and was mindful of an unnamed brigade commander who had committed such an error and destroyed a battalion. At the same time there is reference to 21 Pz Div advancing west of Caen although his account seems to claim that he heard this at about the same time as he has established his headquarters at Hermanville town hall.[17] His justifications seem to have ignored the information available to him at the time. As one example, he blamed the congestion on the decision to land on beaches there were only 30 to 40 feet in depth, prevailing winds and exceptionally rough seas; in reality their restricted size was a detail known throughout the planning process when he had an opportunity to forcefully voice any concerns he held but there is no evidence that he did.[18] Smith's order certainly served to dilute the forces he had available to him. Thinning the Warwicks of one company – D Company being sent to support the paratroops and glider-borne troops holding the ground against a developing German counter-attack – and delaying the movement of the follow-up forces would almost certainly, have left some doubt in the minds of his battalion commanders. This approach would also have highlighted that the strategic priority was the Orne and holding the bridges captured by 6 AB Div.

What becomes clear from his post-war account is that HILLMAN dominated his thinking and entirely undermined his ability to function at the required operational level of command.[19] Scarfe was not alone in his conclusion that "there can't be much doubt that it would have been better if Tom Rennie had sacked KP [Smith] on the spot. Better still if Monty had replaced him during his celebrated weeding of senior officers on his return from Italy at the turn of the year".[20] When he was finally relieved some days later a junior officer who had served as a Smith's staff captain watched him as he travelled back to the beachhead, his "pitiful face" revealing "the bitter journey home" that he faced. It left him wondering if he had stayed with the Brigadier, as opposed to joining the staff at divisional headquarters, his support might have given him "that minute piece of

17 Ibid., pp.105-106.
18 Ibid., p.107.
19 Smith, *Adventures of an Ancient Warrior*, p.103.
20 Scarfe to Lummis, 11 July 1994, Lummis 6/6, LHCMA.

extra confidence he might have needed to take risks at a moment when perhaps he fatally hesitated?"[21] As Smith concluded in his own account, "Lebisey being my Waterloo, as Napoleon was banished to St Helena, I was, metaphorically, banished to Madagascar, although as a commander and not as a prisoner!"[22] In noting that it had taken three divisions to capture Caen when he had been expected to capture it in a day with elements of a single brigade, he did accept that it could have been done. There were, however, four prerequisites: MORRIS and HILLMAN needed to have been captured "fairly quickly" by the assault brigade; the supporting armour for his brigade push needed to have disembarked in time; his brigade and its supporting armour would have had to have reached the city before the German Panzers had arrived; finally, there had to be no unexpected heavy opposition, particularly around Lebisey. Clearly these caveats were so broad and far reaching as to be neither practical or, indeed for that matter, reasonable. Particularly when the Brigadier added to them the impact of the chaos on the beaches which he put down to heavy weather and exceptionally high tides and a lack of intelligence about enemy movements and the layout of the countryside. The information was available but for inexplicable reasons Smith does not appear to have used it to best effect.

One of the chief omissions in terms of gaining an understanding of what happened is knowing what General Rennie thought about how the day developed. Having already been wounded in North Africa, following the D-Day landings he was wounded again on 16 June and evacuated to England. Having recovered from his injuries he was next made General Officer Commanding 51st (Highland) Division, but on 24 March 1945, after crossing the Rhine during Operation PLUNDER, at the age of just 45 years old, he was killed by mortar fire. His corps commander, General Crocker, later wrote that:

> I believed at the time and still do think that had 3 Div been able to land with [brigades] up it might have helped them to get further and faster on D-Day. A good deal of the lack of complete success on [its] sector must be attributed to slowness in deploying the follow-up [brigades] which the one-up plan was the root cause.[23]

His assessment would appear to have been that the chief weakness was that the plan that had been adopted by COSSAC and SHAEF teams who considered Sword had been forced upon them due to the shortage of landing craft for two assault brigades, a lack of room and practicable exits from the target beaches and a desire to keep well away from Ouistreham which was believed "to be a tough place".[24] One of Rennie's brigadiers, Copper Cass, later wrote to the journalist-turned-historian Cornelius Ryan, then conducting the research for his 'The Longest Day', that the assault divisions of I British Corps had faced the most formidable challenge on D-Day.[25] Across the entire NEPTUNE area they had been the last to land, and on the most exposed beaches, from which they had the farthest distance to then go forward, against what was potentially believed to be the strongest defending force. Landing 90 minutes after dawn there was

21   Woodrow Wyatt, *Confessions of an Optimist* (Collins; London, 1985), p.98.
22   Smith, *Adventures of an Ancient Warrior*, p.109.
23   General Sir John Crocker to Ellis, 9 June 1958, CAB101/309, TNA.
24   Alexander McKee, *Caen – Anvil of Victory* (Souvenir Press: London, 1964), p.53.
25   Cass to Miss Isaacs, 8 September 1958, 87/28/1, IWM.

in fact a real potential that the enemy could have used the warning that was likely to have followed the news of the landings elsewhere to have prepared reserves for a forceful response. Cass concluded that for Crocker to have had any chance of even 'effectively' masking Caen, the instruction that had been issued to 3 Br Inf Div, his forces would have "needed smooth landings, maximum fire support and swift penetration of the Atlantic Wall". The city, as he put it, "could be captured on D-Day only by a stroke of luck".

Perhaps the most well-known of the post-war assessments is that to have emerged from General Dempsey who later wrote that he had not wanted:

> … to get involved on too broad a frontage, because that would have consumed two-thirds of their [the assault troops] strength … I was worried about the Germans on their left and on their front … I wanted to be able to push 3 [Br Inf Div] as far south towards Caen as I could and still keep sufficient troops in reserve to be quite sure of holding this flank … I needed to have plenty of troops in reserve to defend the line of the Orne if that were attacked. I never expected 3 [Br Inf] Div to get Caen on the first day, and I always said that if we didn't get it the first day it would take a month to get it afterwards. The important task on this sector was not deep penetration but strength on the flank, for it was against this flank that we felt sure the Germans would make their major effort.[26]

In correspondence with Ellis as he produced the official history, he did, however, also recognise that many had thought Second Army's objectives were too optimistic and he had "withstood many strong attempts to cut them down".[27] Landing on a single brigade front to allow his forces real depth, was based on experience gained during the invasions of Sicily and Italy and the lessons he had learnt, "…D-Day is the attacker's day, when he has all the advantages of planning and surprise … it will take days or weeks to capture the ground that has not been taken on D-Day … troops must only be stopped on D-Day by the enemy or by exhaustion". Yet he also wrote that he had known from an early stage of the invasion that Caen could not be captured on 6 June "directly I got the information about the movements of 21 Pz Div". As he put it, "if the Germans had done something different, we might have snapped Caen"; they did not and the British position would be fixed on ground well suited for the defender fighting a series of costly battles that wore down the already fragile strength of its army.

As for Monty his biographer makes scant reference to events that took place in and around Sword sector. The message he sent Eisenhower at 2000 on the day of the invasion included at its end reference to the city still being held by the enemy and that plans which had been outlined to the supreme commander that day would be pursued vigorously.[28] While Dempsey was still apparently working on the idea of capturing the city within a few days, on 8 June the Allied Land Forces Commander was writing back to Major-General Sir Frank Simpson, Director of Military Operations in the War Office, that, with the German's apparent determination to hold the city he had "decided not have a lot of casualties by betting against the place, so I have ordered Second Army to

---

26 Dempsey to Liddell Hart, LH15/15/130/8, LHCMA.
27 General Sir Miles Dempsey to Ellis, 23 May 1960, CAB101/309, TNA.
28 Hamilton, *Monty: Master of the Battlefield, 1942–1944*, p.627.

keep up a good pressure at Caen, and to make its main effort towards Villers Bocage and Evrecy and then S.E. towards Falaise".[29] The noted British historian Alistair Horne, writing in Montgomery's defence, summed it up:

> His grand strategy, as he had expounded it with utmost clarity back in April and even earlier, was to draw the enemy panzers to the British front on the east end of the line and wear them down, preparatory for the American 'end-run' breakout from the west. And he kept to it. The capture of Caen would have been a bonus, but it was certainly not essential to success of the invasion ... Montgomery's great error was not his failure to take Caen but his prediction of its capture in the initial assault.[30]

D+1 was in many respects just as important for his old division as there still remained some possibility for 3 Br Inf Div to push on towards Caen. The Warwicks, Monty's own regiment, were given the responsibility of trying to capture the high ground overlooking the town in and around Lebisey, known to the troops as STOUT from the bogus maps. They had been selected to lead the attack as the battalion had suffered fewer casualties than the other two in the brigade. It was thought that the wood was not held in any considerable strength but the anti-tank ditch meant that there could be no guarantee of armoured support. For the Warwicks there were only three rifle companies available for the initial attack one of which was to capture the wood on the right with a second moving on the left and the final one, C Company, planned to pass through and complete the assault. The start line was a stream which passed roughly midway between Blainville and the objective and 0845 was the proposed time for the attack to begin. Although the orders had been issued at 0730 there was some delay in moving forward from snipers; worse was to come as the marshy ground prevented the armoured carriers and six pounder anti-tank guns from being deployed in support. The commanding officer, Lieutenant-Colonel Herdon, therefore decided to delay by an hour and called off the artillery fire support which had been planned to include bombardment by a cruiser lying offshore. He could not, however, make contact with B or C Company and they moved forward as previously ordered with only two self-propelled guns providing any cover. Theses troops approached to within a couple of hundred yards at which point defending German force opened up with small arms fire.

Unbeknown to the Warwicks overnight a battalion of 125 Pz Gren had moved into the area and it was well dug in by the morning with defensive positions that had sufficient depth so that when the British infantry tried to rush forward they virtually all became casualties. The three companies found themselves pinned down along the fringes of the wood where they hung on until 1500 without having made any real impact. At this stage the fourth rifle company, D Company, arrived and was able to make some inroads into the wood but the enemy responded by bringing up tanks. At 1600 the Norfolks, who began the day from its overnight position around ROVER and spent most of it holding the line and covering the left forward flank of the brigade, were sent to help and they

---

29 Ibid., p.631.
30 Alistair Horne, 'In Defense of Montgomery', *Military History Quarterly* (Vol.8, No.1; Autumn 1995), p.61.

managed to move through the cornfields up to the wood and into a position where their own anti-tank guns and mortars could provide some support. Once again, as had been the case the day before, with the light fading the decision had to be taken about whether to withdraw or to hang on and wait for further support the following morning. The commanding officer of the Norfolks made the decision and the troops were pulled back; shortly after they had left the Germans shelled and mortared the area but there were no British casualties.[31] The Warwicks continued to hold their position near the edge of the woods until 2230 before managing to successfully withdraw and take up position at Blainville. By the day's end the battalion had lost 10 officers – including Herdon who had been shot through the head and killed – and 144 other ranks and most of their transport had been destroyed.[32] Lebisey was eventually captured by the Norfolks on 8 July and as the regimental history notes "one surprising result of the attack was the discovery of how far the men of the Battalion had penetrated into Lebisey Wood during the operations of June 7th. The position of their bodies, and the abandoned vehicles of the Warwicks, showed the distance they had advanced".[33]

It is perhaps worth considering the comments of one of the company commanders about the events of 7 June 1944:

> Thus the first battle of Lebisey was lost. It was galling that the great prize of Caen had so nearly fallen into our hands. Lebisey could in all probability have been captured if a properly coordinated attack had been put in instead of battalions being committed piecemeal: first a battalion on the evening of D-Day, secondly our own on the morning of D+1, and thirdly by another battalion on the evening of D+1. Even then it might still have succeeded if our attack had not gone off at half cock. It failed because the start line has not been secured and the attack went in without fire support. But in fairness to those who launched the attacks it must be remembered that it was not known that [21 Pz Div] had moved on to the feature, indeed information was to the contrary. Risks had to be taken in order to get on and establish as big a bridgehead as possible before German resistance hardened and their reserves could intervene. Those behind, quite rightly urged those in front to 'get on'. We were sadder but wiser after the dawn of D+2.[34]

An opportunity had been lost but this was the price of battle. For one of those from the Norfolks who had been involved, the failure to capture the objective provided clear evidence of the lesson that "you can do with a platoon on 'D' Day, what you cannot do with a battalion on 'D'+1 or a division on 'D'+3", echoing the conclusion also provided by Dempsey. This much more junior writer, a young lieutenant in June 1944, held both Smith and Rennie accountable, more so the latter, for not having committed greater forces to the battle on the evening of 6 June when the German defences were still weak.[35]

---

31 *History of the 1st Battalion The Royal Norfolk*, pp.21-22.
32 'War Diary – 2 Warwicks', June 1944, WO171/1387, TNA; Cunliffe, *History of the Royal Warwickshire Regiment*, pp.82-87.
33 *History of the 1st Battalion The Royal Norfolk*, p.45.
34 Illing, 'No Better Soldier, 1939-1945', p.24.
35 Dunn, *Sword and Wig*, p.64.

The final comment should be left with Scarfe who so painstakingly examined the battle, one in which he had participated. With the fiftieth anniversary he and Eric Lummis, the Suffolk infantrymen who had been at HILLMAN, exchanged correspondence on the events of D-Day as the latter prepared to have published a second article defending both his regiment and his division.[36] The two old soldiers had slightly different conclusions in terms of what might have happened but Scarfe seemed better able to consider the military imperatives: whilst he was willing to accept that some troops might have been able to reach Caen this "did not mean we could all have got there" and even then it was unlikely that the Germans would have simply withdrawn but they would instead have made "savage armoured counter-attacks…".[37] In truth there is still some work to be done to say what might have been but a poor plan, over-ambitious objectives, indecisive leadership and the 'fog of war' can all be said to have contributed. Eisenhower secured his lodgement and Monty may well have been able to claim with some veracity that the plan had gone how he envisaged but the final positions occupied by 3 Br Inf Div on the evening of 6 June 1944 were not those that had been hoped for and the prize of Caen would take several more weeks to be secured.

---

36 Lieutenant-Colonel Eric Lummis, 'Caen and D-Day', *Journal of the Society for Army Historical Research* (Vol.LXXIV, No.297; Spring 1996), pp.39-49. The early article exploring broadly similar themes was 'D-Day, 6 June 1944: The Truth About 3 British Division', *Army Quarterly and Defence Journal* (Vol.199, No.4; October 1989), pp.393-407. They both remain required reading for Staff College students visiting the D-Day battlefields.

37 Scarfe to Lummis, 22 June 1994, Lummis 6/6, LHCMA; ibid., Scarfe to Lummis, 17 August 1994.

Bibliography

PRIMARY SOURCES

The Royal Regiment of Fusiliers Museum, Royal Warwickshire (Warwick)
Imperial War Museum (London)
Joint Service Command and Staff College (Shrivenham)
The Duke of Lancaster's Regiment Lancashire Infantry Museum (Preston)
University of Leicester Special Collections, David Wilson Library (Leicester)
Liddell Hart Centre for Military Archives (London)
National Army Museum (London)
A Soldier's Life, Discovery Museum (Newcastle Upon Tyne)
Staffordshire Yeomanry Archives, Staffordshire Record Office (Stafford)
Suffolk Records Office (Bury St Edmunds)
The National Archives (London)
U.S. National Records and Archives Administration (Maryland, US)

SECONDARY SOURCES

The History of the 1st Battalion The Royal Norfolk Regiment, During the World War, 1939-45 (Jarrold and Sons Limited; Norwich, 1947)
The History of the Corps of the King's Shropshire Light Infantry Vol.3: 1881-1968 (KSLI, 1970)
The Story of the 79th Armoured Division (Hamburg, 1945)
Stephen E. Ambrose, *D-Day: June 6, 1944 – The Battle for the Normandy Beaches* (Pocket Books; London, 2002)
Rick Atkinson, *The Guns at Last Light – The War in Western Europe, 1944-1945* (Little, Brown; London, 2013)
Roderick Bailey, *Forgotten Voices of D-Day – A New History of the Normandy Landings* (Ebury Press; London, 2009)
C.C. Bates and J.F. Fuller, *America's Weather Warriors, 1814-1984* (Texas A&M University Press; College Station, Texas, 1985)
Antony Beevor, *D-Day: The Battle for Normandy* (Viking; London, 2009)
Major-General David Belchem, *Victory in Normandy* (Book Club Associates; London, 1981)
P.M.H. Bell, *Twelve Turning Points of the Second World War* (Yale University Press; London, 2011)
Raymond Birt, *XXII Dragoons 1760-1945, The Story of a Regiment* (Gale and Polden Limited; Aldershot, 1950)
Horst Boog et al, *Germany and the Second World War: Volume VII, The Strategic Air War in Europe and the War in the West and East Asia 1943-1944/5* (Clarendon Press; Oxford, 2006)
Anthony Cave Brown, *Bodyguard of Lies* (Bantam Books; New York, 1975)

John Buckley (ed.) *The Normandy Campaign 1944: Sixty Years On* (Routledge; London, 2006)

Paul Carrell, *Invasion – They're Coming!* (George G. Harrap & Co. Ltd.; London, 1994) [Trans: E. Osers]

David G. Chandler and James Lawton Collins Jr (eds.), *The D-Day Encyclopaedia* (Helicon; New York, 1994)

Sir Winston Churchill, *History of the Second World War: Vol.V, Closing the Ring* (Cassell and Co.; London, 1951)

Lloyd Clark, *Orne Bridgehead* (Sutton Publishing; Stroud, 2004) [Series Editor: Simon Trew, Battlezone Normandy, No.1]

Jean Compagnon, *6 June 1944 – The Normandy Landings* (Editions Ouest-France; Rennes, 2011)

Terry Copp, *Fields of Fire: The Canadians in Normandy* (University of Toronto Press; Toronto, 2004)

Marcus Cunliffe, *History of the Royal Warwickshire Regiment 1919-1955* (William Clowes and Sons Ltd; London, 1956)

Norman Davies, *No Simple Victory – World War II in Europe, 1939-1945* (Penguin Books; London, 2007)

Patrick Delaforce, *Monty's Iron Sides – From the Normandy Beaches to Bremen with the 3rd Division* (Sutton Publishing Limited; Stroud, 1995)

Patrick Delaforce, *Smashing the Atlantic Wall – The Destruction of Hitler's Coastal Fortress* (Pen and Sword; Barnsley, 2005)

Robin Dunn, *Sword and Wig – Memoirs of a Lord Justice* (Quiller Press; London, 1993)

Carlo D'Este, *Decision in Normandy* (Konecky and Konecky; Old Saybrook, 1984)

Denis Edwards, *The Devil's Own Luck – From Pegasus Bridge to The Baltic, 1944-1945* (Pen and Sword; Barnsley, 2001)

David Eisenhower, *Eisenhower At War 1943-1945* (Random House; New York, 1986)

Dwight D. Eisenhower, *Crusade in Europe* (Little, Brown and Co.; Boston, Massachusetts, 1950)

Major L.F. Ellis, *History of the Second World War: Victory in the West – Volume I, The Battle of Normandy* (HMSO; London, 1962)

R.C.K. Ensor, *A Miniature History of the War – Down to the Liberation of Paris* (Oxford University Press; London, 1944)

David Fletcher, *Swimming Shermans* (Osprey Publishing; Oxford, 2006)

Ken Ford, *Sword Beach* (Sutton Publishing; Stroud, 2004) [Series Editor: Simon Trew, Battlezone Normandy, No.2]

Ken Ford, *D-Day 1944 (3) – Sword Beach and the British Airborne landings* (Osprey Publishing; Oxford, 2002)

Will Fowler, *Pegasus Bridge – Bénouville D-Day 1944* (Osprey Publishing; Oxford, 2010)

James Gleeson and Tom Waldron, *Now It Can Be Told* (Paul Elek; London, 1952)

John Golley, *The Big Drop – The Guns of Merville, June 1944* (Jane's Publishing Company; London, 1982)

Nigel Hamilton, *Monty: Master of the Battlefield, 1942–1944* (Hamish Hamilton; London, 1983)

Gordon Harrison, *Cross Channel Attack* (Office of the Chief of Military History; Washington DC, 1950)

Max Hastings, *Overlord – D-Day and the Battle for Normandy 1944* (Papermac; London, 1993)

F.H. Hinsley (ed.), *British Intelligence in the Second World War – Its Influence on Strategy and Operations: Vol 3/Pt II* (HMSO; London, 1988)

History of the 2nd Battalion the Royal Ulster Rifles in North-West Europe 1944-1945 (The Regiment, n.d.)

John Keegan, *Six Armies in Normandy: From D-Day To The Liberation Of Paris* (Pan Macmillan Ltd; London, 1995)

Lieutenant Commander P.K. Kemp, *The Staffordshire Yeomanry (QQRR) in the First and Second World Wars* (Gale and Polden Ltd; Aldershot, 1950)

Lieutenant Commander P.K. Kemp, *The Middlesex Regiment (Duke of Cambridge's Own) 1919-1952* (Gale and Polden Ltd; Aldershot, 1956)

David Lee, *Beachhead Assault – The Story of the Royal Naval Commandos in World War II* (Greenhill Books, London; 2004)

Joshua Levine, *Operation Fortitude – The Story of the Spy Operation that Saved D-Day* (Collins; London, 2011)

Jon E. Lewis, *Eyewitness D-Day* (Robinson Publishing Ltd; London, 1994)

John Lincoln, *Thank God and the Infantry: From D-Day to VE-Day with the 1st Battalion, the Royal Norfolk Regiment* (Sutton Printing; Trowbridge, 1999)

Lord Lovat, *March Past – A Memoir by Lord Lovat* (Weidenfeld and Nicolson; London, 1979)

Paul Mace, *Forrard: The Story of the East Riding Yeomanry* (Pen and Sword; Barnsley, 2001)

Lieutenant-General Sir Frederick Morgan, *Peace and War: A Soldier's Life* (Hodder and Stoughton; London, 1961)

Brendan A. Maher, *A Passage to Sword Beach – Minesweeping in the Royal Navy* (Naval Institute Press; Annapolis, 1996)

Alexander McKee, *Caen – Anvil of Victory* (Souvenir Press; London, 1964)

Major-General Charles Miller, *The History of the 13th/18th Hussars (Queen Mary's Own) 1922-1947* (Chisman, Bradshaw, Ltd.; London, 1949)

Samuel W. Mitcham Jr., *Retreat to the Reich: The German Defeat in France, 1944* (Stackpole Books; United States, 2007)

B.L. Montgomery, *The Memoirs of Field-Marshal the Viscount Montgomery of Alamein* (The Companion Book Club; London, 1960)

Montgomery of Alamein, *Normandy to the Baltic* (Hutchinson; London, 1947)

Montgomery of Alamein, *El Alamein to the River Sangro / Normandy to the Baltic* (Barrie and Jenkins in association with the Arcadia Press; London, 1973)

Williamson Murray and Allan R. Millett, *A War to Be Won – Fighting the Second World War* (The Belknap Press of Harvard University Press; London, 2000)

Colonel W.N. Nicholson, *The Suffolk Regiment 1928 to 1946* (The East Anglian Magazine Ltd.; Ipswich, 1948)

Lieutenant Colonel P.R. Nightingale, *The East Yorkshire Regiment (Duke of York's Own) in the War 1939/45* (Mr Pye (Books); East Riding, 1952)

David Orr and David Truesdale, *'The Rifles Are There' – 1st and 2nd Battalions the Royal Ulster Rifles in the Second World War* (Pen and Sword; Barnsley, 2013)

T.B.H. Otway, *Airborne Forces: The Second World War 1939-45* (Imperial War Museum; London, 1990)

Major-General R.P. Pakenham-Walsh, *History of the Corps of Royal Engineers, Volume IX, 1938-1948* (The Institution of Royal Engineers; Chatham, 1958)

G.L.Y. Radcliffe, *History of the 2nd Battalion, the King's Shropshire Light Infantry (85th Foot): in the campaign in N.W. Europe, 1944-1945* (Basil Blackwood; Oxford, 1947)

Winston G. Ramsey, *D-Day: Then and Now* (After the Battle, 1995, 2 volumes)

Michael Reynolds, *Eagles and Bulldogs in Normandy 1944* (Spellmount Limited; Staplehurst, 2003)

Andrew Roberts, *Masters and Commanders: The Military Geniuses Who Led the West to Victory in World War Two* (Penguin; London, 2009)

Andrew Roberts, *The Storm of War – A New History of the Second World War* (Allen Lane; London, 2009)

Nick Smart, *Biographical Dictionary of British Generals of the Second World War* (Pen and Sword; Barnsley, 2005)

Brigadier Kenneth Pearce Smith, *Adventures of an Ancient Warrior in Peace War and Revolution* (Stones Printers; Milford-on-Sea, 1984)

Colonel C.P. Stacey, *Official History of the Canadian Army in the Second World War: Volume III, The Victory Campaign, The Operations in North-West Europe 1944-1945* (The Queen's Printer and Controller of Stationary; Ottawa, 1960)

J.M. Stagg, *Forecast for Overlord* (Ian Allan; London, 1971)

Andrew Stewart, *A Very British Experience – Coalition, Defence and Strategy in the Second World War* (Sussex Academic Press; Eastbourne, 2012)

John Terraine, *The Right of the Line – The Royal Air Force in the European War 1939-1945* (Hodder and Stoughton; London, 1985)

Warren Tute, John Costello and Terry Hughes, *D-Day* (Pan Books Ltd; London, 1975)

Major D.F. Underhill, *Queen's Own Royal Regiment, The Staffordshire Yeomanry: An account of the operations of the Regiment during World War II 1939-1945* (Staffordshire Yeomanry Museum; Stafford, 2000)

Flint Whitlock, *If Chaos Reigns – The Near-Disaster and Ultimate Triumph of the Allied Airborne Forces on D-Day, June 6, 1944* (Casemate, Newbury, 2011)

Olivier Wieviorka, *Normandy – The Landings to the Liberation of Paris* [Trans. M.B. DeBevoise] (Harvard University Press, London, 2008)

Chester Wilmott, *The Struggle for Europe* (Wordsworth Editions; Ware, 1997)

Alan F. Wilt, *The Atlantic Wall 1941-1944 – Hitler's Defenses for D-Day* (Enigma Books; New York, 2004)

Woodrow Wyatt, *Confessions of an Optimist* (Collins, London, 1985)

Christopher D. Yung, *Gators of Neptune – Naval Amphibious Planning for the Normandy Invasion* (Naval Institute Press; Annapolis, 2006)

Major General David T. Zabecki, *Chief of Staff: The Principal Officers Behind History's Great Commanders, Volume 2* (Naval Institute Press; Annapolis, 2008)

NEWSPAPERS/JOURNALS

The Guardian
The Independent
The Daily Telegraph
The Times (UK)
UK regional newspapers
Historica (France)

Le Figaro (France)
King's Shropshire Light Infantry Regimental Journal
The 13th/18th Royal Hussars Journal

PHOTOGRAPHS

'War Office Second World War Official Collection', No.5 Army Film and Photographic Unit
    (Public Relations Unit), Ministry of Defence
Eric Lummis Papers (Liddell Hart Centre for Military Archives/Suffolk Records Office)
Author's own collection

Index

Page references in *italics* indicate an illustration. Page references followed by 'n' indicate a footnote.

PEOPLE

PLACES

MILITARY UNITS

MISCELLANEOUS

Related titles published by Helion & Company

D-Day – The Last of the Liberators. Some of the
last veterans of the Normandy Landings retrace
their steps seventy years later
Robin Savage
ISBN 978-1-909982-31-4 (hbk)

Mettle and Pasture: the History
of the Second Battalion the
Lincolnshire Regiment during
World War II
G.J. Weight
ISBN 978-1-909982-14-7 (hbk)

Waffen-SS Armour in
Normandy. The Combat
History of SS Panzer
Regiment 12 and SS Panzer
Jagerjäger Abteilung 12,
Normandy 1944, based on
their original war diaries
Norbert Számvéber
ISBN 978-1-907677-24-3
(hbk)

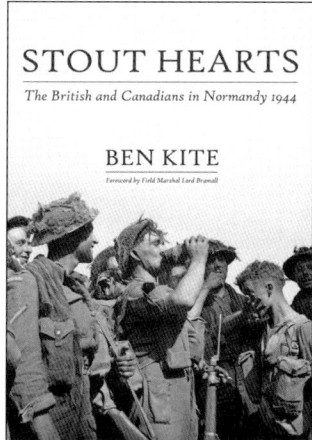

Stout Hearts: The British
and Canadians in
Normandy 1944
Ben Kite
ISBN 978-1-909982-55-0
(hbk)

Destination D-Day.
Preparations for the Invasion
of North-West Europe 1944
David Rogers
ISBN 978-1-909982-05-5
(pbk)